Ambition and Social Structure

Ambition and Social Structure

**Educational Structure and
Mobility Orientation in the
Netherlands and the United
States**

Cornelis J. Van Zeyl
Columbia University

Lexington Books
D.C. Heath and Company
Lexington, Massachusetts
Toronto   London

Library of Congress Cataloging in Publication Data

Van Zeyl, Cornelis J.
  Ambition and social structure.

  Bibliography: p.
  1. Social mobility. 2. Social classes. 3. Social classes-United States—Case
studies. 4. Social classes—Netherlands—Case studies.
I. Title.
HT608.V35   301.44'044   73-11649
ISBN 0-669-89524-5

Published simultaneously in Canada.

Printed in the United States of America.

International Standard Book Number: 0-669-89524-5

Library of Congress Catalog Card Number: 73-11649

To
Catherine and Nicholas Van Zeyl

Contents

List of Tables   xi

List of Figures   xiii

Preface   xv

Acknowledgment   xvii

Chapter 1   **Theoretical Background**   1

The Extent of Association Between
   Class and Culture   3
A Brief Critical Analysis of
   Cultural Theories of Social Class   7
Class Culture and Mobility   11

Chapter 2   **Social Selection and Educational
     Structure**   29

The Subculture and Dominant Value
   Hypotheses   31
Mobility and Class Values   32
Social Selection as a Framework for
   the Analysis of Social
   Stratification   34
The Structure of Social Selection
   in England and the United States:
   The Contest and Sponsored Models   41
The Dutch School System and
   Sponsored Norms of Selection   48
Mechanisms of Socialization
   Appropriate to a Contest System   57
A Comparison of Mobility
   Orientations and Socialization
   under Sponsorship and Contest:
   Expected Findings   66

Chapter 3	**Some Methodological Notes**	77
	The Sample	77
	The Indicator of Social Class Employed in This Study	84
Chapter 4	**Mobility Aspirations and Sponsorship**	89
	Aspirations and Realism	89
	Occupational Aspirations	91
	Educational Aspirations	94
	Mobility Orientation as the Relation Between Class and Aspiration	99
	Desired and Expected Occupation and Background	105
	School and Mobility Aspiration	106
	School Type and Occupational Aspiration	108
	School Type and Educational Aspirations	112
	The Indices of Preferred and Anticipated Status	115
	A Causal Model of the Determinants of Mobility Aspiration	115
	The Relative Effects of Class Background and School on Mobility Aspirations	118
	Chapter Summary	124
Chapter 5	**Social Selection and Value Orientations**	129
	Previous Comparative Research on Value Differentiation	129
	The Selection of Value Orientations	132
	The Selection of Specific Achievement Value Measures	135
	Recapitulation of Theory and Hypotheses	141
	A Causal Model for the Determination of Adolescent Values in a Sponsored System of Education	144

The Construction of Indices   146
The Structure of Determination for
    Value Orientations   147
Analysis by Value Dimensions   155
The Degree of Association Between
    Stratification and Values   162
Chapter Summary   163

Chapter 6   **Conclusion and Overview**   167

The Comparative Analysis of Social
    Selection   167
Social Selection and Aspiration   169
Social Selection, Socialization,
    and Achievement Values   173

Appendix   177

Notes   189

Bibliography   197

Index   203

About the Author   209

List of Tables

3-1   Mean Background Index of Sample
Schools Stratified by School Type
and Social Rank of School
Neighborhoods   82

3-2   Distribution of Father's Occupation
for Sample Schools Classified by
Census Categories   83

3-3   Occupational Distribution of Sample
and 1960 Dutch Census   84

3-4   Educational Level of Sample and
1960 Amsterdam Census Population   84

4-1   Background and Occupational
Aspirations   92

4-2   Educational Background and
Aspirations   95

4-3   Mean Occupational Background and
Aspirations   106

4-4   School Type and Desired Occupation   109

4-5   School Type and Expected Occupation   110

4-6   School Type and Desired Education   113

4-7   School Type and Expected Education   114

4-8   Zero Order Correlation Matrix of
Stratification Variables,
Aspiration Variables, and Other
Control Variables   119

4-9   Direct Effects of Four Variables
on Aspiration   120

4-10	Indirect Effects of Class Background on Aspiration	121
4-11	A Partitioning of Variance for the Determinants of Mobility Aspiration	123
5-1	Correlation of Individual Value Items with Background, School, Age, and Aspiration Indices	148
5-2	Direct Effects of Five Variables on the Value Indices	148
5-3	The Indirect Effects of Class Background on the Value Indices	150
5-4	The Indirect Effects of School Level on the Value Indices	151
5-5	A Partitioning of Variance for the Determinants of Value Orientation	154

List of Figures

4-1   Path Diagram of the Effects of
Class Background, School, Age,
and Grades on Mobility Aspiration   117

5-1   Causal Paradigm on Assumption That
Aspirations Determine Values   145

5-2   Path Diagram of the Effects of
Class Background, School, Age,
Preferred Status, Anticipated
Status on the Composite Value
Index   150

Preface

The relation between social class and cultural values has been a persistent object of sociological research over the last few decades. In this volume a serious attempt is made to provide a new approach to the study of class culture as a supplement to this tradition.

In previous research a strong emphasis has been placed on the conservative impact of class values in maintaining the stability of social stratification systems. The separation of classes into separate cultural enclaves is seen as providing a kind of social inertia which makes it difficult for individuals to move from their class of origin. Typically, the mechanism which is seen as producing this inertia is familial socialization of the individual to the values of his parental class group. This learning, it is asserted, makes it unlikely that he will ever come to appreciate the values embodied in the life style and occupational activity of other strata.

This conception of class culture is difficult to reconcile with the shape of stratification in modern society. In most industrial countries the rate of interclass mobility is so high that class groups cannot be seen as having a stable membership composed of continuous family lines. Over the long run the majority of class incumbents will be composed of individuals who have moved from other levels. Such large-scale mobility makes it difficult to conceive of class culture exclusively as a product of transmission from generation to generation. If it is true that class cultures maintain a continuous identity for longer than a single generation then we must ask the questions: How do upwardly and downwardly mobile individuals acquire the values of the classes to which they move and why do they do so? To answer these questions requires that we consider in a comprehensive way the role that values play in promoting and determining social mobility. It is this problem to which we will address ourselves in the following pages via theoretical speculation and the presentation of empirical data.

Because we will proceed in several stages, not all of which are self-evident, it becomes necessary to lay out in advance the plan of the book.

In Chapter 1 existing conceptions of class culture, social class, and socialization to class values are critically examined. Many of the notions employed by those who have written about class culture in the past are so well entrenched that it was necessary for the author to refute them in detail. In addition many of the issues that emerged from a discussion of class culture were found to be hopelessly entangled with complementary issues in the area of social stratification. An important example of this is the tendency in current stratification literature to equate high rates of mobility with a decline in cultural and interactional barriers between social classes.

Chapter 2 deals with two closely interrelated topics: (1) the formulation of a theoretical alternative to those propositions criticized in Chapter 1, and (2) the design of an empirical study that the author conducted to test his own and other competing theories. The pursuit of a new and dynamic approach to class culture required an altered and expanded conception of social stratification which the author termed "social selection." The broad scope of this theoretical reformulation required that it be tested in a comparative fashion. To accomplish this aim two ideal type descriptions of social selection were constructed, one of which applied to the United States and the other of which applied to the Netherlands. These were termed respectively, "contest" and "sponsored selection." These two modes of selection were compared both in terms of their hypothesized impact on status allocation, and on socialization to class values.

The data for this comparison were derived from two sources. Evidence establishing the impact of sponsorship was sought from a study of Dutch adolescents conducted by the author in 1968. In this investigation a sample of students was chosen from public secondary schools in the city of Amsterdam. A questionnaire that was administered to these subjects during schooltime inquired into their social origins, mobility aspirations, and values. Because the study dealt with secondary school students, our hypotheses dealt only with the implications of the educational structure and social processes taking place in the school for social selection and socialization to class values.

Evidence establishing the impact of contest selection was obtained by reviewing similar studies of adolescents conducted in the United States. By comparing the results of these studies with his own, the author was able to evaluate the differences between these two systems of selection, and their respective impact on class values.

Chapter 3 deals exclusively with certain methodological aspects of the Dutch study such as sampling, translation of questionnaire items, and the categorization of variables.

The remaining chapters deal with the presentation and evaluation of the results. Not all the hypotheses could be evaluated in a comparative fashion, because of the lack of available data. As a consequence they are frequently confirmed or rejected only in terms of our theory. Chapter 4 deals with the impact of sponsorship as reflected through the educational system on the mobility aspirations of our students. In Chapter 5 inferences regarding socialization are derived by comparing the relative impact of stratification variables on various value constellations which previous research has shown are related to social class. Chapter 6 summarizes the overall implications of the findings reported in Chapters 4 and 5.

Cornelis J. Van Zeyl

Acknowledgment

In conducting the study upon which this book is based I received assistance, inspiration, and criticism from many persons and organizations. While I cannot acknowledge all of the help I received, there are those to whom I owe a special debt of gratitude. The Ford Foundation provided financial assistance. I am especially grateful to Ralph Turner, who provided early encouragement and inspiration and assisted me in all phases of the work. A number of Dutch sociologists gave generously of their time, especially H.M. Jolles, A.N.J. Den Hollander, C. Vervoordt, and J. Goudsblom. The staff of the Sociological Research Center at the University of Amsterdam assisted me with countless details and made my field work in the Netherlands a pleasant experience. The dedicated assistance of Gerard Bos, Nicolene Meiners, Cornelis Middendorp, Liesbeth Noordijk and Katrien Hoefnagel made the task of administering and coding the questionnaires considerably lighter. James Bruno provided critically important help with the computer programming and other methodological aspects of the study. Donald Treiman and Vincent Jeffries provided criticisms of earlier drafts which were incorporated into the final version.

Ambition and Social Structure

1

Theoretical Background

The differences between men created by social inequality have been evident to social thinkers throughout the course of history. Many have been concerned with substantive disparities, noting that some men are poor while others are rich, that some men are powerful while others are subjected. But such objective differences have never received the weight of commentary that has been aroused by the impact of classes, castes, or status differences on the personal horizons, character, and personalities of men.

Indeed, it has frequently seemed to many thinkers as though social ranks have been peopled by different species of human beings, so forcibly are men molded by social station. Aristotle was convinced that classes were divided by natural human differences, and, therefore, he asserted that those of superior character ought to be placed above others. The New Testament praised the virtues of the poor, while the established church of the reformation singled out the economically privileged as the chosen of God.

The emergence of the social sciences has marked a change in our assumptions about the "natural" character of differences between men of different status. The notion of fixed character has been replaced by the idea that the circumstances of social deprivation are connected with cultural and psychological differences between men.

Although cultural differences between classes have been accepted as axiomatic since the emergence of social science, the precise nature of this phenomenon and its genesis have never been agreed upon, and appears to be a component of a continuous theoretical debate.

One particular facet of this debate is represented by the Marxian conceptions of false consciousness and class consciousness. Marx asserted that all cultural phenomena were reflections of the objective class structure of society, determined in turn by its modes of economic organization. Under capitalism the culture of the working class was merely a reflection of its economic suppression by the dominant bourgeoisie, and, therefore, a negative form of culture, a false consciousness. The emergence of authentic proletarian culture would be dependent upon the emergence of class consciousness, or a true realization by the proletariat of their economic power and its political significance. Thus the working class would only become a real entity (a class for itself) when men became aware of their common situation and saw themselves as belonging together both in terms of life chances and what they needed to do for themselves to speed the course of historical evolution. Such collective self-awareness is the most explicit or self-conscious level of culture.

1

In contemporary political sociology, arguments are still brought forth for the presence of political class identification, and an attempt has been made to keep this concept alive by stripping it of its dialectical and historical meaning. But it no longer has a wide acceptance among sociologists. In the current context class consciousness appears to be empirically undemonstrable and theoretically ambiguous. As Ginsburg has pointed out, "It is very hard to tell what one is conscious of when he is class-conscious."[1] Faced with the impossibility of demonstrating self-conscious class awareness, sociologists have not abandoned the concept of class culture, but they have recast it in different form. The most general approach to the study of class culture in current sociology is to look for differences in subjective orientation between strata that require a somewhat lower order of individual self-awareness but that, nonetheless, circumscribe a distinct set of world views and norms of behavior. This general point of view has been articulated by Dennis Wrong in a recent essay.[2] Referring to the requirement of class consciousness as the "realist" position (borrowing a term from the ancient philosophical debate) he writes:

Critics of the realist conception of social classes have attributed to it the necessary implication that members of a society must be fully aware of the class system and that its nature can therefore be determined by a simple opinion poll. Surely, this is a specious argument. To assert that social controls and expectancies are present in the minds and sentiments of the people whose conduct they influence is not to maintain that these people can readily put them into words. Consider social norms in primary groups, which are clearly operative influences on behavior; those who conform to them are not always able to provide a coherent account of the codes that guide and restrain them in their day-to-day interactions with others. The kind of awareness-in-behavior that frequently characterizes social class relations may involve still less self-consciousness since classes (except in small isolated local communities) are not even potential primary groups; hence the frequent use of the term "quasi-group" to describe them.[3]

Intuitively, sociologists have followed the spirit of the above statement. In actual fact the notion of class as a subcultural or metacultural entity is the one implied in the major part of the contemporary sociological literature.

The other side of the debate regarding the relation between class and culture has been stated primarily in subcultural terms. Reversing the Marxian formulation this point of view holds that it is the cultural differences (or sometimes intellectual) between class milieus which account for the objective inequalities, rather than the other way around. Proponents argue that the value systems of the various classes place differential emphasis on competitive striving and other personal qualities requisite for upward mobility in our society. Allocation of social positions in society is assumed to be meritocratic, based on the matching of objective qualifications of individuals and functional requirements of social positions. The inertia of lower-class culture, however, and its low "achievement" emphasis are seen as preventing capable individuals from achieving what they otherwise could. This interpretation has been predominant in the so-called "culture of poverty" literature produced in recent years.

However, the Marxian conception of the relation between class and culture can also be recast in subcultural terms. A small but growing body of literature emphasizes that social inequality has direct cultural consequences. The reasoning is that objective deprivation, both material and experiential, is likely to produce adaptive images of life, or rationalizations, in the lower-class individual. From this point of view it is not sufficient to assert that certain values are not properly learned. These values are simply not internalized or disseminated in the lower-class environment because under the circumstances the range of actions and or experiences expressing these values is also limited. The lower-class man does not desire an education, for example, because in the context of his day-to-day economic problems it yields him nothing; he does not have the resources to acquire it (resources conceived as both material and experiential) and he cannot calculate a meaningful economic return. Furthermore, he cannot see education as a means to an end either, for he perceives that those who do acquire an education already have the rewards or status to which it leads. If the reward is not present as an object in one's experience, then perhaps the achievement sequence is also meaningless.

The Extent of Association Between
Class and Culture

The question discussed in the foregoing pages (the nature of the relations between stratification and culture) is undoubtedly the most fundamental theoretical issue. The theoretical controversy that has provoked the most interest among sociologists, however, is the degree of cultural variation between classes. There are very few who would deny that there are some cultural differences between classes, however, their relative importance has been consistently debated. Predominantly this argument has been articulated in terms of two distinct positions: The first has been termed by this author as the "dominant culture" approach; the second has been referred to in sociological writings as the "subcultural" view. The basic assumptions and advantages of both approaches are discussed under the headings below.

Class as Subculture

A succinct statement of the subcultural theory of social class, a theory that has emerged largely by default, has been given by Reissmann:

+ contrast

The theoretical basis for the formulation of a class subculture is that the values, life styles, goals, and behavior of the several classes are distinct and different. Even further, the assumption is made that the cultural expressions with any one class are sufficiently cohesive and consistent to distinguish them from those of any other class. The class subculture, then, is a cultural unity and there arises the distinct reality of a middle class culture, an upper class culture, and a lower class culture—or as many other variations as can be found and identified.[4]

This new concept of class represents more than just an adjustment of old notions to fit changed conditions. To refer to classes as separate subcultures is to transform the very concept of class itself. The subcultural concept of class has had much popular currency because it permits one to study class without making rigorous assumptions about individual social psychology or about economic and political interest. To speak of social classes as subcultural entities, however, has far-reaching methodological and theoretical implications that are frequently not elaborated upon in current discussions of class structure.

The change in theoretical focus from economic and political structure to subculture has freed the researcher from the use of independent standards set by the theorist—such as the insistence of Marx and contemporary political sociologists upon such political dimensions as ownership vs. nonownership, ownership vs. control—or of psychological dimensions—such as class consciousness and subjective self-identification. Methodologically the researcher is freed from theoretical constraints: the criteria or cutting points for delimiting specific class groups are no longer fixed according to theoretical limitations upon the types of appropriate evidence for demonstrating class differences. The criteria for delimiting class levels become a matter of "operational" determination. It is not important to consider what means or indicators are used to arrange individuals hierarchically according to class position as long as the indicator or classification schema employed is capable of uncovering or predicting important subcultural variations. The content of these subcultural variations can be very broadly defined: They can consist of artifacts, life style, belief systems, rates or frequencies of certain behavior. The list can go on indefinitely.

In this endeavor, statistics have come to the aid of the sociologist. A battery of quantitative indicators has been developed which can be located on continua and combined in various ways to provide an operational assessment of class position. It does not seem to be a topic of great controversy that different indicators are used or that they are segmented in different ways. Whether one cuts three ways or five ways seems to make no differences in the results. The major advantage seems to be that the necessity for clear theoretical conceptualization of the nature of social inequality or cultural pluralism is deferred, until "all the evidence is in."

The widespread use of socioeconomic indicators as variables in survey research has led to a vast proliferation of knowledge about the "correlates of social stratification." The range of phenomena which can be demonstrated to vary with social class is truly remarkable. Without reviewing the literature extensively, let us cite a few of these: mobility rates, child-rearing practices, life styles, occupational and educational aspirations, mortality rates, fertility rates, sex codes, family organization, political beliefs, psychological orientations, moral codes; all have been shown to vary by socioeconomic level.

The accumulation of such research has not led to any significant new conceptual integration of the meaning of social class. Theoretical notions at the most primitive level of elaboration are used as explanations for diverse findings. A single concept is used to explain the significance of a wide variety of findings: the notion of class culture. Value differences between classes are made to carry the weight of causal imputation. Nevertheless, such differences are rarely investigated directly. There is a certain circularity in the majority of descriptions of cultural differences between classes. Values are inferred from behavior and then used to explain that same behavior, although the degree of subjective interrelatedness between the two has not been demonstrated. Whether or not a subjective value orientation accounts for the behavior in question cannot be verified directly. But such a mode of explanation does provide the social researcher with protection from possible contradiction, and absolves him of the necessity of looking for other causes. The subcultural theory of social class, in its most extreme form, has no way of accounting for the many features of modern social structure which weld a society into a single unit. Societywide political and economic forces or institutions which affect class distinctions (or variations in behavior) are explicitly overlooked.

The persistence of the subcultural view is based, to some extent, on its close affinity with a particular explanation of social inequality, which we presented in the foregoing section. The majority of research and theoretical commentary on subcultural differences between classes has emphasized that they are to some degree responsible for the inferior economic position of the lower classes. The postulated relationship of class differences in power and life chances to cultural variations resembles quite closely the earlier arguments for social inequality put forth by Social Darwinism. In this case it is not biological variations but cultural and "motivational" differences which are put forth as criteria of superiority and inferiority.

Dominant Culture Theory

The dominant culture approach appears to be closely intertwined with the functionalist theory of stratification. A number of theorists whose work deals with social stratification have abandoned the stratified or layered conception of class entirely and replaced it with the notion of a classless or open society. They have taken very seriously the evidence of high-mobility rates and of overall consensus in occupational prestige ratings found in empirical studies. The former is regarded as a manifestation of the fact that everyone is striving for very similar cultural goals; the latter is regarded as a manifestation of the fact that there is a single dominant hierarchy of cultural values which determines what these goals should be. It is generally asserted that comprehensive cultural differences between classes have been replaced or subordinated by dominant national cultures. The residual variation in values is largely the product of imperfect permeability. From this point of view, social inequality is no longer the product of political or cultural dissensus but rather the product of generalized consensual judgments of social esteem; i.e., everyone basically agrees about who is to be superior and inferior.

The most prominent representatives of point of view are Parsons, Merton, Davis, and Moore.[5] The basic position has been stated best by Parsons, who defines social stratification as "the ranking of units in a social system in accordance with the standards of a common values system." This dominant hierarchy of values has been variously defined by these theorists as "universalistic achievement," "generalized emphasis on success," or "functional imperatives." The specific content of such value orientations is not as important, however, as their basis in societywide consensus. Under such a system the differential ranking of "subunits," which by strong implication are occupations, occurs as the result of differential embodiment of the basic values of the society.

The unequal reward given to various occupations in industrial societies is not based on a differential distribution of power or economic resources but rather on their prestige as assessed according to basic values, since basic values are described as being achievement-oriented. In fact, there are two characteristics related to the amount of reward a position receives: its difficulty and its functional importance. The former characteristic is probably most closely related to skill level or education; the latter seems to imply the level of authority or responsibility involved in a position.

This new model of social stratification is based on the status-order characteristic of the modern bureaucracy. The institutionalization of the achievement ethic in such organizations represents, in large part, a justification for a hierarchy of status based on skills. The functionalist theory of differential rewards is based primarily on such unidimensional criteria, or value orientations. From this point of view in such a system economic inequalities are important no longer for themselves but for what they convey symbolically. The important thing is the cultural superiority of one man's work over another.

Under such a system individuals differ not so much in terms of their basic values but rather in their ability to realize such values. Parsons has suggested that the adequacy of socialization and personal capabilities may be two important variables in "value acquisition." Merton explains individual variation in ability as a consequence of discontinuity between socially structured opportunities and universally inculcated goals.[6] Put more simply, the social structure is seen as allowing some individuals access to the means of achieving culturally defined aspirations and as restricting such means to others.

A Brief Critical Analysis of Cultural
Theories of Social Class

The most important failing of the dominant culture approach is the specification of an overall consensus whose content and structure have not been demonstrated empirically. It is perhaps doubtful if such consensus can ever be demonstrated, since it depends primarily upon an artificial separation between culture, social structure, and the individual for the purposes of a "technical theoretical" analysis whose correspondence with reality is questionable. Modern society is characterized by unparalleled complexity and change, producing individual value hierarchies that are both subjective and situational in character. It would seem that under current conditions the conception of culture as an entity *sui generis* amounts to platonic idealism. Subcultural approaches, of course, are not immune from this criticism either. Those who view the separate classes as subcultures also assume cultural consensus. However, convincing empirical demonstrations of cultural homogeneity seem to be lacking on both the subcultural and societal level.

Small-scale technologically primitive societies have frequently been utilized as examples of cultural integration and "unreflective conformity." Nevertheless, anthropologists have failed to find such consensual integration in even the most isolated communalities. Florence Kluckholn, in a recent work, goes so far as to say that all societies, whatever their scale, are characterized by systematic cultural variation, and presents comparative evidence in support of this contention.[7]

In modern societies the assumption of cultural homogeneity becomes even more dubious. Contemporary social structure is characterized by an associational network of many independent institutions or groupings that, as tangible social entities, are frequently embodied in formal organizations. Such entities do not maintain subjective value orientations similar to those of individuals. But, as E. Lemert has pointed out:

It is possible to show that groups, through social interaction and control, can determine that certain values will necessarily be satisfied by members before others, or that certain values will be maintained in a dominant position in group interaction. Furthermore, it is possible to show with factual data a series of interlocking or intermeshing groups, which, due to their positions in relation to accessible means of power and social control, can determine that certain values will be dominant, i.e., satisfied first by various persons in constituent groups.[8]

This kind of accommodative ordering of values, frequently the outcome of ideological compromise, does not, of course, find much expression in theory oriented towards cultural consensus.

The extent to which associational networks are characterized by relations of submission and domination is a separate issue. Nevertheless, the very complexity of modern organizations produces irresolvable tendencies towards cultural heterogeneity, both in terms of subjective attitudes and behavioral expression. This is still true even if we assume early childhood socialization of most individuals to a general set of cultural values. The associational complexity of modern society and the consequent overlapping institutional involvements necessitated by adult roles would tend to produce a general modification and reordering of values acquired via early conditioning. Lemert has proposed a theory of "contingent valuation," which describes this process quite well:

Values are defined as factors that, within physical and biological limits, affect choice. As such, they are abstractions inferred from acts. However, in making such inferences, it is mandatory to distinguish between the act of valuation by an individual and the observable pattern of action which demonstrates the position of a value in a hierarchy order. The act of valuation is a sorting out or ordering process . . . which results in preferences for various courses of action.

Valuation immediately precedes action to a greater or lesser degree in all societies because individual members seldom are supplied with means for satisfying their values at costs which correspond to their wishes. The concept of costs here is taken to mean those other values which must be sacrificed in order to satisfy any given value. It is assumed that costs can be at least as roughly gauged by the amount of time, energy and psychic stress required in order to reach a chosen goal. Costs are important variables in analysis because changes in the costs of means can modify the order of choice, even though the "ideal" value order of the individual remains constant.

The order of value satisfaction in groups must be understood as the product of the interaction of many individuals, each pursuing his hierarchy, sacrificing something of lesser value for something of greater. In so doing the individual frequently sees the group as a means to ends; he is adjusting to the fact that services of others, whose value hierarchies differ from his own, become means whereby he can achieve his own ends. For this reason the pattern of his choice in a group setting may not correspond to his subjective hierarchy.[9]

The notion of contingent valuation expressed above implies that in modern society the individual is "cross-pressured" by a number of conflicting allegiances which he must compromise either willingly or unwillingly in many ways. Such compromise may involve change in subjective orientation or in overt behavior and in the long run perhaps both. When valuation is viewed in this manner as a process, rather than as an expression of fixed tendencies, it becomes clear that one cannot deduce precisely from a particular performance its meaning in terms of valuation, since outward form and inner orientation do not always necessarily coincide.

The notion of contingent valuation is not completely new to sociology. Max Weber long ago emphasized that one of the most salient characteristics of the modern legal-rational social order is the interchangeability of means and ends

with respect to such rational considerations as cost or profit. The notion of means-end interchangeability implied in contingent valuation has frequently been brought forth as a criticism of theories that postulate the existence of a dominant value hierarchy. In modern society, it is not possible to determine from the intrinsic nature of a value whether the individual is employing it as a means or as an end. Therefore, critics argue, such means-end distinctions cannot be legitimately employed in describing an overall value system. The average individual will consistently modify ends according to the cost of achieving them and will accordingly also consider a number of means as functional alternatives to ends. The means-end interchangeability of values is frequently cited as a reason for abandoning the concept of value entirely, as an unreliable and vague empirical or analytical tool. Such interchangeability merely points, however, to the nature of the social process in which valuation itself occurs, and begs that we examine that process in more detail. Occupational success, for example, may be regarded as a means to the more general aim of forming a respectable social image and an elegant life style. There is also strong reason to believe, however, that manifesting certain "respectable" character traits such as lack of absentee-ism, or elegance in speech and manners, may serve as the means to social ascent. This does not imply that the overall goals are an inadequate description of the individual's behavior. Rather, it points to the fact that the social climber's values are contingently ordered according to the types of audiences he is likely to encounter. These contingencies and their implications for his values can frequently be quite clearly described.

Dominant value theory requires, by contrast, that all actions be interpreted as instrumentalities for achieving some ultimately sacred and internalized goal. That this sometimes involves rationalization can be seen if one considers that almost any action can be retrospectively interpreted as conforming to a value when that value is stated at a sufficient level of generality. Let us assume, for example, that a dominant American value is "achievement." If we examine the content of achievement-oriented behavior in different groups, however, we find profound differences. Lower-class males, for example, may value achievements that reinforce their masculinity, such as skill in street fighting, whereas middle-class males may be more concerned with writing poetry or with educational achievements in general. Both of these concerns involve rational pursuit of achievement. When the abstract value of achievement is said to account for these diverse types of behavior its logical content seems to be reducible to the statement "All human beings are motivated."

Such discrepancies between behavior and generalized cultural emphasis are frequently described in terms of the differences between goals and values. William James once referred to one aspect of such a distinction as the difference between the desired and the desirable. Clearly, in a general sense there are sets of values that everyone considers desirable or admirable. Yet we do not all possess the means for achieving such values and, therefore, do not establish them as goals for our own behavior. For example, when lower-class parents are asked to indicate what sorts of occupations they would like their sons or daughters to enter they invariably express high aspirations. On the other hand, when asked what types of occupations they realistically anticipate their children will have they revise their aspirations downward, for they realize that neither they nor their children possess the requisite advantages in competing for such high positions.

Goals differ not only in terms of their relevance, however; they can be systematically differentiated in terms of their content. In a recent study by E. Mizruchi it was disclosed that subjects from both middle- and lower-class backgrounds tend to endorse "the value of getting ahead in life" with about equal frequency.[10] When this investigator queried his subjects further, however, it was discovered that not everyone had the same mental picture of what he or she had endorsed. When asked to indicate what they had in mind as symbols of success the lower-class subjects responded that homeownership and secure income were their primary goals, whereas the middle-class subjects tended to emphasize the acquisition of education.

There is no doubt that such distinctions between values and objects are useful; nevertheless; they point to a crucial weakness of dominant value theory. The separation of generalized values from more specific goals is simply another way of indicating the difference between universals and unique occurrences. When it comes to the question of assessing cultural differences between groups the very phenomenon that can be demonstrated to vary are *objects*. This may be one of the reasons why anthropologists concern themselves so much with the description of artifacts and traits in describing cultural variation. For when we wish to place specific behaviors or objects in more abstract categories we frequently end up describing universals. Thus it seems very unlikely that there is any culture which does not value achievement, or courage, or skill; on the other hand, specific definitions of behaviors that fall into these categories vary widely. As C. Wright Mills once pointed out, almost every social theory operates with certain hierarchies of specificity.[11] One of the major problems with dominant value theory seems to be a lack of awareness of such hierarchies and their implications.

Above we discussed two of the major problems inherent in dominant value theory: (1) that the nature and form of cultural integration in units as large as total societies have never been dealt with systematically; and (2) that the basic unit of analysis, the value orientations, can only be used as an analytical component when the specific empirical objects or social processes to which it refers have been carefully delineated. Furthermore, the structural and cultural heterogeneity of modern society renders a dominant value order highly implausible. Dominant value theorists, in their efforts to describe all-pervasive cultural regularities, ascend to such a high level of abstraction that they must frequently abdicate the task of description.

By contrast, subcultural theory gives a picture of social classes as constituting one of the major sources of cultural differentiation in modern society. It views the several classes as distinguishable cultural worlds, characterized by sharp differences in attitudes, goals, and behavior. The subcultural approach, while giving us some latitude to describe cultural differences between classes, also has distinct limitations. Like dominant value theory it simplifies the complex nature of modern society and ignores the institutional structure which shapes its distinctive form of social inequality. It breaks up society into unitary cultural complexes that are to some degree isolated from each other, thereby, neglecting such society-wide processes as contingent valuation and ideological accommodation. All the criticisms applicable to dominant value theory are recapitulated in subculture theory, only in plural. Both approaches make the crucial assumption of cultural homogeneity, which, as we have indicated, seems to break down upon closer analysis. The most serious problem with both theories is the specification of a unitary set of values which presumes to account for a large portion of the behavior of individuals. Contingent valuation implies, on the other hand, that competing sets of values are present in a society and that some type of weighing of different value alternatives takes place in determining which shall be given priority in a particular course of action.

Class Culture and Mobility

As we have emphasized in the foregoing discussion, cultural differences between classes have received fairly extensive theoretical and empirical attention. Yet the relationship of social mobility to class culture has been almost totally ignored by sociological literature on stratification. A small body of literature has appeared on the "consequences" of mobility, some of which deals with psychological problems experienced by the mobile individual in making the transition from one class culture to another. But no comprehensive discussion has appeared.

Nevertheless, the author feels that this is not really too surprising or inconsistent, in light of the current state of stratification theory. The lack of literature on culture and mobility is symptomatic of a broader problem. In addition to the classical debates over the justice and inevitability of stratification, contemporary sociology is also enmeshed in a controversy over the reality of class differences in themselves. The phenomenon of social mobility has never been thoroughly integrated into theoretical discussion of stratification. In the current context, however, the meaning and functions of social mobility have been further confused by the tendency to equate mobility with social fluidity or the open society. In current commentary, mobility is not interpreted as connected to the stratification process (as a mode of allocation) but rather as a symptom of the general decline of class differences or as a force undermining stratification. Hence, the great concern in modern sociology with empirical research on the rate of mobility.

Before we can speak meaningfully of the relation between culture and mobility, therefore, we must attempt to clarify this controversy regarding its role in contemporary stratification. This task shall be undertaken in three steps: In the following pages we shall discuss (1) the state of current stratification theory and its approach to mobility, (2) the author's own approach to the relation between mobility and stratification, and finally (3) the relationship of mobility to class culture and to class barriers. Hopefully, as we proceed, the reader will understand the need for this lengthy and polemical preface to our substantive discussion of mobility and culture. There is a great deal of ground which must be cleared in order to place our own efforts in clearer perspective.

Current Stratification Theory

"It is both remarkable and slightly ludicrous," T.H. Marshall once stated, "that it should prove necessary to carry out the most elaborate research in order to discover what the shape of stratification is in modern societies."[1][2] Marshall, like other students of stratification, seems to be referring to some hypothetical time in the past when class barriers were more rigid and when the standing of a man with respect to others could be determined in a simple and unproblematic fashion. And he, like many others, has compared present society to some previous period when the lines of demarcation between classes, based on wealth, power, and life style, were presumably matters of common knowledge. Our knowledge of the past is probably poorer than that of the present, however. And such statements may stand up better as a symptom of intellectual confusion than as a defensible generalization about social history. Whatever may have been the "shape of stratification" in past societies, it is manifestly clear that there is little consensus, either among laymen or sociologists, about the meaning or "tangible" social reality of class differences in contemporary society. There is in some quarters a nagging suspicion that we are trying to apply outworn words or concepts to institutions that have changed their fundamental character and that we can no longer fully understand by using older terms.

One would anticipate that sooner or later students of stratification will produce some analyses of those processes of social change which have rendered older notions inadequate. Currently, however, most analyses of social stratification still retain a taxonomic character, being based on description of static processes rather than on an explanation of those forces which bring about changes in the nature of stratification. The major effort of contemporary stratification theorists has been focused on amending or modifying older ideas based on classical theories, rather than on attempting a comprehensive reformulation of concepts. As a consequence, current images of social class are highly ambivalent. On the one hand, it is stressed that the classical conception of sharply layered differences between classes is no longer relevant; on the other hand, it is held that class still "makes a difference" for a wide range of attitudinal and behavioral phenomena. In contemporary sociological literature the most widely presented picture of social class is that which portrays class differences as located on a continuum. Sharp unidimensional cleavages between classes based on economic interest are seen as being replaced by multi-dimensional "hierarchies of status," in which a number of important criteria contribute to a single assessment of social positions. Modern society has become far too complex and pluralistic, it is argued, and competing loyalties have become too demanding to allow the use of any single, or simple calculus for determining one's social class. It is further asserted that the ties that may have previously bound men to distinct class groups, which maintained common norms, values, and identities, have been frayed by the social changes accompanying the later stages of industrial development. Various social forces have been cited as contributing to this development: the gradual abolition of any residual legal distinctions between classes, i.e., the evolution of the concept of citizenship, and the increasing importance of educational credentials. Many other factors associated with modernization have been pointed out as influencing the disintegration of class. All these changes taken together, it is asserted, have tended to increase the mobility and permeability between classes, thereby also reducing the social and attitudinal distance between them.

Despite the wealth of commentary of a general nature, however, no comprehensive analysis of the significance of these separate phenomena and historical occurrences has appeared in the sociological literature. Instead the major part of our energies as sociologists has gone into a debate about the "reality" of class differences—a debate that appears to be irreconcilable on the theoretical level and untestable on the empirical. In the context of this debate the classical concept of class has been reified to the extent that it is regarded as the only point of departure for a discussion of social stratification or social inequality. Few, if any, critics have considered other points of departure. The form of this debate has been most succinctly described by Dennis Wrong, who borrows some terms from a philosophical argument of far older vintage, which once served as a time-consuming preoccupation for medieval scholars:

Sociologists who argue that social class is no longer a useful concept take what has been called a "realist" position regarding the existence of classes. They are committed, that is, to the view that, in the words of one of them, social classes "are groups possessed both of real and vital common economic interests and of a group-consciousness of their general position in the social scale." Their contention that social classes are disappearing in industrial societies rests on the failure to locate such groups. The opposing "nominalist" point of view regards classes as a useful classificatory concept for grouping together for purposes of analysis individuals who possess certain attributes in common, whether or not they feel any unity or are even aware of having something in common with their fellow class members. The sociologist, in effect, creates the "class structures" he describes which are no more than a means of organizing his data on variations in human behavior. He may find several different class systems or pyramids of stratification within a society, none of which are perceived or experienced as collective realities, as real social groups, by their members.[13]

In general the realist vs. nominalist debate described above has led sociologists away from the enterprise of uncovering the *structural* bases of social stratification or social inequality. As Wrong suggests above, neither position in this debate contributes anything towards such a goal. The modern apparatus of survey research, when employed in the service of the nominalist (or operational) point of view, has done nothing to clarify the conceptual status of social classes. The realist position, on the other hand, is far too rigid, acknowledging only one particular form of social inequality in contemporary society,—in the absence of which society becomes "classless" or egalitarian.

Marxist theory emphasized that classes must have a certain type of group structure. Therefore, stratification was defined as the hierarchical ranking of collectivities that have certain specified organizational characteristics. At least four important structural characteristics of such groups were distinguished: (1) They had differential amounts of control over the distribution of those scarce social and material resources which formed the basis for privilege and power; (2) they were structurally continuous and remained in the same hierarchical order for several generations; (3) the social mechanism that insured the structural continuity of classes was hereditary transmission of power and privilege; (4) the members of each specific class group were conscious of their common position and aware of their collective identity as distinguished from other classes. Each facet of the above definition was to some degree equally important, since together they constituted a comprehensive explanation for the structure of social inequality.

Contemporary empirical research, however, has failed to substantiate the existence of at least two of the above prerequisites. First, self-awareness of class position has been almost impossible to establish as classically defined. Second, the current, empirically demonstrated high rates of intergenerational mobility between classes have made it difficult to support the notion that class structure is maintained solely by inheritance of either economic or occupational position. The structural continuity of class groups from the nineteenth century to the present has not been challenged, although historical trends towards stratum mobility of the agricultural working class and the entrepreneurial middle class have been noted.

The empirical invalidation of certain aspects of the concept of social class has left stratification theory in a somewhat schizophrenic state. The failure to locate all the specific characteristics of social class outlined in classical theory seems to have led to a general abdication of the search for group structure as operative in the stratification process. Current research and commentary attempts to distinguish class groups according to external outlines, emphasizing description and neglecting structural supports. Class boundaries are used in a heuristic fashion to organize data on variations in attitudes and social behavior; and the literature is replete with generalizations about the so-called effects of social stratification. But the underlying structure that actually stratifies these effects, or social artifacts, remains hidden. The vast amount of empirical data gathered in this manner are doubltess not without significance. However, the failure of contemporary researchers to locate the structural prerequisites set out by classical theory does not mean that the accumulated evidence cannot support alternative theoretical assumptions about the structure of the contemporary stratification system.

Most important, from our standpoint, though, are the implications of this impasse in stratification theory for the study of mobility. In current thinking, mobility is associated with the reduction of inequality and the leveling of cultural barriers between classes. A positive analysis of mobility as a regular component of all stratification systems becomes very difficult when such a point of view is maintained. From such a standpoint mobility always has a negative impact on stratification.

For classical theory the major axis of stratification was to be found in a hierarchically arranged series of integral class groups. Current evidence regarding class consciousness and mobility, as we have already emphasized, makes it difficult to support the existence of such autonomous groups. However, social inequalities do persist. Although trends towards equalization have been noted, the distribution of income, occupation, and political position retains a pyramidal profile. We may refer to the groupings or aggregates thereby produced as classes for convenience. But the concept of class does not adequately portray the social reality referred to. In an attempt to bridge the gap between current social reality and classical theory Dennis Wrong has suggested that inequality persists in modern society without social stratification.[14] However, social stratification has a more general meaning, and his statement might be more acceptable if reformulated to say that social inequality persists in the absence of social classes. The concept of a stratum certainly does not imply the necessity for self-conscious awareness by its incumbents, nor does it exclude the idea of permeability. It is this concept of stratum which we will employ throughout this volume (even when the term "social class" is used).

We could proposed several alternative explanations of stratification in modern society. For example, rather than being rooted in autonomous class groups, stratification in modern society is based, we might assert, on broader institutions—institutions that are, although societywide in scope, themselves not strata, but that operate to distribute positions, individuals, and rewards. This type of explanation has been proposed by Dahrendorf, who refers to the basic locus of stratification in modern society as the "imperatively coordinated association," a term first employed by Max Weber to refer to large scale groups.[15] However, the task of elaborating a theory of stratification is beyond the scope of this volume. The point of the foregoing discussion has been to illustrate the place of mobility in current thinking about stratification. As we shall see in the following pages, once social strata, or social inequalities, are accepted as the framework for discussion, mobility can be seen not as a contrary force to social stratification, but as one of its major supporting elements in modern society.

Mobility and Social Stratification

There was never, of course, any real logical contradiction between high rates of mobility and pronounced status inequality. "The class systems of the past," writes Wrong,

have undeniably been hereditary, though permitting sufficient mobility to justify distinguishing them from caste systems. But need this be so in the future? Historically, biological continuity has been the major means of preserving internal solidarity and the distinctive ethos of classes from generation to generation, but is it necessarily the only possible means? George Orwell wrote: "the essence of oligarchical rule is not father to son inheritance, but the persistence of a certain way of life imposed by the dead upon the living. A ruling group is a ruling group so long as it can nominate its successors. Who wields power is not important, provided that the hierarchical structure remains always the same." Orwell was writing of political elites, but his point that the permanence of structure need not depend on biological continuity may well have a broader relevance.[16]

In a stratification system dominated by a high degree of bureaucratization, mobility reinforces the stratification process. For under such a system the more mobility, the more power that the system has for introducing social distinction based on nonhereditary characteristics. Even certain nonbiologically transmitted attributes of the individual are suppressed. The personal needs, social origin, and personality of the individual are all ultimately subordinated to the institutional "need" of large scale organizations for an efficient means of staffing personnel.

From the standpoint of organizational imperatives, expedient recruitment must insure the maintenance of both hierarchical rank and social differentiation. Social differentiation refers to that division of labor which is essential to insure the coordination and specialization of work—which in turn enables the completion of a complex series of tasks, either productive or administrative. In the past and in the present the most efficient way of doing this has been to differentiate occupational roles. The higher the degree of differentiation in the occupational structure, however, the greater the problem of recruitment. Given demographic fluctuation, changes in instrumental technology, and other sorts of organizational problems, hereditary allocation of occupational roles and familial socialization become completely inadequate to handle the selection of individuals for specific positions. Because of current organizational imperatives the most efficient means of recruitment to such roles is through postfamilial socialization to their technical and social requirements, without regard to biological continuity. Mobility is thus efficient from the standpoint of the work organization, which is concerned, as a whole, with insuring that individuals fill appropriate roles and that they perform predictably in them.

The need of large-scale organizations for hierarchical staffing or lines of authority also stems from the requirement of administrative expediency. Such expediency involves centralization of decision making and the extension throughout the organization of delimited areas and levels of authority and responsibility. Here again the most efficient method of allocation or recruitment to hierarchical roles is through postfamilial socialization. Various human products of such socialization, such as the corporate man, are no doubt already familiar to the reader from literary descriptions. The emergence of such types illustrates that predictability and compatibility are more important requirements for recruitment than is technical competence. But these requirements, too, can be learned. For this reason mobility, as opposed to hereditary allocation, is frequently the most efficient method of staffing hierarchical roles. The mobile man is frequently the one most loyal to his office, or position, and least likely to respond to the outside loyalties of family, peer group, or class. An excellent example of this principle is the history of the Jannisaries, the elite guard of the sultans under the Ottoman empire. They were recruited by being kidnapped from their families in rural Greece and were as adolescents trained under the tutelage of the palace. Not surprisingly they rarely wavered in their loyalty to the sultanate throughout the history of the empire.

Mobility is one response to large-scale and regular dislocations in the occupational structure. Drastic changes in the division of labor, whether due to modifications in technology, political imperatives, or demographic changes, frequently have a direct and negative effect on the allocation process. A technological innovation frequently renders whole categories of individuals unemployable and they may subsequently be defined as unskilled. Moreover, this can occur at both the top and bottom levels of the status hierarchy. As an example one need only look to the rapid rise and decline of needs for engineers in the 1950s and 1960s. When an individual via his ability, skill, or former occupational role has no claim on a position within some institutional setting in our society, he thus becomes structurally marginal and must be allocated somewhere else.

According to prevailing American ideology, structurally displaced persons are capable of exercising individual initiative in finding new positions, and ideally they should. Nevertheless, however much we believe in them, individual solutions cannot be relied upon to deal with collective problems of such magnitude. Structural displacement of old positions and structural creation of new positions are not random phenomena which are due solely to fluctuations in the economic cycle and which will correct themselves over the long term: Structural displacement of unskilled manual labor by skilled manual and white-collar labor has occurred systematically throughout the course of the industrial revolution and especially within the last 60 years. The staffing problems posed by such structural dislocations have not been solved by the accumulation of individual initiative. On the contrary, this problem has been dealt with by the evolution in industry and government of institutional arms which are primarily concerned with allocation. In industry such allocation arms are referred to as "personnel departments." These undoubtedly play an important role, but the major proportion of occupational allocation (insofar as differentiation of skill and recruitment for hierarchical positions are involved) has been carried out increasingly by educational institutions. Work organizations must rely upon the educational process for comprehensive minimal socialization to job requirements such as functional literacy. Tests of competence and the training involved in the educational process are not as important, however, as the institutionalization of allocation as a separate and functionally isolated sphere. It has frequently been held that the educational credential conveys nothing about the individual's competence to perform a given task, and frequently bears no relation to his performance on the job for which it qualifies him. On the other hand, educational credentialization does solve the allocation problem by giving certain individuals the exclusive right to compete for a range of positions and to legitimize their claims to specific occupations.

Credentialization, therefore, reduces the complexity of the allocation problem. The institutionalization of allocation as a separate arm permits great flexibility in meeting the staffing needs of a wide variety of institutions. Within each work organization decisions regarding claims of individuals to given occupational positions do not need to be solved independently. Large-scale changes in technology, such as the recent massive increase in agricultural and industrial productivity, have had numerous effects on the staffing of work organizations. Such changes can be accommodated easily by processing large numbers of individuals through educational institutions that prepare them for the differentiation of function and the hierarchical positions they will occupy when employed. The flexibility of the educational credential and its vagueness are in large part responsible for the success of the educational institution as an allocative mechanism. The credential satisfies the need for organizational mobilization of individuals, but it does not establish absolute skill requirements for occupations or absolute claims to specific positions. In other words, the credential is like a market commodity that acquires more or less value according to fluctuations in demand and supply. Should the supply of individuals for certain occupations exceed the demand, the credential can be devalued or be replaced with less widely distributed criteria. On the other hand, should the demand for some positions exceed the supply, either existing credentials can be revalued or new ones created. Thus the structure of credentialization is always hierarchical, but in a relative sense—it is a rehearsal of the distributive inequality of the occupational structure.

The purpose of the foregoing analysis was simply to illustrate the close connection between mobility and the structural characteristics of those institutions peculiar to modern industrial societies. We did not disprove the assumption that mobility may, to some extent, weaken the barriers between classes or otherwise reduce class distinctions. We only tried to demonstrate that high-mobility rates do not necessarily result in the reduction of inequalities. The relatively unequal distribution of psychological, material, and social rewards may remain largely unaffected. Mobility may actually serve the function of making these inequalities more palatable. Furthermore, the parameters of inequality may be more important than class barriers, as conceived of by classical theories of stratification, in describing our contemporary stratification system.

The relative lack of class consciousness, as we have already observed, is frequently commented on by sociologists and other commentators of the American scene and cited as evidence that some of the "group properties" of social class are absent in our society. What has been overlooked in such commentary is that people in most industrial countries are oriented not toward separate and distinct class groups of which they count themselves members, but rather towards the prevailing system of inequality. This prevailing system of inequality undoubtedly includes mobility.

In modern society, intergenerational continuity of occupation, the primary determinant of class position in traditional social structures, is a relatively rare phenomenon. At the very least, almost every individual must expect some degree of lateral mobility relative to his parents, due to the complexity and instability of the contemporary occupational structure. Vertical mobility is less frequent but still very important. Because of the pyramidal structure of the stratification system, large numbers of the incumbents of a particular stratum will, by the simple laws of social circulation, have been recruited from other strata. Statistically, inheritance of class position and mobility both play relatively equal roles in determining social position between two generations. But over the long run, say three to four generations, projections of current mobility rates show diminishing influence for the process of inheritance; over this time span almost every family line shows signficant discontinuities.[17] Since generalizations concerning the functioning of stratification systems in industrial societies should run over the entire period of development, we must pay some attention to such statistical formulations. Even in the short run, however, the social psychological impact of mobility should not be underestimated. Inheritance is important in determining class position between generations. However, individual consciousness may be oriented most strongly to that aspect of the stratification system which is both most problematic and a source of instability in one's personal career or in that of one's children. Specialization and continual shifts in the occupational structure make direct inheritance of occupations in nonproprietary areas difficult to guarantee. In the popular conception, distinctions between lateral and vertical mobility are not so finely drawn. The lack of assured inheritance of parental occupation and class position taken together forces the individual to consider a variety of career alternatives as opposed to a fixed continuous pattern. Thus the individual is naturally oriented to the most uncertain aspects of the allocation process. Even if inheritance of class position is possible it is rarely secured before one's perception of the class system has congealed.

Thus it may be said that individuals are oriented to the entire mobility process itself—rather than to class of present membership as determined by parental status—and to the distributive inequality which is the outcome of that process. The personal orientation of the individual is focused upon obtaining a competitive advantage in the recruitment process, rather than on inheriting a specific position. Considerable inheritance is achieved because the family provides a base for informal advantages and socialization. Still there are few who would consider inheritance as automatic. The son of a professional, for example, must partake of a long and frequently rigorous formal education in order to inherit a position of comparable social standing to that of his parent. Even then, changes in the occupational structure may reduce his chances, and dislocations are difficult to forecast. Furthermore, while there are many institutionalized channels for mobilizing individuals needed for newly created occupations, these avenues are generally based on intergenerational mobility (via education, for example). Also, there are few mechanisms for facilitating the maintenance of class position by those who are directly dislocated: It may be difficult to recuperate from the interruption of a specific career, for either because of advanced age, or advanced specialization in occupational role, displaced individuals are frequently poor candidates for other positions.

The great changes in the occupational structure which have marked the course of the industrial revolution have involved considerable mobility. A large portion of that movement has been lateral rather than vertical—involving, for instance, structural elimination of agricultural occupations and their replacement with employment in the manual sectors of industry. Even so, the impact of such changes on popular perceptions of stratification has been profound. They are certainly an important component of the average man's view of the occupational structure as a fluid entity, involvitg competitive rather than secure claims to positions. The conventional expectation of instability also works to the advantage of a highly industrialized, technologically advanced economy. Without such instability, the mobilization of large numbers of individuals into new occupational roles created by technological changes or by new allocations of economic surplus would be relatively difficult.

Self-awareness of class position, a feeling by the individual that he shares common interests, life chances, and fate with his fellow class incumbents, cannot come about if a class is not a stable membership group over the span of at least three or four generations. Under conditions of moderate to high mobility the objective conditions for such communal sentiments are easily destroyed. Classical theory presented social-class groups, or at least the working class, as collectively entrapped in their positions; this was both evidence of their oppression and the source of their potential strength. Only because a class group was collectively entrapped could the political solution of collective enfranchise-ment become the logical historical outcome of their position. Structurally, the common identity of social classes was based not so much on common institutions, but on inescapable positions of individuals within the economic and political hierarchy.

The maintenance of inequality in modern society does not depend on the cross-generational maintenance of class membership through collective entrap-ment. Inequality in contemporary society is distributive. That is to say, it is of little consequence which individuals are occupants of specific groups of positions as long as the hierarchical distribution of economic, political, and psychological rewards remains the same. There is no contradiction between high rates of intergenerational mobility and high levels of distributive inequality. From this standpoint, stratification can be likened to a massive sorting process wherein individuals are selected for hierarchically arranged positions. The reason that sociologists have clung to inheritance as a mechanism for explaining inequality is that within the context of classical theory it was the only logical way of explaining the persistence of class distinctions, and one aspect of the basic confusion in *contemporary* stratification theory results from the failure to consider supplementary modes of allocation.

Mobility and Class Culture

Large-scale mobility is not inconsistent with the maintenance of sharp class boundaries based on cultural distinctions or status characteristics. Whether mobility tends to weaken such boundaries depends entirely upon the character of the mobility process and how it is institutionalized. In many stratification systems there is only a single avenue to mobility, carefully controlled by a dominant elite. In such a system individuals are selected for interstratum mobility according to a rigid and unified set of criteria, which are designed to sift out all those not possessing the desired "elite" traits. Under such circumstances distinctions between class groups will be conspicuous and easily maintained. As we have already pointed out, the maintenance of cultural barriers between classes does not require that individuals be selected according to background.

If, on the other hand, large-scale mobility is accompanied by a relaxation of the standards of selection for class membership, then the cultural characteristics that differentiate classes may undergo a leveling process. This was clearly the case in seventeenth-century France, where most noble titles could be obtained by purchase as well as by birthright. Leveling of class distinctions is thus facilitated by the introduction of multiple criteria for class membership. If high income as well as distinct life style or education were to enable one to enter the upper class, then the force of any one of these distinguishing criteria would be diminished. In any stratification system, however, there seem to be observable limits beyond which the process of leveling cannot extend. Wherever there is a small number of highly ranked positions there is a tendency to introduce selective criteria of a fairly unitary nature in order to maintain social control.

Undoubtedly mobility, as a mode of allocation, has a profound impact on cultural stratification in all stratification systems. The consideration of mobility as an important aspect of stratification has many further implications for an analysis of class differences. Mobility is a dynamic phenomenon, involving changes in the ranking of positions, aggregates, and persons. The conception of class culture presented in the beginning of this chapter implied a static perspective on social class. Those who view objective inequalities as the source of cultural differences are inclined to emphasize the collective entrapment of the class group from the Marxian perspective. Those who see differential socialization as the source of subculture, or cultural, variation are likely to emphasize inheritance and familial socialization. Both perspectives involve a somewhat static view of social class. If we wish to consider the impact of mobility, we must inevitably adopt a more dynamic conception of class culture and the institutions supporting it, since existing theories make it difficult to talk about mobility.

The differential socialization hypothesis is undoubtedly the consensual view among sociologists of class culture. The majority of descriptions, whatever their level of theoretical sophistication, emphasize that the distribution of values in different classes comes about by early learning in the family context. Thus it may be best if we focus our analysis of mobility and culture on the problem of socialization.

As pointed out earlier, a theoretical concomitant of the early socialization hypothesis is the conception of culture as an external and compulsive entity. From this view the child is born into a world which he has not made, as an amorphous, pliable entity. As he moved toward maturity his early experiences shape him in an irrevocable fashion:

In the conventional development model, the very young organism is presented as a fluid, polymorphous, multi-potential and perverse, susceptible to suggestion and rudimentary of will. Each interaction between organism and environment modifies the shape the organism takes into the next encounter. The earlier a situation imposes itself, the more likely it is to add an enduring element, partly because early learning is general enough to escape outright contradiction in subsequent particular experience. ... Thus the organism acquires an adult's efficiency at the price of adult versatility. New ideas compete on unequal terms with old ones, because the latter have a place in the structure and have been used to direct behavior.[18]

From the standpoint of both dominant value theory and subculture theory it is the early socialization process which insures the primacy of a unitary hierarchy of values in determining the later behavior of the individual. Dominant value theory would argue that basically everyone is socialized to similar values at an early age. Although the individual may encounter obstacles in achieving those values, his behavior will generally be explicable in terms of the conflict between his values and the means available for attaining them. Similarly subculture theory would argue that the observed differences in behavior between classes are the result of differential socialization in the family context, and that because of the primacy of family socialization over later experiences the individual will manifest both behavior and values congruent with his early experiences. Although the reference to the family context occurs most frequently in the literature, it is rarely included in explicit formulations. The theory as a whole is never explicitly formulated and constitutes a kind of "middle range" conception.

Early crystallization of personality is an impediment, however, to the explanation of social change. In a relatively unchanging traditional society, family socialization might be very adequate to prepare the individual for adult life, for the very stability of social arrangements would allow the family to articulate the socialization process with the requirements of the adult role. In modern society, however, the discontinuity between family and occupational structure, which has become extremely complex, is too great to permit it to function in this way. In a rigid system of stratification, where movement between strata is at a minimum, the family would probably provide effective socialization for the limited variety of statuses available to the individual. For in this case each class would be, to a large extent, a "separate world," within which the major social process (including the processes of status allocation and socialization) would be carried out independently. Modern society, by contrast, is characterized by relative permeability of barriers between strata. Movement from class to class is not only possible but very frequent.

Mobility statistics indicate that a large number of the incumbents of any particular class level were recruited from other levels. A large number of studies, conducted in many different industrialized societies, report consistent correlations of .4 to .5 between father's and son's occupation.[19] In another type of study, researchers have recently employed Markov chain projections to determine the precise consequences of a given mobility rate over a three-generation period.[20] When, for example, the generational transition matrix corresponding to a .5 correlation coefficient is multiplied by itself n times, the effect of parental status disappears almost entirely in the generation corresponding to great grandchildren and is barely noticeable in the generation corresponding to grandchildren ($r = .12$). Further empirical examples would be redundant. It suffices to say that, in terms of the available statistical evidence, in the long run, everyone is mobile.

The prevalence of large-scale social mobility makes the question of class differentiation in values much more problematic. If value cleavages between classes do exist, then one must ask: How do upwardly and downwardly mobile individuals acquire the values of different strata? Under such circumstances, it becomes important not only to provide descriptive evidence regarding the prevalence of class values but also to establish the social mechanisms by which such differences come into being.

It is clear that if individuals move relative to their stratum of origin, primary socialization in the family context cannot be the total determinant of cultural differences between classes. If the turnover of class incumbents is as high as our statistics would suggest, then in the long run some other mechanisms may be instrumental. That cross-sectional studies have indicated some differences in cultural orientations by social class does not imply that these differences were produced by transmission from generation to generation in the family context.

Once the primacy of early socialization in generating value differences is questioned there are a number of other alternatives which come to the fore. One of the more plausible of these is that the objective circumstances of a man's work and his occupational career will effect his values or general orientation towards life. Given the increasing number of highly specialized occupations the individual is rarely if ever completely prepared or knowledgeable about the work situation he will enter as an adult.

By far the most important force in maintaining the cultural segregation' of social classes, however, are the changes in the relative weight and role of various agencies of socialization which have taken place in industrialized societies. The family's role in the socialization process, as Parsons has commented, has been largely supplanted by the school on the "formal level and the peer group on the informal level."[21] Indeed, the impact of the shift from the family to the school of a major portion of the responsibility for childhood socialization has received considerable comment in sociological literature. Yet, the weight and function of such secondary mechanisms of socialization (school and peer group) has not been so thoroughly evaluated. In the great proportion of writings primary socialization (or those patterns laid down at the earliest stage of life in the family context) is given the central role. Secondary socialization, on the other hand, is frequently conceived of as supplementary to, or expressive of, earlier experiences. Many researchers, for example, have described the high-achievement emphasis of middle-class families and the subsequent high performance of their offspring in school as parts of a single continuous pattern in which earliest conditioning plays the most important part.

But the school, the peer group, and other intermediary agencies of socialization do carry considerable independent weight. The impact of these types of secondary socialization lies primarily in the essential discontinuity between the world of discourse of the adult and that of the family. The former is organized on the basis of extrafamilial solidarities and achievements. Consequently there must be some effective mode of transition between the two, since the family is generally not equipped to prepare the child for all the roles he must play in the larger society. The school as a socializing agency that reaches from early childhood to early adulthood must fulfill the focal socializing function.

The cumulative weight that has come to rest upon the educational process is summarized in the following statement by Parsons:

To assess the significance of this pattern, let us look at its place in the socialization of the individual. Entering the system of formal education is the child's first major step out of primary involvement in his family of orientation. Within the family certain foundations of this motivational system have been laid down. But the only characteristic fundamental to later roles which has been clearly "determined" and psychologically stamped in by that time is the sex role. The postoedipal child enters the system of formal education clearly categorized as boy or girl, but beyond that his role is not yet differentiated. *The process of selection, by which persons will select and be selected for categories of roles, is yet to take place.*[22]

It must be said, of course, that the influence of the family does not end here, and that there are always important predispositions laid down in the family context that will affect the child's career in school. But the most important thing is that the family can no longer monopolize the socialization process; the influence of the family and the school must be conceived of as being interactively related. That the school is a selective and evaluative agency independent of the family and that educational achievements are a powerful determinant of subsequent social status give the school considerable power of determining the nature of cultural segregation in future cohorts of adults.

The school serves two types of socializing functions which might be termed as *instrumental* and *moral.*[23] The instrumental role of the school is that which one encounters most frequently in sociological or pedagogical descriptions. The school is instrumental because modern-day society requires large numbers of individuals with special skills acquired only through extended education. The moral role, on the other hand, involves the development of character and other qualities or values considered desirable. Formally, the technical and social aspects of learning are kept separate, but in reality they are closely related. There is no doubt that learning in the cognitive sense involves implicit commitment to certain kinds of values.

Both the learning of values and the learning of instrumental skills take place independent of the family. The family can provide important reinforcement, but on the whole it is relatively powerless to alter the character of the socialization process except through some kind of political action. For imposed upon children within the context of the school is a common set of tasks and activities which is, as Parsons has commented, "compared to other task-areas, strikingly undifferentiated." The family, though, can contribute significantly to the child's performance by providing needed motivation or cultural environment, but it cannot provide a similarly intensive learning experience.

Sociologists are fond of commenting that the middle and upper classes avail themselves far more frequently of educational opportunities in this country than do the lower classes—a fact which is frequently cited as evidence of class selectiveness inherent in the educational system. One must not overlook, however, that the lower strata are more populous than the upper ones. While the lower classes are underrepresented relative to their size they constitute a large proportion of college students in absolute numbers. Current statistics indicate that approximately 40 percent of the students in American universities are from manual-labor backgrounds. Considering the superior cultural advantages of having been born in a family where both parents are highly educated, it would seem that the school is remarkably effective at equalizing these differences to the point that the majority of the students receiving elite education in our society are in fact not from elite backgrounds.

Parsons and other authors have characterized the educational process as part of the "general cultural upgrading" of our society and see it as leading to a general commitment to a common set of cultural values shared by the majority of citizens.[24] Within the context of the school they see selection and differential reward of ability. But these processes, they assert, can only operate in an homogenous value climate, in which everyone values achievement. Thus it is implied that, while considerable selection of individuals takes place on the basis of their instrumental skills, people are not sifted and sorted according to their values. Their "capacity to act" according to these values may differ but not their degree of endorsement.[25]

Such a point of view overlooks the implications of the close relationship between the evaluative and technical aspects of the learning process to which we have already referred. The social values so frequently described as conducive to achievement also appear to be a part of the normative description of that same activity, and thus subject to the same processes of sorting and sifting as academic ability. For example it may be argued that such values as individualism, self-reliance, and deferred gratification are part of the overall value climate which stimulates academic achievement in our society. However, it seems equally plausible that the individual who is a high-academic achiever would endorse all of these values to a greater degree than the average. By selecting for academic achievement in the schools, we are also selecting for a broad range of attendant behavior and auxiliary values. In actual fact the school does not merely select for scholastic ability alone but for a whole host of cultural and social characteristics present in those who see academic achievement as meaningful. Academic ability may be only the most external manifestation of such characteristics. Such values, of course, may be acquired through familial socialization. Nevertheless, the school does provide a separate base for the internalization of values and for the evaluation of those "performances" important to determining the individual's selection for future occupational status. The oft replicated research-finding that upwardly mobile lower-class individuals and their families overconform to middle-class values may be, in fact, primarily due to their desire to come favorably through the cultural aspect of the selective process as instituted by the school.

Thus it is the school and other agencies of secondary socialization which exert the strongest influence on the values of the mobile individual. Primary socialization for mobility is also an important factor. Lower-class families, for example, frequently manage to impart both aspirations and values appropriate to higher-class membership. Such efforts, however, are successful primarily because the school exists as a separate basis for evaluation, and indeed the strivings of lower-class parents frequently take into account the availability of education as an intermediary step to mobility.

Yet, the relative impact of competing agencies of socialization in promoting the cultural segregation of classes has not been put to any rigorous empirical test. We have little if any evidence about psychological and social mechanisms which produce differential learning of cultural values within the school itself. In attempting to isolate secondary mechanisms of socialization which could account for the values of mobile as well as stationary individuals we have concentrated on the school environment. The reason for this emphasis was not the fact that the school has demonstrably greater impact on cultural values than any other agency of socialization. Nor has it been shown either empirically or theoretically that most students do not enter school with many of their cultural predispositions already determined, although it may seem more plausible that they do not. Rather, the primary reason for our emphasis on the school is its decisive impact of social selection. The school is the primary formal agency of status allocation in our society. The individual's performance in school and the amount of education he acquires are important determinants of his class membership.

Most studies of stratification variables conclude that in the long run educational attainment is the most important determinant of occupational position. Thus, the types of values or achievements selected in the school context are more likely to be associated with subsequent class differences than those which the educational process does not favor. Insofar as there is a lack of value consensus within classes, individuals may be marked for mobility because they possess divergent values favored by the educational system. On the other hand, the values that the individual derives from his class of origin may be renounced in favor of others which will enable him to fulfill his aspirations for educational attainment. By setting up its own set of priorities the school can force the mobile individual to accommodate his values to those favored by social selection.

2 Social Selection and Educational Structure

A number of basic theoretical issues in the area of social stratification have been presented and discussed. The reader is now aware of several areas in this body of theory which have been inadequately conceptualized and inadequately researched. The basic purpose of this volume is presentation of the results of an empirical investigation in which the competing aspects of current theories are evaluated. The task of an original synthesis of theoretical constructs is outside of the province of a research report. This author realizes the need, however, for close interaction between theory and empirical research. And, wherever the research results justify reevaluation of existing theory an attempt will be made to provide a plausible scheme of interpretation. Since the research design utilized in this study brings together some competing propositions that, in previous research, have been segmentally investigated, there is no doubt that the pattern of the results will enable us to make some redefinition of current theories based upon the weight given by the empirical evidence to one or the other set of theoretical constructs.

Earlier it was emphasized that the usefulness of class as an object of sociological investigation seems to rest very heavily upon the hypothesized relationship between class and culture. The basic focus of this study is the investigation of the relationship between social class and values (as the differentiated component of culture). In this investigation we are not interested, however, in social class merely as a static entity, for any investigation of the relationship between class and culture must incorporate the process of mobility as an axis of value formation. Because of the larger turnover of class incumbents in modern society the proposition of class cleavages in general culture cannot be supported without showing that upward and downwardly mobile individuals acquire the values of the classes to which they are moving. It is also incumbent upon the researcher to show that such value acquisition is the result of stable processes of socialization or selection.

The ideal way to examine the relationship between class, mobility, and values would be through a longitudinal investigation, that is, where the individual is followed from birth to adulthood. Since mobility encompasses the entire life cycle, only in this way could we hold constant its effects and separate them from those of class as a static membership group. It would then also be possible to determine to what extent class cleavages in value orientations are the result of passive transmission from one generation to the next, and to what extent such cleavages are the result of later socialization or selection for mobility.

29

Unfortunately such longitudinal studies are rarely feasible. The alternative adopted in this study was to examine in the life cycle of the individual that stage which was most crucial from the standpoint of mobility: the period of adolescence. The study reported in the following pages deals with a group of Dutch secondary school students whose median age is approximately sixteen and who are all approaching the termination of their school careers.

There are several advantages to studying individuals at this stage of their life careers. At this period many of the major mobility determinants—school, family, ability, personal aspirations—are not yet disentangled from each other, enabling us to examine the interaction and relative impact of these factors. Also, this is the stage when an individual must both manifest those attributes which will make him mobile and make the crucial decisions which will affect his future career. The decisions he makes at this stage of his life will have permanent and inescapable consequences.

There are, though, disadvantages to the choice of an adolescent sample. Since the adult status has not yet been assumed, objective mobility cannot be studied directly. Under such circumstances future mobility can only be examined in terms of aspirations or ambitions. Similarly the interaction of cultural values with the mobility process can only be observed in terms of their relationship to projected future status. The impact of later experiences of success and failure cannot be established.

Such limitations and their influence upon the range of generalizations we can make will be discussed from time to time as it becomes appropriate. The remainder of this chapter, however, will be taken up with the presentation of the research design.

Questionnaire methodology was employed in this study. The limitations and advantages of the questionnaire method have been well documented and there is no need to elaborate upon them here. Specific descriptions and justifications of questionnaire items used in this study are deferred until the presentation of the research results in the following chapters; nevertheless, at this point it *will* be useful to delineate the general categories of variables used so that they can be referred to meaningfully in the presentation of the research design.

Three major categories of variables were measured by means of the questionnaire: social-class position, values, and mobility aspirations. The interrelationships between these variables in various contexts form the main theme of our analysis.

Social-class position was measured in terms of the occupational and educational level of the student's parents. These two variables were used to assess the impact of the student's milieu of origin. The social group or social reality to which the variables correspond will be referred to as "class of origin."

· *Values* were measured in the same manner as has been employed in the past in many attitude or opinion scales. Statements that tapped a specific value dimension were assembled from various sources. Students were asked to indicate their opinions about these statements in the questionnaire. There are, of course, many ways of measuring social values. Values may be inferred from other cultural objects or from behavior. A few of the limitations and advantages of our specific methods are discussed in Chapter 5.

Mobility aspirations were measured by direct questions concerning the student's desired level of material, educational, and occupational achievement. These queries were intended to tap the student's assessment of his future class position. It is difficult to know how realistic such aspirations are at this age. Internal evidence from analysis of our results indicates that the aspirations of Dutch student's were indeed oriented toward concrete possibilities. Other longitudinal studies, also, have indicated a high correlation between such aspirations and subsequent occupational status. It should be mentioned in passing, though, that all measures of subjective class position at any stage of the life cycle have important sociological implications, however unrealistic they may seem in terms of objective life chances, for the subjective class assessment of an adult, as pointed out by Hyman and others, frequently has more influence on his behavior and attitudes than does his current objective position. The lower-class parent, for example, may instill in his children the attitudes appropriate to mobility even though his own opportunities are limited. Thus the impact of social class can never be explained totally in terms of objective position.

The major portion of the analysis is concerned with examining the effect of social-class background (class of origin) and aspirations (class of destination) on the students' value orientations.

The Subculture and Dominant Value Hypotheses

Two theories regarding the extent of relationship between social class and values have been stated. The first of these we have termed "dominant culture theory." Its major proposition is that modern society is characterized by an overall cultural consensus which transcends class boundaries. A corollary of dominant value theory even holds that the class system itself is an expression of consensual values which determine the social esteem accruing to various positions in our society. The second or competing theory was referred to as "subculture theory." From the viewpoint of the subculture approach each class is, to a large extent, a separate cultural world in which the major social processes are carried on separately and in which behavior is a reflection of qualitatively different preconceptions. It follows, therefore, that objects and goals which are evaluated positively by one class subculture may be negatively evaluated by another.

The extent of relationship between social class and values is the major issue of concern in this study; it is also the most difficult issue to evaluate empirically. When two theories expressing this relationship are stated as polar opposites they can be tested without ambiguity. For example, low or insignificant correlations of value items with social class would lend support to dominant value theory, whereas high correlations would lend support to subculture theory. Such clearcut results, however, have not been obtained by researchers. The majority have found some support for the class value hypothesis, but the degree of association reported has always been moderate. The preponderance of empirical evidence, therefore, seems to point to a pluralistic value structure, in which both consensus and divergence of value orientations seem to play an important part. As a consequence both the dominant value and subculture approach are usually stated in less dogmatic form. Subcultural differences are depicted by most writers as being of degree rather than of kind. Classes differ more, it is asserted, in their degree of emphasis on a specific value than in terms of their rejection of it. Dominant value theory, on the other hand, is usually presented as allowing considerable latitude for variance of values within a general climate of consensus. Florence Kluckholn has even asserted that within all cultures the model values of a society are almost always partially dominant rather than consensual, and that all social groups, however small, are characterized by cultural variation.[1]

When the two theories (or hypotheses) are stated in such an amended form it is clear that moderate correlations between social class and values will support both of them. It would be wiser if we were to obtain such results, to reject both the polarized formulations in favor of a pluralistic conception. If indeed the pluralistic pattern of value distribution were supported by our evidence, then any attempt to make an overall assessment of the validity of class subculture or national culture would be relatively fruitless, since both patterns would express only a segment of the entire picture. A more useful effort would be to render a thorough description of those specific categories of values which appear to be class- or nonclass-linked, and then proceed to isolate the types of social contexts which are responsible for different portions of the value constellation.

Mobility and Class Values

Most of the research on the relationship between social class and values has focused on a single dimension of stratification, namely, the objective class position of the adult male. In studies of adolescents, who have not yet committed themselves to the job market, class position is measured by parental occupation and education. The impact of mobility on the class structure, however, demands that we consider at least two principles of stratification—of which both operate throughout the individual's life cycle in various ways: stratification of origin and stratification of destination.

Stratification of origin refers to the class position of one's parents. Its impact is limited to the advantages accruing from one's parental status throughout his lifetime, and to the effectiveness of one's family experience in shaping his subsequent attitudes.

Stratification of destination, on the other hand, refers to that class position at which the individual arrives via upward or downward mobility. Its impact on the individual's subsequent attitudes or behavior is largely dependent upon the degree to which his postchildhood experiences are capable of modifying or replacing his earlier conditioning.

For the students who are the object of this investigation both these principles of stratification are equally relevant. Most of them are about to commit themselves to some future adult status. Yet they are still involved in their family groups and their social interactions are still restricted by their parents' statuses. Aspirations of our students will probably already be considerably at variance from their parental positions. Insofar as their aspirations are still anchored to their class background, stratification of origin will still be the relevant dimension of social class affecting their attitudes. Insofar as their aspirations differ from the class level of their parents, however, stratification of destination may already be affecting their behavior and outlook. A major goal of the data analysis will be to determine the extent of harmony or cleavage between class background and aspirations.

Discontinuity between aspirations and origin should also lead to a cleavage between the value orientations of the mobile and nonmobile. Students whose aspirations are still closely aligned to their class of origin should reveal value orientations appropriate to their background. Students whose aspirations depart from their background should reveal value orientations appropriate to their class of destination. Such a pattern of results is crucial to the demonstration of subculture theory, for if new recruits to the various class groups did not realign their value orientations then in-group cohesion of cultural attitudes would eventually disintegrate. Dominant value theory also requires a similar pattern of results for its validation. If values are unrelated to class of origin, then they should, similarly, show no cleavage with class of destination.

The principles of origin and destination operate throughout the individual's life cycle to determine the nature of his class consciousness. For our subjects the more subjective assessment of class position is the one based on destination. Later in the life cycle one's origins may function in a more subjective way to determine his identity and life style even though his economic position will determine his life chances. The retention of subjective identification with class of origin may account for the frequent finding that downwardly mobile parents frequently produce upwardly mobile offspring. The interplay between origin and destination is indeed far more complex than simply a relation between generations, however. One's class consciousness may undergo drastic alteration without any change in objective class position. This can be seen in the case of the highly ambitious individual—especially one who has passed a number of crucial mobility tests—who is handicapped in early adulthood by a deficient opportunity structure produced, for example, by an economic upheaval such as the great depression of 1929. This type of individual is also likely to pass on his earlier ambitions to his children.

The notion that either class of origin or class of destination may be the subjective focus of class identification refers to actual social processes which encompass a large proportion of individuals in our society. The weakness of previous descriptions of subjective class identification based on questionnaire research is that no actual social process was referred to which could account for the disparity between subjective and objective evaluation of class position. Class of origin and class of destination refer to two distinct events within the life career of specific individuals—events of which both may have some impact on the individual's subjective attitudes.

Social Selection as a Framework for the Analysis of Social Stratification

In order to speak meaningfully about the relation between stratification and values, we must employ a broader conception of status transmission than currently in use. Also, before we can investigate class values among Dutch secondary school students we must have an analytical framework adequate to the task. As we have emphasized, the impact of stratification is not sufficiently portrayed by considering only the influence of parental origins, since the class situation of many is expressed only by their destination. In order to resolve this difficulty a new concept, the "system of selection," is proposed. *A system of selection* refers to the entire process whereby individuals are sorted and selected for status across generations. This concept is intended to provide a broader framework wherein both inheritance and mobility are conceived of as part of a single phenomenon. The purpose of this section is to sketch the basic theoretical parameters of social selection in a very general way. We shall then proceed with an analysis of the specific structure of social selection which is relevant to an investigation of the class situation of our students.

Origin and destination are but reference points for an overall dynamic or overall process, a process that determines the selection and recruitment of individuals for their position in the class hierarchy. Mobility, after all, is an abstract concept, defined by sociologists as the difference in position of a generation of offspring from that of their parents. The average man does not think of mobility as a mathematically defined net difference; he thinks of it in terms of opportunities and obstacles determining his personal advancement. He is concerned with the sacrifices to be made and the personal resources he must accumulate, such as education or money, in order to meet the demands that society makes on him before it permits him to change his status. When he does these things he relates his thinking to some prevalent system of social testing which determines the criteria for status acquisition.

What conventional wisdom takes into account, however, the sociologist frequently overlooks. Sociological analyses are focused on individual movement abstracted from the "hydraulics" of mobility. In a society where inheritance is the primary form of allocation for social position, the specification of a system of selection is not so problematic. But when there is widespread mobility, as there is in many class systems, the question of cross-generational staffing of different levels of the class hierarchy becomes a problem and must be insured by institutional provision. Contemporary ideology frequently makes it seem as though all of the mobility which takes place is a product of the accumulated initiative of individuals or of some kind of natural competition. American mobility ideology in particular perceives all institutions of selection as facilities for the equalization of opportunities. Later on we shall have occasion to comment on the discrepancies between this manifest belief and the latent structure of selection in American society. For the moment, let us take note of the fact that any theory of behavior which is based on individual initiative alone does not meet the criteria of a sociological level of explanation. Although mobility is predominantly measured as the sum of individual "moves," this does not imply that it can be explained only as a function of the relation between specific qualities of individuals and the number of vacant statuses in any society. Surely one must posit the existence of some kind of agency of social selection which intervenes between the individual's desires or qualities and his ultimate social status.

For purposes of the subsequent analysis let us proceed to define, in a formal way, the characteristics of a selective system. A system of social selection will be referred to henceforth as that social process which sifts and sorts individuals to staff the various strata or positions in a system of stratification according to institutionalized criteria. Studies of intergenerational mobility have dealt only with rates of movement between strata and not with the institutional structures that control and facilitate individual movement. It is only by correcting this balance that we can begin to provide causal explanations of the flow of mobility. P. Blau and O.D. Duncan underscore this point in their introduction to *The American Occupational Structure:*

The tendency to conceive of mobility as a single variable and examine it largely without relating it to other variables has severely restricted the fruitfulness of mobility research. After all, the purpose of a scientific inquiry is to establish, and then to explain, general relationships between variables, and not merely to delineate the population distribution of a variable, regardless of how important this variable may be.[2]

The specification of causal processes generating rates of mobility should assist us in the illumination of another process of major concern to us in this study: the socialization of the individual to class values. If we are to explain the continuity of class culture it is incumbent upon us to provide some explanation of the process of socialization whereby individuals come to acquire the values of strata to which they will move. That we observe high correlations between mobility and change in value orientation is not sufficient to establish a causal connection between the two; some intervening process of learning must be hypothesized to account for this phenomenon. One frequently hears individualistic explanations of mobility behavior which describe changes in value orientations as the natural product of high ambition. Such explanations are ex post facto in character and they overlook a basic sociological axiom: All recurrent (social) behavior is to some degree a consequence of stable and institutionalized processes of learning in particularized social contexts.

The basic mechanism of socialization which accounts for internalization of values within each individual's class of origin has been thoroughly described in the literature. The majority of authors have argued that the observed differences in attitudes and behavior within classes are the result of differential socialization in the family context. It is generally asserted that because of the primacy of early conditioning such socialization has an enduring effect upon the individual's personality throughout his lifetime. This process was termed earlier "primary socialization" to indicate its position in the life cycle, without making any commitment as to its relative weight.

It was implied in the previous chapter that socialization for mobility was secondary socialization, or learning, which is chronologically later than early childhood and takes place outside the family. Mechanisms of secondary socialization have received only meager descriptions in the literature. This may be in part because the theoretical stance of writers on socialization conditions them to look at personality rather than at macroscopic social structure, wherein secondary socialization plays a greater role. The cause of this neglect may also be found in the fact that the role of secondary socialization is infinitely more complex to trace and, therefore, difficult to describe in an axiomatic theory. When tracing the evolution of individual personalities from childhood one may regard the earliest socializing experiences as a kind of seedbed, which unfolds rather than changes. This facilitates single factor, or reductionist, explanations. In explaining the myriad types of social experience and learning which account for the complexity of role and structure in modern society such axiomatic theories are, however, simply not adequate. The consequence of relying on a simple theory of primary socialization for the explanation of cultural stratification, as some writers have done, is the unwitting acceptance of an oversimplified theory of stratification. Implicitly they must accept the notion that the major portion of status transmission is hereditary.

In general, there is no explicit description in the stratification literature of the relation between processes of status transmission and socialization. Any explanation of how individuals acquire the necessary social and technical education for highly differentiated roles, whether divergent or similar to their social origins, must include some explanation of how individuals are sorted into these roles. When status transmission is hereditary, successful early socialization leads to successful transmission of status. In modern society, however, successful primary socialization is by no means sufficient to insure successful status acquisition. Those who acquire supplementary socialization, via education, for example, quite frequently move into positions divergent from their origin. Therefore, one must posit that there is some overall selective process that is both nonhereditary in character and conducive to the process of secondary socialization.

Before we can proceed to describe the process of socialization by which the mobile individual acquires the values of the class to which he moves we must outline the mode of social selection prevalent within a particular system of stratification, of which the manner of socialization is a logical component. In much of the sociological literature we encounter descriptions that make it seem as though successful mobility is the outcome of a natural competition in which talented individuals win out over others. From this standpoint, selection is not social but self-selection, and socialization is not regulated by norms, but becomes self-socialization. In reality, competition always occurs within limits, for the terms deciding who wins and who loses must be based on normative criteria of success. Talent can never be universally defined, for the qualities considered admirable or essential in one social structure may be considered irrelevant in another. Even within a specific society, selection must proceed by limiting the range of socially recognized talents or qualities. It is frequently asserted that the purpose of social selection is just the opposite of this: i.e., the maximization of individual talents available to society. It is further asserted that the optimal distribution of talent is necessary if the society is to survive. No doubt this is true to some extent. However, an equally great threat to any social order is the appearance of individuals and groups with alternate definitions of "talent" which challenge those established by prevailing elites. Social selection, whether based upon inheritance of family position or mobility, is inevitably intertwined with social control.

Even when there is relative consensus regarding the qualities or talents which those individuals who are to be upwardly mobile must possess, the control of the selective process is by no means unproblematic. The tests of competence employed must necessarily be few in number, otherwise too many individuals gain credit for competence, and they must not be overly difficult, otherwise too few individuals will move. Nevertheless, it is still possible that too many people will pass these tests and thereby gain legitimate claims to higher status which cannot be satisfied. Thus it seems likely that inevitably some arbitrary, ascriptive, limitation must be employed.

Because any system of social selection sorts and sifts individuals only according to particular socially recognized talents, or qualities, it must, as an inevitable consequence, also distinguish them in accord with their value orientations. Thus, for example, within feudal society one important mode of social ascent was prowess in battle, for the system of feudal obligations required that a lord reward his armed retainers. Once a knight came into possession of a fiefdom his administrative ability would probably determine whether the income from his lands was sufficient to pay his own armed retainers and, therefore, whether he would hold on to his power. But, however important administrative ability may have been in maintaining the continuity of power, it was never the basis of the system of social selection. An armed retainer was rewarded for his commitment to the primary values of feudalism. In most cases the explicit basis of selection is rather precise, such as an educational diploma, a particular set of accomplishments, or any other generally recognized credential for social advancement. However objective or precise the test of competence or any other required quality, it almost always involves a latent commitment to a diffuse set of value orientations. Thus a student who is graded on academic ability must also endorse the value of deferring important alternative gratifications in life in order to devote time to his work.

Personal characteristics that favor mobility do not appear spontaneously, and they are usually not exclusively based on biological inheritance; indeed, the values and capacities singled out by the process of social selection are almost always socially learned. Thus, the process of social selection is always closely articulated with the process of socialization that produces individuals with the desired characteristics. Such control over socialization is necessary, first of all to insure a proper supply of individuals with the desired qualities, and secondly, to have some mechanism for limiting their number. For example, the Janissaries were required to have the quality of absolute loyalty to the Ottoman emperor under all circumstances and conditions, and the mode of selection employed to recruit them insured that this would be the case: They were taken from the homes of Greek families at an early age and brought under the tutelage of the palace. Thus they had no competing family or regional loyalties to which they could refer other than the court itself. This manner of selection also facilitated their indoctrination in loyalty to imperial rule since they had no opportunity to acquire alternative values.

Therefore, not only is membership in a specific social class limited to those who have been socialized to those capabilities and values which the selective process favors, but also to those who have had access to the appropriate socializing experiences and institutions. Overproduction of elites, as we have pointed out above, is a serious threat to their legitimacy. Therefore, some process which limits the acquisition of elite characteristics is almost universally found. In his classic work, *Social and Cultural Mobility*, P. Sorokin points to such a phenomenon as operative in medieval social structure.

What the sieve is the flour will be. Take further the medieval church and school. The people with strong bodily proclivities, especially such as the sex impulse, the people with an independence of opinion, with anti-dogmatic mind, and so on, as a rule, could not pass through this "ascetic, dogmatic, intolerant" sieve; such people were left either at the bottom of society or were put down, or had to find other social channels for their elevation.[3]

The modern school as a selective structure is usually thought of as giving freer access to all individuals. It is seen as a sorter and sifter of "talent" but its function in distributing or selecting individuals is ideologically underplayed. However, the equal opportunity afforded to talent in the modern school is equal opportunity only to compete and not to succeed. As Tawney has put it so eloquently, the "credit" of the equal opportunity system is good "so long as it does not venture to cash its cheques."[4] Any undue pressure on such a system reveals its covert selective function. As long as a "talent scarcity" prevails, according to accepted definitions of socially needed skills, the system works without contradiction. However, a "talent surplus" would require a restructuring of the system to make it more selective.

This can be seen most clearly when one observes the application of the criterion for equal opportunity in the school system, ability, as measured academically. If the object of the system were to give reward to talent, then it would be possible to establish a rational standard, however crude, for distinguishing such talent and sending it to its proper place. A standard of selection which can be shown to have a *functional and rational* relation to job requirements can be seen as an arbiter of talent. However, a criterion which is disproportionate and even spurious with regard to the needs of a position can only be seen as a means of selection and distribution for scarcely distributed positions. Although the raising of educational standards is frequently viewed as a means to insure the levels of competence required by our technologically based societies, such movements are, as Max Weber so astutely commented, actually based on a "desire for restricting the supply for these positions and their monopolization by the holders of educational certificates."[5]

Thus, in many European school systems, children are channeled at the age of eleven or twelve, via tests and previous school performance, into various levels of schooling which will prepare them for divergent social destinations. This selection is regarded as egalitarian in character because it is based on ability rather than on privileges. Yet, under this system it is never any absolute level of intellectual ability which gives one a claim to superior education—for there are only a fixed number of places for children in elite schools. Thus ability is always differentiated on a relative basis, which means that arbitrary rather than rational cutting points are used. Should the entire population of eligible youth raise its intellectual capacity by a considerable increment there would be no difference in the number of people acquiring elite education.

In American schools access to most levels of education is not limited by ability, whether defined in an absolute or a relative sense. Individuals are differentiated for occupational positions primarily according to the length of their education. That this also involves arbitrary limitations can be seen in the fact that there is no absolute level of education in America which gives one a claim to a particular social position. If too many individuals attempt to gain access to elite status via educational credentials, the educational ceiling is usually raised until the supply of individuals is suitably restricted. Therefore, the arbitrary nature of the competence criterion can be seen from the constant need to reassert the selective function of the system. Differentiation is a far more important consideration in its survival than is mere competence.

Social selection as depicted above refers to a process even broader than social stratification as normally conceived of—a static analysis of the parameters of inequality in a single society. Social selection refers to dimensions that are typically thought of as varying between stratification systems. When we compare stratification systems we most frequently make reference to two criteria that are aspects of social selection: (1) the relative openness of a system, or the frequency of mobility within it, and (2) the manner in which individuals are sorted and sifted (e.g., ascription vs. achievement). The degree of hierarchy or inequality and, in quantitative terms, the overall height of the stratification pyramid are aspects far less frequently mentioned in such comparisons. It is more or less implied in many presentations, although it does not necessarily logically follow, that the mode of social selection stands in a functional relationship to the structure of a stratification system. This author prefers to think of social selection as a dimension that is analytically separable from the degree of hierarchy involved in stratification.

So far we have emphasized how the structure of a particular system of selection determines the nature of channels for mobility and the number of people who will be mobile. Conversely, a system of selection also determines the prevalence of and mechanisms for social inheritance. In modern class society, as we have emphasized, individuals possessing certain qualities, attributes, or values are likely to be selected for mobility. The criteria of selection employed also determine the opportunities and strategies open to individuals who wish to maintain their status of origin; the two things are cut, as it were, from the same cloth, and they stand in reciprocal relation to each other.

In the context of early capitalism the most important criterion for middle-class status might have been the possession of investment capital or wealth. When such criteria prevailed, the inheritance of status was, to a large extent, dependent upon the inheritance of wealth or upon political advantages. Conversely, mobility was dependent upon the individual's ability through enterprise to make a small fortune into a substantial one, or upon his marriage into a family with money. In modern business the entrepreneurial classes have been largely displaced by the managerial elites and the criteria of selection have been changed from wealth to the personal qualifications and cultural accomplishments of candidates. When these types of criteria prevail, the mechanism whereby an individual can inherit his parents' status is less direct but not necessarily less effective. Under these circumstances the major portion of selection for occupational position is carried out by institutions such as schools, as separate agencies of selection and testing.

To summarize the foregoing: The explanation of how mobile individuals acquire the value orientations appropriate to their destinations requires reference to the structure of the process of social selection within a particular society. Although the entire question of the socialization of the mobile individual has been dealt with only sparsely in the literature, prevalent points of view take a somewhat different approach. Most of the literature which deals with this question asserts that the mobile individual moves between two groups, his class of origin and his class of destination, each of which is characterized by a homogeneous set of values, and in the process of moving the individual emulates or learns the values of the groups to which he moves and unlearns his previous ones. The approach taken by this author contrasts sharply with this point of view. The "social selection approach" presented above implies, in fact, that within a class structure it is not just upwardly mobile individuals who must be tested for conformity to values but also downwardly mobile and, most important, the nonmobile individuals. Everyone must be seen as passing through a kind of giant sieve.

The foregoing discussion, or polemic, on "social selection" has been rather abstract. We have made reference to a process that embraces all the major institutions of society, without giving a concrete description of how it operates in any one of them. Before we can illustrate the impact of this process on the values of those students who are subjects of this investigation, we must show how they are involved in it.

First, however, let us break the general question up into more specific components. These are as follows:

(1) What is the structure of the process of social selection, and how does it determine the values to be satisfied in the selective process?
(2) How do individuals acquire or learn those values favored by the selective process?
(3) What is the relation between (2) and (3)? To what extent is the process of socialization to class values integrated with the selective process?

These questions shall be dealt with in sequence throughout the remainder of this chapter.

The Structure of Social Selection in England and the United States: The Contest and Sponsored Models

The structure of the process of social selection can be broken down into two further components for purposes of empirical analysis. The first of these is the specific institutional structure whereby a society sorts individuals for social status. The second is the ideological framework wherein individuals are reconciled to the social differences thereby produced. Both are essential to a full exposition.

To show that the subjects of this study are affected by the general process we have referred to as social selection we must establish first that they are involved in an institution that performs such a function. This was insured by drawing a sample of secondary school students. The school, as we have already argued, is distinctly the major institution of social selection in modern society. Therefore, the attitudes and behavior of students ought, in some partial degree, to reflect this screening function.

Secondly we must show that our students, as well as the members of the larger society, are oriented subjectively to the selective process as a feature of social reality. We could imagine a system of social stratification where individuals are selected according to their hair color. Unless we had some evidence, however, that individuals accepted this mode of stratification and had incorporated it into a system of beliefs which established its legitimacy we would have no firm basis for concluding that it exists, for hair color could be epiphenomenal with relation to the true criterion of stratification. But if we had evidence that the individuals in this society regarded hair color as a sign of mystical leadership qualities or intelligence we would then be able to render a fuller interpretive substantiation.

This author needed a theoretical framework that meets the above two requirements and would be readily applicable to Dutch society. Since the relevant unit of analysis is an entire society, however, those features of ideology and institutional structure which could be generalized would only emerge with a comparison of two or more societies. The socially situated properties of a particular ideology, for example, would not be apparent when looked at from the inside, from which standpoint many socially variable formulations could be regarded as universal.

The appropriate comparative perspective was suggested to the author in an article by Ralph H. Turner entitled "Sponsored and Contest Mobility and the School System."[6] In this work he presents a paradigm for the explanation of differences in patterns of mobility and their relationship to the structure of the school system. He applied this paradigm to an empirical review of mobility channels and school structure in the United States and England. Turner's framework was sufficiently general, however, that there was good reason to believe, before this study was prosecuted, that it might also be applicable to a comparison of the United States and Holland. A thorough review of Dutch literature on school structure and history (the results of which are presented in the following section) and a series of informal interviews with Dutch sociologists and educators confirmed this initial conviction and it was decided to utilize Turner's theoretical framework to evaluate the impact of the Dutch school system on the major variables of interest in this study. Turner's scheme is not completely applicable to the Dutch school system and therefore we must introduce qualifications at many points, but it provides a useful starting place and overall metaphor for our general analysis. The following pages will be devoted to an exposition of the major ideas in Turner's article and some critical examination of them, and then, in the next section, we shall consider their applicability to Dutch society and school structure.

Turner's main thesis is that "the accepted mode of upward mobility (in a society) shapes the school system directly and indirectly through its effects on the values which implement social control."[7] He isolates two major modes of upward mobility, organized by contrasting "folk norms" or value assumptions. These patterns are based on English and American society. In England the organizing folk norms produce a system of "sponsored mobility" and in the United States they produce a system of "contest mobility."

Turner characterizes the "organizing norms" governing sponsored and contest mobility as follows:

Contest mobility is a system in which elite status is the prize in an open contest and is taken by the aspirants' own efforts. While the "contest" is governed by some rules of fair play, the contestants have wide latitude in the strategies they may employ. Since the "prize" of successful upward mobility is not in the hands of the established elite to give out, the latter are not in a position to determine who shall attain it and who shall not. . . . Contest mobility is like a sporting event in which many compete for a few recognized prizes. The contest is judged to be fair only if all the players compete on an equal footing. Victory must be won solely by one's own efforts. The most satisfactory outcome is not necessarily a victory of the most able, but of the most deserving.[8]

Under sponsored mobility, elite recruits are chosen by the established elite or their agents, and elite status is given on the basis of some criterion of supposed merit and cannot be taken by any amount of effort or strategy. Upward mobility is like entrance into a private club, where each candidate must be "sponsored" by one or more of the members. . . . In this process the elite or their agents, who are best qualified to judge merit, call those individuals to elite status who have the appropriate qualities. Individuals do not win or seize elite status, but mobility is rather a process of sponsored induction into the elite following selection.[9]

These metaphors describe two distinctive systems of mobility characterized by completely different forms of normative legitimation, each of which can be spelled out somewhat further. The sponsorship norm states that society must make the best use of the limited talents at its disposal by sorting and sifting people into appropriate statuses on the basis of their capabilities. Since society is composed of individuals of different ability only those who are demonstrably superior, or the social elite, are considered qualified to guide the selection process. The best method that the elite has at its disposal for solving the general "talent scarcity" is some process of controlled selection whereby talent is discovered and nurtured. This requires that those who would have the necessary qualities for elite status be separated out at an early stage so that their development will proceed in the right direction. In general, it is asserted, that all elite candidates must be selected and instructed very early for their leadership roles, so that they will be prepared for the responsibilities and tasks facing them later in life.

Contest norms, on the other hand, state that personal ability, whether random or hereditary in origin, plays a relatively small role in determining who is fit for elite status. Higher status is to be won in a competitive struggle with others. In this struggle the only rule which should govern selection is: "the survival of the fittest." A major purpose of society is to keep this struggle as open as possible and insure that no one has an uncompetitive advantage. Everyone has potentially equal opportunities to compete for elite status. Should he fall by the wayside it is not due to lack of ability alone but rather to lack of ambition, enterprise, or initiative. An individual of only moderate ability who exercises "craft, enterprise, daring, and successful risk-taking" is likely to win out over others who possess only native intelligence. Low native ability is a sort of environmental obstacle that can be overcome by education, the purpose of which is not so much to discover ability as to awaken one's dormant talents and his motivation to learn. The primary criterion for elite status, in any case, is not intelligence but effort. Those who fail in the struggle for status are never permanently disqualified. If they manifest sufficient ambition at some point in the future, they may reenter the competition and succeed.

Turner makes no explicit commitment regarding the causal role of such organizing norms in the mobility process, describing them alternatively as having independent, interactive, and dependent relations to social structure or to the stratification system. They are also conceived of as "ideal-typical" constructs, which are abstractions from a considerable range of empirical variation.[10] Despite all such extensive qualifications, however, the norms *do* exert a "strain towards consistency upon relevant aspects of the society."[11]

The most important macroscopic structural feature related to the formulation of mobility norms is the overall stratification system of a society, which is referred to by the author in terms of the divisions between "elites" and "masses," although intended to apply to more continuous conceptions of the class structure. The most important features for distinguishing between societies that espouse one of the two norms are (1) the structure of the elite and (2) the degree of elite control over its own selection and recruitment. Under the sponsorship system, society is dominated by an established elite, who determines both the credentials and the qualities that potential recruits must possess in order to obtain admission to elite circles. Such qualities are generally related to a high degree of competence in the practice or appreciation of artistic, literary, or intellectual spheres of endeavor. Therefore, as a consequence, only trained members of the elite are competent to judge whether the individual possesses such qualities or skills, since only they, it is argued, have undergone the long period of training and cultivation themselves. The elite in such a society monopolize both the credential granting and the credential validating process.

The metaphor of sponsorship suggests a dominant elite; conversely the metaphor of contest implies the lack of one. Under a contest system, society is dominated by "multiple elites," none of which have exclusive control over the process of selection. The granting and validation of credentials must come from many different groups or, as Turner suggests, from the masses themselves, who have a certain wide power of investiture by virtue of a power vacuum created by the lack of a dominant elite. Consequently, the types of achievements that count as credentials for higher status are highly diverse and no single standard exists for judging them. As Turner points out, however, whatever credentials the individual claims must be "highly visible and require no special skill for their assessment, since credentials are presented to the masses."[12] Turner cites money and mass popularity as ideal credentials under the contest system.

The most dramatic (or perhaps the clearest) institutional reflection of the organizing norms, however, is to be found in the process of formal education, which, in modern society is a major instrument of elite recruitment. And, in the latter half of his paper, Turner sketches the relations between school systems, class structure, and mobility norms. He picks two empirical examples to illustrate his discussion: the respective school structures and class systems of England and the United States. The following summary of this analysis is somewhat extrapolated to facilitate relevant comparisons with Dutch society, but on the whole it should be relatively consistent with Turner's intentions.

Under the sponsorship system the educational structure tends to be highly centralized in administration and selection procedures are highly standardized. The major object is the passive induction of those few people with appropriate capabilities into elite status. Therefore, the ideal way of proceeding is to introduce early differentiation and specialization into the school system so that individuals may be separated according to their destined occupational statuses. Those bound for elite membership can then be given special training in elite skills and cultural attributes. Early selection allows a single set of standards or credentials to distinguish the elite, because others who have not met the initial test are disqualified from later competition.

This mode of "controlled selection" is clearly institutionalized in the English school system. One of the governing philosophies behind English education is "to sort out early in the education program the promising from the unpromising so that the former may be segregated and given a special form of training to fit their adult years."[13] In England this system is implemented by having students take a series of examinations at the approximate age of eleven. These exams are the primary determinant of who will go on to college preparatory schools. Those who do not qualify at this age must attend secondary schools or technical schools of relatively poorer quality—schools from which there is little chance to obtain admission to colleges and universities. Once the student enters the university the major task of selection is presumed to be complete and rigorous elimination is not practiced. In fact, the majority of British university students (in contrast to their American counterparts) finally obtain a degree. The general features of the British educational system can be seen, therefore, as satisfying the logic of sponsored norms of selection.

Under the contest pattern of social mobility the educational structure is much less likely to be characterized by those features which distinguish sponsorship: a high degree of centralization, early differentiation of educational routes, standardization of selection procedures. Centralization of the educational structure is not necessarily incompatible with a contest system, but if a centralized structure exists, the potential for standardizing selection procedures and implementing their control by a single elite is, of course, greater. The existence of a decentralized educational system implies that no single dominant elite has been able to gain control of the selective process. Decentralization permits the coexistence of heterogeneous standards of selection.

A decentralized school system, such as one finds in the United States, reinforced by contest norms, is characterized by the absence of sharply differentiated educational routes in the early stages of the student's school career. The governing philosophy behind American education is to maintain the features of an open contest in which all have an equal chance. Every attempt is made to keep "slow starters" in the race until the very finish, and to "avoid absolute points of selection." In the United States every attempt is made to defer the final selection until the very end of the educational process. Students are not differentiated in any formal way by ability in the secondary school, and in many states the high school diploma of a "C" student is just as effective in meeting admission requirements as that of an "A" student. In other states where higher grades are required for university admission, the student is still allowed to avail himself of a junior college education, and, eventually transfer back into the mainstream. Within the university, competitive standards prevail. Exams are set at very short intervals, and a bad performance on one is never irrevocable. Even graduate schools will not evaluate an individual on his total record. Frequently only the last year or two of college, or an entrance exam score, are taken into account. In lieu of uniform and standardized criteria of selection, American schools employ the most external and competitive standard available: they differentiate between the length of an elite aspirant's education rather than the quality. Thus they can be seen as operating to support contest rather than sponsored norms of selection, since the logic of a "race" in which one runs further than other contestants is clearly implied.

So far we have discussed only one side of Turner's analysis: his description of the two ideal-typical mobility norms and their institutional reflections. In his article there is another line of analysis which concerns itself with the ideological role of mobility norms and, consequently, their functions in the maintenance of social control.

The type of ideology implied is close to Mannheim's conception of total ideology.[14] Mannheim distinguishes this notion from that of the "particular conception of ideology," which refers to conscious disguises and deceptions made by political opponents and is similar to "the common sense conception of a lie." The conception of *total ideology* refers to the "total structure of the mind" of a particular age or social group. Such structures of thought transcend political boundaries since they contain common criteria of objective validity, i.e., criteria that are shared even by partisan interests. Only a broad historical or comparative analysis reveals the structure of distortion involved. From the standpoint of a particular society they are consensual formulations.

The ideological functions of the two organizing norms are discussed by Turner in terms of their implication for social control. Every society, he asserts, has the problem of maintaining the loyalty of those groups relatively less well endowed by the prevalent system of stratification. This function is carried out somewhat differently within the context of each organizing norm. Thus, in a contest system, he states,

This is accomplished by a combination of futuristic orientation, the norm of ambition, and a general sense of fellowship with the elite. Each individual is encouraged to think of himself as competing for an elite position so that loyalty to the system and conventional attitudes are cultivated in the process of preparation for this possibility. It is essential that this futuristic orientation be kept alive by delaying a sense of final irreparable failure to reach elite status until attitudes are well established. By thinking of himself in the successful future the elite aspirant forms considerable identification with elitists, and evidence that they are merely ordinary human beings like himself helps to re-inforce this identification as well as to keep alive the conviction that he himself may some day succeed in like manner.[15]

Turner observed, however, that

These social controls are inappropriate in a system of sponsorship since the elite recruits are chosen from above. The principal threat to the system would lie in the existence of a strong group the members of whom sought to *take* elite positions themselves. Control under this system is maintained by training the "masses" to regard themselves as relatively incompetent to manage society, by restricting access to the skills and manners of the elite. The earlier that selection of the elite recruits is made the sooner others can be taught to accept their inferiority and to make "realistic" rather than phantasy plans. Early selection prevents raising the hopes of large numbers of people who might otherwise become the discontented leaders of a class challenging the sovereignty of the established elite. If it is assumed that the difference in competence between masses and elite is seldom so great as to support the usual differences in the advantages accruing to each, then the differences must be artificially augmented by discouraging acquisition of elite skills by the masses. Thus a sense of mystery about the elite is a common device for supporting in the masses the illusion of a much greater hiatus of competence than in fact exists.[16]

Turner's comments regarding the social control implications of mobility norms, as well as the formal descriptions of the norms themselves, can be regarded, when taken together, as implying a certain definition of a "total mobility ideology." Following Mannheim we might formulate this definition as follows: A mobility ideology is a parable, or social fiction, which incorporates a series of "exaggerations" or assertions that "structurally resemble lies" concerning the mobility process.[17] There is no malevolent conception of lying intended in this definition (such as is incorporated in the Marxian conception of false consciousness). This conception merely refers to a system of beliefs which is held in common by a number of people in a society, adherence to which necessarily involves a selective interpretation of reality.

In this study we emphasize both the normative and ideological side of the sponsored-contest paradigm as a framework for interpreting our data. The ideological emphasis facilitates certain kinds of analyses which might otherwise be overlooked. It is specially from the standpoint of individual social-psychology that a specification of the function of mobility ideologies could lead to some clarification, by explaining how individuals, as well as groups, are consensually integrated into a stratification system. Henceforth, for convenience, we refer to sponsored- and contest-organizing norms as ideologies or systems, depending upon whether the reference is to attitudes or institutions.

A mobility ideology and its institutional reflections taken together constitute a broader reality that we have referred to as a "system of selection," or that aspect of stratification systems which accomplishes cross-generational staffing of strata. While Turner focuses primarily on the legitimation of upward mobility, it can be seen his generalizations apply to status transmission, which involves downward mobility or inheritance of parental status. The norms and institutions described by him, although they focus ideologically on upward mobility, also serve to structure the attitudes and strategies of those who are not upwardly mobile. Whatever the fate of an individual within a given system, all use the same logic or structure or rationalizations in explaining it.

Now that we have outlined the theoretical paradigm used in examining the process of social selection, the next step is to determine its applicability to Dutch society, educational structure, and mobility norms. Once we have established its suitability we can move on to the more important task of projecting, or analyzing, its implications for socialization and value acquisition.

The Dutch School System and Sponsored Norms of Selection

The Dutch school system is clearly organized along sponsored rather than contest lines, and in our comparisons with the United States, the Netherlands will be placed on this side of the ideal-typical dichotomy between the two systems of selection. There is not a complete "fit," however, between the ideal type of sponsorship and the Dutch school system, but the basic organizational features of an educational system organized to facilitate sponsorship are present:

a high degree of centralization, early differentiation of educational routes, and standardization of selection procedures.

Moreover, its historical evolution and morphology still reveal sufficient variation from the English model to warrant separate consideration. One important difference, which was unfortunately difficult to research, is the structure of elite control in Dutch society. The Dutch aristocracy were not incorporated into the industrial elite as in England, and aristocratic life style or culture never formed an important basis for elite identity as it did in England. Nevertheless, the lack of a conspicuous elite identity did not prevent the formation of a distinct and centralized structural elite, lending credence to the assumption that "folk norms" which support elite selection are somewhat similar in content. Political forces peculiar to Dutch society have resulted in a school structure more bureaucratic—coming somewhat closer to a "meritocracy"—and a little less paternalistic than the British system. The following historical and structural analysis will, hopefully, serve to elucidate some of these important features.

The Dutch school structure began to take form in the middle of the nineteenth century in the context of an early industrial-class system.[18] The class structure, or *standenhierarchie*, was generally referred to by writers of the period in unambiguous terms. One of the most frequently made distinctions was that between the *geleerde stand*, or learned class, and the *burgerij*, or citizenry. Such a distinction referred primarily to the level of cultivation and education of these two groups, the latter corresponding to our contemporary middle class, and the former to the upper class. The lower or working class was rarely mentioned in the context of cultivation and were referred to from time to time only as the "masses" or the "common people."

Education for the learned class was based upon the literary-humanistic tradition, which the Netherlands had retained largely unchanged since the Renaissance. The majority of children of professionals and business leaders attended Latin schools, where they studied languages and classical topics. The better situated and the nobility hired tutors to provide such an education. Later in the century the government started building grammar schools, *gymnasia*, also founded upon classical principles. These were distinguished qualitatively from other types of "practical" secondary education existing in that period. The gymnasium was considered the first step in the entire process of higher education, which culminated in the university, and its purpose was to provide character formation or cultivation for a leisure class.

The secondary schools served primarily to distinguish the elite from the middle class and to distinguish both from the *volk* or masses. In them, the *burgerij* received an education with more practical content. They were called the *hogere burgere scholen*, which can be translated only as "middle-class schools." The description of such schools in the parliamentary proceedings notes that they lacked "the foundation and formative powers provided by classical learning."

Yet, the basic intent behind the establishment of these schools was to "provide some of the general knowledge of business skills and other subjects and some rudimentary cultivation which was needed in the business world." These schools stood at the "entrance to the world of work of the middle class."

Technical schools were always provided largely as an afterthought and in a patchwork fashion. Towards the end of the nineteenth century and prior to World War I, however, the Netherlands industrialized rapidly and the demand for skilled workers grew. Private foundations began to establish craft schools and other types of academic preparation. No systematic provision of large-scale secondary education for manual workers was provided, however, until 1920.

During this formative period of Dutch secondary education, a dual educational philosophy emerged. One of these philosophies, based upon the classical literary-humanistic tradition, argued that the purpose of education was basically self-enrichment and the formation of character and morals. The study of classical and contemporary languages and culture was held to be of fundamental importance in the formation of the intellect and personality. Such education was specifically devoid of practical content, for as its proponents argued, once a man's character and intellect were formed in the proper manner, he could deal with any practical problem. The basic purpose of such an education, at any rate, was the maintenance of a rich cultural tradition embodied in a self-conscious intellectual elite. Such education, it was argued, could not be provided for the masses because they had neither the time and leisure nor the freedom from spiritually deadening and demeaning labor which would enable them to cultivate their intellect. As the century wore on, this argument was replaced by a genetically based Social Darwinism, which argued that the masses were not sufficiently endowed in general to benefit from "high culture," or *beschaving.*

The other and contrary philosophy of education was termed *adaptive pedagogiek,* adaptive education. Its basic tenet was that the function of education was to prepare the individual for life, the world of work, and other sorts of practical endeavor. The learning of any subject which could not be justified in terms of practical purpose or did not increase one's knowledge of the world about him was regarded as an ascetic, introverted, and basically useless discipline.

The evolution of these two philosophies may be regarded, in large part, as a manifestation of the struggle for supremacy between the commercial middle class and the upper and aristocratic class. In this struggle both philosophies were used as ideological weapons. Numerous compromises and adjustments occurred throughout the century. Technical colleges and institutes were established in competition with the universities. The *gymnasia* were split into classical and scientific curricula and, in other ways, were "leveled" through the introduction of more practical subjects such as modern languages. Eventually the *hogere burgere* schools were upgraded and joined the *gymnasia* as college preparatory institutions, and new types of secondary schools, such as the *lyceum,* were founded to combine the features of both classical and business education.

The final compromise reached in this struggle involved the establishment of a dual system of education and a dual educational philosophy. The classical ideal of character formation was transformed into the concept of *algemene vorming*, liberal education, in which elements of a classical-literary, scientific, and business curriculum were all combined. This type of education can now be obtained exclusively in one of the many varieties of secondary schools offering a college preparatory curriculum. These are more or less the equivalent of an English grammar school.

The notion of adaptive education, on the other hand, was institutionalized in the form of vocational schools in which it is possible to obtain technical or craft training for almost every skilled manual labor occupation. It is also possible in these schools to be exposed to liberal arts subjects, but little emphasis is placed upon them. Presently the Dutch vocational school system is among the most comprehensive of its type in the world. It is remarkable for the large number of types of training it provides and its close cooperation with industry.

During World War I another type of secondary school was established, one which offers a curriculum similar to that of the college preparatory schools but considerably diluted and less demanding. It is commonly referred to in the Netherlands as the U.L.O. (*uitgebreid lager onderwijs*). Since World War I this type of education has grown enormously until it now encompasses at least a third of the school population. The introduction of this form of education was the final phase in the "leveling" of the classical tradition and the extension of liberal education to the general populace. In actual practice, however, the basic purpose of this type of school is to develop a form of high-grade literacy or a set of business skills, such as typing or bookkeeping. It is from these schools that the majority of clerical and lower-grade white-collar workers are recruited. The curriculum is much narrower than the college preparatory schools. Such subjects as higher level mathematics or literature are specifically not provided. Furthermore, the teachers at these schools are not required to have the same level of academic preparation as the college preparatory school instructors.

Thus, at present, there are three major types of secondary schools in the Netherlands: the vocational schools, the U.L.O. schools, and college preparatory schools. Because of the cumbersome length of their original Dutch names, these three types will be referred to henceforth as (respectively) technical schools, clerical schools, and grammar schools.

The new schools introduced in the course of the nineteenth and early twentieth century have resulted in the extension of secondary education to the general populace. In many ways, however, the stamp of the nineteenth century can still be seen. The three major school types discussed above, the grammar school, the clerical school, and the technical school, are hierarchically ordered with respect to the social prestige and life chances of their graduates. The grammar schools, as the direct descendants of the Latin schools, retain their position as the mode of education for the cultural and social elite. The clerical and technical schools are ranked respectively second and third and provide, as is generally acknowledged, a poorer quality of academic preparation. Students in the three schools differ sharply with respect to their potential occupational destinations. Access to white-collar occupations, for example, is restricted to those who have at least a clerical school education. Access to higher-level professional training is restricted to those who have a grammar school education.

Before we provide a full description of the structure of the Dutch high schools, however, another historical occurrence which had a profound impact on their development must be discussed. Johan Goudsblom presents an admirable short summary of this far-reaching development.[19] "One of the most striking features of modernization of Dutch society," he writes,

has been the fact that the two most important religious minorities, the orthodox Calvinists and the Roman Catholics, were the first to launch a successful emancipation movement some decades before the working classes began to respond to the call of socialism. The immediate cause prompting the religious minorities to action lay in a series of measures initiated in the middle of the nineteenth century, measures by which the ruling liberal bourgeoisie intended to further general education upon a secular basis. Against these attempts Calvinist as well as Roman Catholic leaders insisted upon school instruction with a religious background. Throughout the second half of the century the "school struggle" remained one of the dividing issues in Dutch politics. As the franchise was gradually extended in the interim, national parties and leagues were founded which rallied the voters with an appeal to religious principles. Thus the scene was set for a process of "segmental integration" whereby several blocs of the population, defined by their religion or *Weltanschauung*, strove for fuller participation in society. When toward the end of the century socialism emerged as a political force, it joined the already existing pattern as a full-fledged ideological bloc.

The resultant cleavages are referred to as the *verzuiling*, which means literally "columns" or "pillars." This process resulted in the formation of a number of independent blocs, or *zuilen*. While the *zuilen* were initially political action groups, they have become institutionalized to the point that a wide range of organizations have been established within each bloc. In fact, the majority of educational institutions, communications networks, trade unions, and voluntary organizations are separately organized within each *zuil*. Thus each *zuil* embraces a very comprehensive segment of the social institutions of Dutch society.

The impact of the pillarization process on the school system in the Netherlands was very profound. As part of the political compromise resulting from the "school struggle," separate primary and secondary schools were set up for every religious bloc, at the expense of considerable duplication of effort and expenditure. In towns that would normally justify only one grammar school, three or even four would be established to provide separate instruction. Each of these schools would, nonetheless, be given complete financial parity with each other and with larger schools. The maintenance of this "separate but equal" system involved extensive centralization and formalization of a school system that, under the liberal bourgeoisie, had been very loosely administered. Each of the separate blocs wanted a specific religious (or nonreligious) emphasis in curriculum. However, the school struggle also had a class character in that the largest minority, the Catholics, were largely lower class and rural. Thus there was also strong pressure to maintain equal academic standards and uniform curricula in nonreligious areas to insure that graduates of specific denominational schools would have equal life chances. In order to accomplish this it was necessary for the central government to take over the role of coordination of curriculum requirements and teacher qualifications. In addition, a national system of school "inspection" authorities and standardized national examinations for all schools insure that there is little deviance from these basic criteria. Finally a national system of government certified diplomas, which has been imposed upon industry and civil service, guarantees the rights and privileges associated with a specific level of education.

Despite all the foregoing changes, however, the hierarchical grading of school types established in the latter part of the nineteenth century has emerged largely unaltered. From the standpoint of basic structure, the Dutch school system resembles very closely the model described by Turner as being conducive to the norms of sponsored mobility. The Dutch school system, like the English, is characterized by "controlled selection" and early formal differentiation of educational and occupational avenues. The aforementioned political movement resulted in the introduction of "meritocratic" selection procedures, elimination of tuition, and the extension of the school-leaving age. It did not result, however, in the elimination of status distinctions between schools.

At the age of eleven or twelve and upon the completion of primary school, students are advised on the basis of school grades, teachers' opinions, and examinations to proceed to one of three basically different types of secondary school (lower technical, clerical, grammar). In this process the examinations probably carry the most weight; however, the parents are required to take the initiative in enrolling their child in the school to which he has been referred. Thus, a particular parent may take the step of enrolling his child in a school that is considered beyond his capacity. A very small minority do this, however, and such attempts generally fare very poorly, since they meet the organized resistance of school officials. At any rate, should the child fail his examinations the first year of secondary school, the parents would have no further recourse but to have him begin again in a less rigorous school. There is good evidence that the system functions very well in terms of consensus between parents and school officials.

The type of secondary school which the child attends has a profound influence on the quality and type of educational preparation that he receives. A minority of children are selected to attend a grammar school, where they are taught only college preparatory subjects. Although the curriculum is no longer exclusively classical in orientation, it is heavily linguistic in emphasis, and the student must learn four languages as well as achieve a relatively high standard of expressive ability in his own language. It is this better command of the language, which, above all, distinguishes him from his fellows by raising his social credit and cultivation. The elite character of a grammar school education is further revealed by the corresponding restriction of educational avenues for other students. Only those who have this type of education may enter a university. With respect to university admission even further rank distinctions are made among grammar schools. The very prestigious curricula of law, theology, and literature are accessible only to those who have a diploma from a classically oriented gymnasium.

Students not selected for grammar school must attend either a clerical or lower technical school. These provide either a very diluted general curriculum or a specific technical education. Such education is openly regarded as either of poorer quality or as an educational program scaled to those of lower ability. The instructional staff is, without a doubt, less adequately trained. A teacher in a clerical school, for example, is not required to have a university education. Technical school teachers need even less formal education, and their occupational qualifications are more closely related to knowledge of the specific craft or technical skill they must instruct. Grammar school teachers, on the other hand, must possess a number of years of university training. Therefore, since all teachers are paid "meritocratically" according to the quality of their training, the clerical and technical school teachers are paid less for their efforts. Teachers of the three types of secondary school are even referred to by different names: the grammar school instructors have reserved for them the higher status title of "teacher," whereas, the others are referred to as "educators" (a less prestigious title in the Netherlands). In view of the above, therefore, it is not surprising that all occupational-prestige surveys in the Netherlands rank the grammar school teacher far above his counterparts in other secondary schools.

In addition to the above status distinctions and restrictions upon university admission, schools are also differentiated in a more comprehensive way with respect to their students' future occupational and educational career. A recent statistical analysis of interschool transfers conducted by the Dutch National Statistical Bureau showed that although crossovers between secondary school types were possible, they occurred very infrequently. Furthermore, almost all postsecondary educational institutions in the Netherlands, such as social work academies or advanced technical schools, are stratified by admission requirements according to previous level of secondary training. Therefore, the school type for which one qualifies at the age of eleven is almost totally determinant of his subsequent educational career.

The type and level of education attained is, in turn, a strong determinant of one's subsequent occupational career. There is evidence that in this respect the Dutch schools conform more closely to the ideal type of sponsorship system than the English schools. In England, too, the grammar and secondary modern schools are differentiated in terms of both prestige and quality of academic preparation. Yet, the barriers between these schools are not completely formal, for the exceptional misplaced student or the late bloomer *can* obtain admission to a university. And, in the business world, it is probably possible for the individual of superior ambition to overcome the initial handicap of a secondary modern diploma. In the Netherlands distinctions between types of secondary education are more formal and legalistic in character and as a consequence occupational life chances are more restricted by education. The government distinguishes, for example, between school types not only on the basis of quality preparation or curriculum differences but in terms of *level of education*. Thus the individual who completes a clerical school education has, in the eyes of those who judge his occupational qualifications, a lower absolute level of educational preparation than the graduate of a grammar school. The national system of government certified diplomas further reinforces such distinctions. The range and specificity of educational qualifications which are legally imposed for specific occupations is wider than in most countries. No skilled craft occupation such as house painter, carpenter, or plumber is accessible through mere apprenticeship alone. A technical school background and a school-supervised apprenticeship are minimum requirements. So comprehensive, varied, and specific are the educational requirements that the average individual is not likely to be familiar with them. Thus voluminous, continually updated "guides" are sold in large numbers or provided free by the government so that the individual can determine what specific occupations he may qualify or what specific additional training he may require. This author made an extensive survey of such guides and was surprised to discover that specific educational training is required in the Netherlands to become a department store sales clerk, a waitress, or a veterinarian's assistant. Advertisements for occupational vacancies always specify very carefully the precise level of education needed. Often the advertisement will first solicit individuals of a specific educational background and then explain that they can be employed with a given firm in a specific function. It goes without saying, therefore, that individuals without the specified education need not apply.

In terms of basic structural features the Dutch school system is clearly organized on sponsorship terms. Nevertheless it is still necessary to show that these structural features are supported by subjective attitudes or "folk norms" conducive to the sponsored patterns. It was not feasible for this author to conduct an additional investigation to determine if such attitudes were prevalent among the general populace. A cursory review, however, of Dutch pedagogical and sociological literature convinced him that ideological patterns which supported the sponsorship system were present.

As Turner has commented,

The most telling observation regarding the direct normative operation of these principles would be evidence to support the author's impression that major critics within each country do not usually transcend the logic of their respective mobility norms in their criticisms. Thus British critics debate the best method for getting people sorted according to ability, without proposing that elite station should be open to whoever can take it.[20]

Dutch educational sociology and pedagogical literature seem to emphasize a meritocratic logic of selection even more strongly than British commentators. A major proportion of research and commentary in the area of education has focused on the problem of a talent scarcity. Recently the University of Leiden conducted a large research project aimed at determining the nature of the sorting process in the schools and suggesting possible means for its improvement.[21] The formulation of the research problem by the investigators and its empirical evaluation reveal very clearly that their assumptions are based on mobility norms similar to sponsorship. To begin with, the social problem situation that had initially stimulated this research was the fact that, in the Netherlands, the lower classes were sharply underrepresented in the grammar schools and universities. The only dimension of this problem which interested these researchers, however, was the potential loss to the society of capable individuals. They were explicitly not concerned with uncovering whether all students were involved in an equal-education contest. The data were collected primarily for the purpose of determining whether there was any class bias in the selection process by which the more promising university-bound students are separated from their less-capable fellows. They discovered, not too surprisingly, that there was little if any bias against qualified students from lower-class backgrounds. They were not concerned with uncovering, on the other hand, the motivational or cultural factors which led to a much lower general rate of academic achievement among the lower class.

One might argue that sponsored or contest structures are the products of a particular set of historical circumstances. For example, it might be argued that a society undergoing rapid changes in its occupational structure would emphasize contest norms in order to mobilize individuals for large numbers of unfilled vacancies, whereas a relatively more stable society would emphasize sponsored norms to insure a smooth and regular succession of individuals. If this were indeed the case, then basic economic transformations and changes in the occupational structure might motivate political reform of the educational system in the appropriate directions. One would expect that in the Netherlands, which has experienced a rapid transformation in its occupational structure in the last two decades, paralleling that of the United States, policymakers would start to call for a system approximating contest. This has not occurred. There has been considerable political debate regarding the school system and numerous changes have been legislated. However all changes have been directed toward the "liberalization" of a system whose basic outlines remain largely unchanged. Approximately ten years ago a piece of omnibus legislation was passed which was intended to reform the Dutch school system in the most radical possible way in order to render it more democratic. That these changes were viewed as radical and comprehensive by everyone can be seen even in the name they were given: The entire reform program was referred to as the "Mammoth Law." As a master plan it is currently intended to guide progress for the next ten years. Yet none of the modifications in the school system planned under this legislation involve any drastic departure from the norms of meritocratic selection.

This would seem to support the notion that mobility ideologies are not mere passive reflections of the existing class structure. They must possess some cultural autonomy, since even those who propose radical changes must couch them in terms that are ideologically comprehensible to everyone.

Mechanisms of Socialization Appropriate to a Contest System

The impact of systems of selection on value orientations has already been alluded to; all systems of selection involve overt and covert use of culturally specific, politically managed criteria of selection. The result of such sorting and sifting over several generations is embodied in the distribution of individuals among social classes. It is also reflected in a differential distribution of cultural orientations within such classes, since individuals are selected in accord with their values. All of this does not occur in a mechanical fashion—involving only the manipulation of differently colored human marbles—but is pervasively and subtly institutionalized. Systems of selection insure the succession of individuals with appropriate values not only by dominating access to the means of selection but also by their control of the facilities available for learning or acquiring such values.

We have hypothesized that the Dutch school system, along with other important features of Dutch society, is organized along the lines of a sponsored system. The purpose of this investigation is to trace the impact of the stratification system operating through sponsored norms of selection on the value orientations of Dutch students. Before we examine the impact of sponsorship on the learning of values, however, we must carefully consider the null hypothesis to be rejected in substantiating our conclusions. Both sponsorship and contest are ideal types, and empirically we shall find not only considerable variation but also intermixture between them. In addition, there is a danger when one considers only the features of one of these two polarized conceptions of overlooking processes and characteristics common to both, or mistaking them as distinctive to only one type. To avoid these problems we must first sketch the mechanism of socialization appropriate to contest and its impact on students involved in a school system organized according to these norms. This sketch can then be employed as a relief against which those processes peculiar to sponsorship will stand out more clearly.

We have implied that within a given system of selection important aspects of the process of socialization are culturally and structurally relative to that system. Not only does the manner in which individuals acquire their class positions differ under different systems, but also the manner under which they acquire cultural attributes and attitudes appropriate to that status. In a sponsored system of selection, students are selected early and inculcated in the values and skills appropriate to their future status. Under a contest system, however, students are never either explicitly selected or eliminated. Thus, explicit provision of socialization for future status would be impossible, since there are no definitive points of selection which would allow one to distinguish successful from unsuccessful candidates. Individuals are, in fact, always in the position of aspirants rather than of candidates.

A formal process of socialization such as elite education would, therefore, be inseparable from formal mechanisms of selection. In order to accommodate a contest model of social selection, socialization must be provisional and informal. It must also be wide enough in scope to be accessible to all aspirants. An exclusive elite culture, which requires long apprenticeship, is anathema to contest. Therefore, whatever cultural distinctions prevail they must consist of qualities or values accessible through emulation by anyone.

Another important different rests with the timing of socialization experiences. As opposed to sponsorship, the learning of values appropriate to future status must occur not only in advance of actual selection but also without guarantee of successful status attainment. Because there is no formal articulation of socialization with selection there may be considerable discrepancy between the values of an individual and his placement. When the opportunity structure is deficient the number of individuals socialized to elite values may be too large. On the other hand, sudden expansion of opportunities under a contest system may result in the advancement of individuals without any selection for cultural attainments. Under contest the advancement of the individual with role specific skills but without other attendant cultural values is much more acceptable. A good case in point is the rapid expansion in the opportunities for programmers during the 1960s. While this expansion proceeded, individuals with the requisite aptitudes who wanted to be programmers were hired wholesale. A good deal of cultural deviation was tolerated in terms of personal habits of dress, norms of social intercourse, and so on. Now, however, that there is actually an oversupply of programmers this is simply no longer the case. One prominent consulting firm in New York City began to use the recession as an excuse to lay off "eccentric" individuals, despite the fact that there was no cutback in its business.

The foregoing is in all probability only a partial listing of the restrictions that must accompany any description of socialization to class values under contest. There has been very little sociological speculation regarding socialization for mobility in the United States. Nevertheless, the best-known theory implicitly acknowledges the major features of a contest. This is the theory of anticipatory socialization developed by R.K. Merton and A.K. Rossi.[22] It is no accident that this theory deals primarily with learning by aspirants—with those who have not been successfully confirmed in their status. There are some crucial weaknesses in this theory, as we shall point out, but it seems to be one of the few really plausible frameworks for examining socialization under a contest system, and a good starting point for our own analysis.

The major propositions of the theory of anticipatory socialization as stated by R.K. Merton and A.K. Rossi can be summarized very simply.[23] Social groups, they point out, are characterized by internal conformity and by sharp differences between them in values and attitudes. However, *individuals* do not always conform to the mores of their own particular membership group. A certain number of individuals are always aspiring to change their membership from one group to another. In the process of facilitating their movement, or their acceptance by the new group, they will have consciously adopted the norms of the group to which they are moving. This process of learning in advance the values, or norms, of the future membership group (or *reference group*) is termed "anticipatory socialization." The type of learning implied is relatively external, involving emulation, or imitation, of the attitudes of the group to which one aspires and rejection of the values of the group of which one is a member.

Merton and Rossi apply the theory anticipatory socialization to social mobility without much modification, changing only the terms and referents. The mobile individual also learns, they assert, in advance, those values and attitudes appropriate for the class to which he aspires, and this helps to ease his adjustment to the new position. They also assert that anticipatory socialization is, indeed, only functional in a society characterized by widespread mobility, where the individual would be readily accepted by the class groups to which he aspires.

For many reasons the theory of anticipatory socialization is not totally adequate to our needs. Therefore, we must proceed with a critical analysis and a presentation of an alternative formulation. However, Merton and Rossi's theory will be employed later at the level of an hypothesis. For this reason we present our criticism in the form of a statement of the conditions that would favor anticipatory socialization and attempt to show that those conditions are not likely to hold for a group of students such as those who are the objects of this investigation.

There are some good reasons to believe that the theory of anticipatory socialization may be relevant to the mobility experience and the microsocial interaction which characterize the secondary school. The student enters secondary school with the major portion of his childhood, or family socialization, completed. Insofar as this earlier experience was affective he will have internalized values appropriate to his social class group. Within the school itself, he will tend to form friendships with individuals of similar backgrounds, either because these friendships are a continuation of earlier relationships, initiated through family contacts and residential proximities, or because he seeks out individuals with attitudes similar to himself. There have been a number of American studies dealing with friendship patterns in the secondary schools, studies that have uncovered some consistent although moderate tendencies for cliques to form along class lines. Since these tendencies are not strong, it seems likely that the individual who has high aspirations would tend consciously to form relations with those who have similar goals and to learn their attitudes as part of the process of becoming accepted by them.

In the situation of the adult who aspires to membership in another class, the learning of values appropriate to future group membership is somewhat more difficult, since his social interaction is generally more limited to his own class group. The adult with high-mobility aspirations would experience some difficulty in internalizing the values and attitudes appropriate to higher-class membership, since he is prevented to some degree from maintaining informal egalitarian social relations, which aid him in the learning process. In high school the individual is in close social proximity to those of dissimilar origins, and he is able to observe their attitudes and behavior as a model from which to judge his own. The presence of other comparison, or audience groups, enables him to internalize the attitudes through social interaction involving cross-class friend-ships.

Although we can hypothesize that the above process should occur to some degree, its empirical confirmation is somewhat more problematic. From a cross-sectional sample, it is not possible to make inferences about longitudinal processes. For example, the process of value change and realignment of friendships essential to anticipatory socialization can only be evaluated in terms of the difference between two states. Even from a static viewpoint, however, there are certain conditions or circumstances which could be described as prerequisite, or favorable to anticipatory socialization. The argument for anticipatory socialization would receive the most support if it could be shown that value orientations show sharp cleavages by social-class background at the same time that a strong alignment with individual aspirations to rise in the class structure is exhibited. The high association of values with background would result in the formation of distinct reference groups toward which the individual could orient himself in learning the values of his class of aspiration. The alignment of values with aspirations would imply that the mobile individual is actually changing his values with reference to his class of destination.

The theory of anticipatory socialization can only be valid, however, insofar as we can demonstrate a certain balance between group cleavages based on origin and other social alignments based on destination. If our students should demonstrate high aspirations relative to their class background, in-group cohesion by class of origin would be relatively weak. Under such circumstances where an entire group of individuals is oriented towards future status, a different pattern of group cleavages would probably emerge. If class of destination were the most important frame of reference for secondary school students, then the major portion of their social alignments and learning experiences, insofar as these are relevant to stratification, would revolve about their future class position. Mutual attraction of individuals with similar aspirations would be the major axis of group formation, and of group cleavage. The process whereby the values appropriate to future class position were learned would also take on a different form. Anticipatory socialization involves rejection of values learned in the context of earlier experiences. If destination *were* more important than origin, however, the relevant process of socialization might involve the initial learning of values in concert with the acquisition of a specific level of aspirations. Rather than reject earlier experiences the individual would tend to take on the values of the group of fellow students who set the norm for his level of aspiration.

The process of socialization whereby class of destination becomes the major focus of value acquisition will be termed "future orientation," to distinguish it from anticipatory socialization. From the standpoint of the variables used in this study, the best evidence for the relevance of future orientation as a mechanism of socialization would be reflected in the pattern of relationships between values, aspirations, and social-class background. If the impact of aspirations independent of background had a greater relative influence on values than does background alone, the case for future orientation would be somewhat stronger. The validity of this pattern of evidence depends, however, upon our total ability to predict the value orientations of the student. The same pattern of confirmation would hold for evidence obtained about the friendship relations of students. If class of destination were more important in structuring group formation, then friendship alignments would be more closely related to the aspirations of the student. Such a pattern of friendship alignments would imply a graded series of audience or comparison groups to which the student could orient himself in forming his level of aspiration.

So far, however, we have produced only an external description of this process rather than a complete explanation of the way it functions. The notion that individuals learn subcultural values in concert with the development of aspirations is something which may emerge as an empirical fact from our investigation, but it is still incumbent upon us to provide some description of the social process that results in the differentiation of both aspirations and values. The most crucial problem is to isolate, in the context of level of aspiration, that social process which results in differential learning of values.

Part of our difficulty in applying the theory of anticipatory socialization is the notion that full crystallization of the value orientations appropriate to future status has already occurred in some groups of individuals, whereas in others the process of changing values to conform with aspirations is presently on-going. Neither group of individuals has actually arrived at their projected future status, since no formal class distinctions are present in the organization of the school system. The questions become: Why do some individuals want to retain their value systems and why are others willing to change? Is there in any school system between those who have arrived and those who have not a strong cleavage which is perpetuated in terms of informal distinctions, so that the individuals in the out-group are willing to emulate the values of the successful?

Such a state of affairs seems highly implausible to this author, for there is in every school some emulation of high-background students, of their values and behavior, in terms of other students' perception of class differences and of the desirability of arriving at a higher level than one's parents. This sort of prestige identification, though, with the values of the highborn is not based upon the knowledge that emulation of such values is likely to lead to their accepting him as an insider. Rather, the values of the highborn are more likely to correspond to those values favored by the selective processes introduced in the school system.

In the previous chapter it was argued that the school was in our society the primary agency of social allocation accomplishing the selection of individuals for future occupational status. It was also pointed out that the educational process provides the most important learning experience for those attributes and achievements employed as selective criteria. It was concluded, therefore, that the school has a profound impact on the socialization process because it supplies the environment where both values and mobility orientations can be learned. Thus, from our standpoint, it is the school which provides the relevant models for specific values toward which the mobility aspirant orients himself. (Some further analysis of the process whereby this occurs is contained in the following section.)

Whether socialization under a contest system tends toward future orientation or anticipatory socialization is not clear to us yet and will require further research. Undoubtedly, there is situational variation. Some high schools may approximate the ideal conditions favorable to anticipatory socialization. Others may be more favorable to the pattern of future orientation. But, however conceived, socialization under contest conditions must incorporate personal aspirations as an important component. The individual, under a contest system, must be thought of as taking an active role in emulating the values of the class to which he subsequently moves.

This does not imply, however, that individual initiative is responsible for socialization under a contest system, but simply that personal aspirations are important as a mode of selection. American sociologists, in their numerous attempts to debunk the classless image of American society, have shown that personal mobility aspirations are strongly determined by social factors such as class, race, sex, school composition, neighborhood, and a host of other things over which the individual has little control. In addition, there are many types of constraints—informal selective processes—which limit the aspirations of Americans. Nevertheless, the decisive characteristic of a contest system, from the structural standpoint, is not the absence of a selective process but rather the lack of one which is uniform and dominant. Because there are no dominant agents of selection there can be no formal and *objective* criteria of selection, such as measured academic ability.

As in all systems of selection, differentiation of candidates is still the primary problem and some kind of common denominator is necessary to sift them out. The selection of candidates by aspiration serves this function admirably. When several competing interests—expressed in divergent criteria for selection—govern the selection process the best common denominator is that which permits the identification of successful candidates irrespective of the kinds of mobility tests to which they have been subjected, or, irrespective of the kind of mobility advocacy they have received from some agent.

The differentiation of candidates by their aspirations does not imply that individuals are selected by their desires or their personal initiative alone. Under a contest system those aspirants who maintain a sustained motivation for success or a sustained performance are selected. That is to say, subjective aspirations must be validated by an objective mobility career. The lower-class youth who desires a college education is not thereby immediately favored for upward mobility. He must persist long enough to make his desire concrete and obtain a degree. That there are no formal barriers to his success, such as stringent academic tests, does not imply that this process is not selective. In addition, that his individual aspiration to succeed is of crucial importance does not imply that he does not need collective support.

In an educational system organized according to contest norms there is, in fact, considerable differentiation of students by ability, although of a less formal character. The individual may be stimulated or discouraged from maintaining his aspirations by his teacher, school counselor, his peers, or his parents, all of whom make some kind of evaluation of his promise. Within the educational structure the relative evaluation of ability occupies a much more important place than in a sponsored system, since the students cannot be treated as a roughly homogeneous ability grouping. There is no segregation of superior from inferior students, in order that judgments about students not be prejudiced by premature categorization. But, such a structure would have little purpose if *no judgments* were made regarding the student's ability. The aim of this suspension of final judgments is to give slow learners, underachievers, and late bloomers a chance to catch up with those of steady promise. At some point, however, these individuals must be identified and their progress noted, relative to others. Since the standard of judgment is always relative, differentiation of ability is a crucial problem.

It is difficult to imagine that a student could maintain his personal aspirations against the organized resistance or support of his evaluators. This does not imply, however, that his aspirations are realistically articulated with his "objective" ability. That there is no objective standard allows many other considerations to enter into the evaluative process. Depending upon the interests of those who judge him, the student may be evaluated upon his academic record, his personality, his conformity to important cultural values, his conformity to the behavioral image of a good student (irrespective of his ability) or his social adjustment. Those American universities for which admission is competitive have long used such criteria to obtain the so-called well-rounded person. At any rate, under a contest system, it is difficult to compare academic performance between institutions because no common standard is imposed on all of them. But most important from our standpoint is the fact that academic ability of the student, whether measured according to relative or common standards (or assessed according to extraneous indicators), does not, in itself, give him a claim to anything. Under a sponsored system the passing of a crucial academic test gives one a noncompetitive claim to an elite education, from which all the less successful are disqualified. In this kind of educational system one must concentrate his efforts on achieving at a certain level in order to come favorably through the selective process at one particular point in his life. The important rewards under a contest system are given not primarily for academic excellence but for the completion of a higher level of education relative to one's peers. The academic attainments of the student do not result in any immediate change in his life chances, and, from the standpoint of mobility, all may come to naught unless he persists in the educational process long enough to realize its fruits. Persistence in the educational process is the crucial test and not a specific mastery of the contents of education. Thus, under contest elite candidates are differentiated, first and foremost, according to their aspirations for higher education.

Yet, in general, the most problematic aspect of mobility within a contest system *is* the persistence of personal aspirations. Because of the importance of personal motivation, aspirations are likely to receive more emphasis than either material resources or academic achievements as a mobility strategy. Academic performance can merely serve as an important guide to one's chances and will determine the kind of encouragement and social support he receives. Frequently it is those who manifest ambition (often indicated by nonacademic accomplishments) who have ability imputed to them. Those of very average ability who make it through a university receive no stigma. In fact, in the past, employers have frequently favored such individuals.

Because of the importance of proceeding on to higher education, those who evaluate an individual's ability, whether on academic or other bases, are likely to devote the most time and effort to strengthening his aspirations. Almost anyone is considered likely to benefit from a college education. Those, in fact, who receive the greatest stigma are the "dropouts" at any stage of the educational process. This type of failure is far more visible in the public mind than academic incompetence. Excessive aspirations are frequently encouraged because it is not the accuracy or appropriateness of the student's goals which is important but his persistence. All evidence of objective ability, whether constituted in formal or informal evaluations, is impotent unless organized into a self-concept of ambition which sustains his progress.

From the ideological standpoint contest mobility is always perceived as individual mobility. Success or failure is seen as an individual matter. Anselm Strauss has commented on the sociological fallacy in such a perception:

An ideal picture of individual mobility would show an individual in complete control of its every feature and phase. Furthermore, he would have neither help nor hindrance from any known agent (friend, kinsman, sponsor, enemy) or from any unknown agent. If fortunate or unfortunate accidents occur, he alone takes advantage of, or succumbs to, or copes with them.[24]

No social action has the above features, much less mobility. Although contest selection is based on personal aspirations these are not necessarily individual. An aspirant's desires are shared or promoted, in most cases, by an agent or a set of agents. Both agents and aspirants tend to be structured as aggregates rather than as individuals. What really makes a contest system or selection distinctive is not the degree of collective support but its structure. Under a sponsored system only one set of agents has the decisive power to further an individual's mobility. Under contest many different types of agents, groups, and experiences may act as the effective agent and their influence may come early or late in the mobility career of the individual. It is they, in fact, and not the individual who are in competition with each other. In large part, some individualistic strategies are possible under contest primarily because of the vacuum left by the lack of dominant agents.

As we have emphasized, a contest, as well as a sponsored system of selection, is supported by a total ideology. One consequence of this is that many features of the system operate in a certain fashion not because they are fully institution-alized, but simply because individuals see the system as functioning in a certain way. One of the premises of the contest ideology is that all individuals have essentially similar starting points in the race for higher status. As much of the literature on the American school has emphasized, such equal starting points are not necessarily institutionalized. However, such a belief in equal opportunity is important in explaining how a contest system works to motivate individuals.

The ideological consistency of the "race model" of mobility has been maintained in recent years despite social pressures which would tend to undermine its credibility. One of the dangers under a contest system is the overproduction of elites through mass higher education. One solution under such circumstances would be to tighten academic standards and institute sponsorship. The actual course followed is more consistent with a contest logic. The oversupply of elites produced by mass education in the United States has been reduced primarily by raising the educational ceiling, a measure which reinforces the race model and reasserts the importance of personal aspiration as a mode of selection. Should further extension of the educational ceiling become infeasible, as may currently be the case, a devaluation of all credentials via market processes may be permitted.

This self-fulfilling prophecy character of ideological formulations must be taken into account in explaining the impact of a contest system on socialization. The learning of cultural attributes appropriate to one's status can be explained in terms of a structure institutionalized to support contest norms, but whatever the structural reality an important component of our explanation must include an account of the impact of popular beliefs about mobility and the learning of values.

A Comparison of Mobility Orientations and Socialization under Sponsorship and Contest: Expected Findings

This study is not in itself intended to be a thorough test of the validity of the sponsored model of mobility. Such a task would require separate investigation of the distribution of supportive folk norms among the general populace and further research into other aspects of social structure. Our decision to study students in Dutch secondary schools makes it necessary to circumscribe the scope of our investigation. In this section we lay out the major features of socialization and selection in the context of the Dutch educational system. We then project their impact on the variables to be investigated via the questionnaire. Finally, the pattern of anticipated findings is codified in a series of formal hypotheses that structure the presentation of the data in the succeeding chapters.

As emphasized in our discussion of socialization under contest, the process of socialization and the structure of selection within any system of stratification are closely intertwined and must be analyzed interactively. This holds also for the empirical confirmation of these two processes. For heuristic, however, purposes we have adopted an arbitrary causal ordering of variables. In most previous investigations of the relation between social stratification and values, class origin is treated as the independent variable and value orientation as the dependent one. The same basic logic will be employed by this investigator. However, in line with the previous discussion the links in the causal chain have become more complex with the addition of intervening variables. System of selection replaces class of origin as the causal agent that stratifies values, and is analyzed not as a single variable but rather as the relation between three variables: class origin, mobility aspiration, and school level. The mechanism of socialization is inferred from the relation between the pattern of variables indicating a specific structure of selection and the value orientations of our respondents. The entire scheme should become clearer to the reader in the following exposition.

Because of the logic of our research design the first order of business is the empirical confirmation of the structure of selection that is affecting the mobility careers of our students. The most desirable way of proceeding would be to observe the impact of educational selection on the subsequent mobility of those under investigation for a significant portion of their life span. However, since our students have not yet even entered the labor market, the impact of a system of selection on status transmission can only be gauged via its effect on their mobility aspirations.

Aspirations also play an important role in our implied comparison of sponsored and contest systems of selection. In a contest system, as we have emphasized, personal mobility aspirations are important both as motivational fuel and as a component of the ideological rationale. The operation of a sponsored system is characterized, on the other hand, by early confirmation of mobility careers. Therefore, personal aspirations, if not completely irrelevant, are at least secondary in importance to formal selection processes within the school system.

The primary dimension of comparison between mobility aspirations in the two systems is the degree of realism they express. Under sponsorship early formal differentiation of educational and occupational paths should produce early crystallization of well-defined and realistic occupational and educational aspirations. The major lines of cleavage in aspirations should be found between the various levels of the "graded" school system. Since aspirations are irrelevant after the initial selective process has occurred they should reflect the student's fate. Competitive aspiration can have no meaning except during the period preceding selection for school types. At that time ambitious parents may push children to overachieve with regard to their native ability. To this aim they may employ such stratagems as cramming or tutoring.

The anticipated pattern of student aspirations under contest, however, would be just the reverse of that under sponsorship. In order to be consistent with contest logic, the collective level of students' aspirations should be higher than the system can reasonably fulfill. This does not mean, however, that their goals are inappropriate or irrational. Such a pattern is perfectly consistent with the requirements of a contest structure. Because no explicit selection has yet occurred there is nothing to restrain a student with poor qualifications from aspiring as far as he wishes, although he may have difficulty translating his ambition into concrete mobility. Therefore, because there are no realistic constraints, aspirations may still be at fantasy levels. This, by itself, would not be enough to raise the collective level of mobility aspiration to an exaggerated height, however. It is not just lack of restraint but also the positive emphasis placed upon mobility aspirations which produces this result. In this context it may be worthwhile to briefly restate the argument presented in the previous section. Under contest the school system possesses few means of formal selection of candidates, therefore, it may rely upon informal means. The internalization of motivation or aspiration for higher status are of primary importance; consequently differentiation of individuals by aspirations is the primary mode of selection. Academic ability is not unimportant as a selective mechanism and it is evaluated competitively, but it functions more as a guide to the individual's evaluation of his potential than as an actual restraint. That individuals of a wide range of ability can enter a university means that the primary mechanism by which they must be differentiated is their own personal aspiration for a college education.

Two other mechanisms producing high aspiration are purely ideological in character. In a contest system, all explicit recognition of failure is avoided and concrete disadvantages such as low ability or inadequate resources are underplayed. The individual is permitted to rationalize his fate by believing that there are no irreparable failures or setbacks and that he need only re-enter competition and exercise sufficient effort to succeed. Therefore, it follows that even the most disadvantaged may have high aspirations and every attempt is made to give them legitimacy. Even those who are too far committed to an adult career to anticipate any substantial mobility may retain the image of a contest for opportunities of their children believing that it was only their personal failure in taking advantage of the system which impeded their mobility.

High aspirations are also stimulated by one of the major contradictions of the contest system. Unlike a sponsored system explicit mobility tests cannot be employed at any point to regulate the number of candidates for elite status. In order to avoid either an oversupply or undersupply of elites the educational credential must be continually revalued or devalued (in the manner of currency) in terms of the specific status level to which it provides admission. The logic of a race is thereby maintained; the winner is decided by the competition and not by some absolute standard. Thus, because one is never sure what level of educational attainment is necessary to enter elite status or, for that matter, any level of the occupational hierarchy, the most secure position is to maintain the highest possible aspirations for oneself.

As part of the task of confirming the presence of a sponsored system of selection, therefore, we will have to examine the degree of realism of students' occupational and, especially, educational aspirations. If our assumptions regarding sponsored selection are correct, then the collective levels of aspiration expressed by students should correspond closely to the opportunities available to them and should reflect, at the very least, the constraints induced by early educational selection on their future careers. If aspirations were unrealistically high, however, we would have to consider the alternative hypothesis of contest.

The most important evidence confirming the presence of a sponsored system of selection however, would be the pattern of relationship between three variables: parental class, secondary school level, and mobility aspirations. In all systems of selection, inheritance of parental position accounts for a substantial proportion of status transmission. Yet, sponsored and contest systems, while they might be characterized by identical rates of inheritance, differ with regard to the social process whereby this occurs. Because of early selection for different occupational and educational paths, the impact of parental status is exhausted early in the educational process. The class background of a student is undoubtedly a powerful determinant of how he fares in the selective process and, consequently, which type of secondary school he attends. However, once selection is over, background would cease to function in discriminating students from each other in terms of ability or aspirations. Therefore, the direct impact of parental class background on the aspirations of secondary school students should be small. Class background would not cease to function as a determinant of future status, but its primary effect would be interactive with that of the school. In our data we might anticipate that school would show a strong effect on school level attended, but when class background is controlled, the primary determinant of aspiration would be the school level of the student. In addition, the impact of class background on school level attended must be moderate rather than overwhelming, since under the latter circumstance the school would function as merely a vehicle for confirming prior selection by class.

Under a contest system of selection, the impact of background on relative levels of aspiration is more direct, being unmediated by any kind of explicit selection. Within the comprehensive secondary school, which is characteristic of a contest educational system, we should find considerable direct impact of class background on aspiration. Under sponsorship, parents are generally forced to modify their aspirations for their children and discontinue their mobility advocacy after selection for secondary school since there is little they can do for them. But under contest, parental pressure and assistance may be important right up until the end of a student's educational career. The foregoing generalizations apply only to the relative levels of aspiration, however, and their correlation with background. Because of the dynamics of a contest system of selection the absolute levels of aspiration in each background group are likely to be unrealistic.

The impact of the sponsorship pattern on the socialization process is undoubtedly quite profound. Since the major process of selection is already presumed to have occurred, the only thing that remains is to guide the child along the path which lies before him. Personal aspirations at variance with this direction would be extremely dysfunctional, since he is already constrained in various formal and informal ways from altering his course. Since the school system itself is future oriented and position within it represents a measure of objective mobility, the future orientations of students are largely superfluous.

Under contest, socialization must be conceptualized as an active process, in which the individual takes some initiative in acquiring the attitudes of the class to which he will move. In an educational system characterized by sponsorship, however, the school system itself is differentiated according to the future class destinations of its students, and their own personal aspirations are less important in determining their life chances. Consequently the process of socialization must also be conceptualized as more passive. The acquisition of values appropriate to future destination must take place largely by means of conformity to the expectations of peers and teachers within a specific school level. This is supported by organizational structure. The cultural attitudes appropriate to future class level are to some degree institutionalized in the educational program of each level of secondary school.

Under a contest system, elite culture is seen as accessible to everyone who may aspire to attain it, consequently, a competitive standard is set for achievement, both in the areas of social and technical learning. Negative and positive evaluations can be attached to varying levels of performance. The overachiever or ambitious individual will receive a favorable response for his efforts. In an educational system characterized by sponsorship, however, such competitive standards have no place. Separate standards of achievement are set for each school level. The individual in a technical school receives a drastically different and considerably less demanding curriculum than the grammar school student. Consequently, there is no mechanism for comparing their performances or for validating them. Should the technical school student be capable of achieving at the grammar school level, there is no means of evaluating his capabilities. The lowest performance of a grammar school student is still, a priori, superior to that of the best technical school student. Thus, since the expectations of teachers and peers are geared to attainment at a specific level, divergent aspirations or capabilities receive little support. The same sponsorship logic applies to the learning of values. The student internalizes a specific set of cultural expectations presumed to be appropriate within the context of his class of destination and appropriate to the exercise of those technical and social skills in which he is being prepared. He is not exposed to divergent values, however, and deviance is not, as under the contest system, explicitly rewarded or institutionalized.

The foregoing analysis implies that the majority of socialization for class values under sponsorship is institutional socialization. By "institutional socialization" we simply mean that the school is oriented towards processing individuals into a relatively similar mold. The student is selected in early adolescence and inculcated in the skills and values felt to be appropriate to his destination. There is little opportunity for contradictory learning to take place, since the primary social facilities for validating important values are vested in the school. Competing agents such as the family or other reference groups are relatively powerless to alter this process once it has begun. Take the example of a child from an upper-middle-class professional family who, because of very poor academic performance, must attend a nonelite secondary school. His parents may continue to assert the importance of middle-class achievement values such as the deferral of gratification, but the situation in which such a value would be expressed via his activity is precisely that which is monopolized by the school.

Deferral of gratification by spending long hours at study is much more meaningful when the academic program is oriented towards intellectual achievement than when it is subordinated to teaching the student automechanics or bookkeeping. Thus the student may eventually begin to feel that his parents' values have little relevance to his current activities and to the future being prepared for him.

Under contest, the student who has internalized divergent values can make up for his low natural ability by turning in nose-to-the-grindstone performances and by exercising persistence in staying in the educational process. The learning of values divergent from one's origin can also stimulate the expression of the student's native ability in line with performances favored by the school. Thus, under contest, the learning of values discrepant with one's origin or academic potential can be translated into selective advantage. This is not as easy under sponsorship. Prior selection and sorting means that the school is much more homogeneous in terms of values expressed via academic achievement and in terms of the expectations of significant others. Parental inculcation of values divergent to the school context can receive no reinforcement in the school itself. Under contest, on the other hand, the school is heterogeneous with regard to the values and ability of its students, and the teaching staff regulates this diversity in a competitive fashion. Thus divergent values can easily receive social support or other reinforcement from models obtainable in the school.

In the Dutch school system the notion of providing a unique elite education, which will develop leadership qualities, is not as explicitly institutionalized as in England. The segregation of students, however, by occupational destination involves the close articulation of curricula with future job requirements. No serious attempt is made to expose every student to a broad general education as in the United States; a specialization is accepted as a matter of course. A student in technical school will receive sufficient verbal training to achieve functional literacy, but the majority of his education emphasizes manual skills. The grammar school student, on the other hand, is offered no vocational subjects, and his level of verbal competence is expected to extend to reading of the Greek, Latin, and Dutch classics. Such differences would suggest that each school, at the very minimum, has a distinct academic subculture which would stimulate the learning of homogeneous values by its students. Such differences would operate to restrict both cultural horizons, as well as knowledge of significant alternatives. There is little sense, for example, in encouraging the student to value achievement in a generalized way when the ceiling on his concrete achievements is to some degree limited.

Such subcultural differences are doubtless supported by many aspects of the pedagogical structure. Under a contest system, the secondary school teacher acts as a mobility agent by differentiating between students and giving reward and encouragement to those of greater ability. The recognition of late bloomers or incorrectly placed individuals by school teachers would tend to disrupt a sponsored system, however. This is avoided, at least in the Netherlands, by giving the school teacher a similar cultural status to that of the student. The technical school teacher never attends a university and his training is definitely inferior in terms of social respect to that of the grammar school teacher. It would be difficult, therefore, for him to presume to be the judge of any student's potential for higher education. On the other hand, the grammar school teacher, who does have university training and who would presumably be able to judge the competence of a misplaced student, is not placed in a position where he could exercise such judgment. All of his students are destined for university if they fulfill the minimum requirements, and he is focused on preparing them for this destiny. The learning of divergent values from those which are considered appropriate to the student's destination, is, therefore, severely impeded by the fact that not only the mobility aspirant but the agents to which he can turn are limited in their horizons.

Under contest, students with divergent mobility destinations are gathered together under a single roof. Although students are differentiated to some extent by ability, and placed in different streams, no confirmation of future status results therefrom. Students are not socially segregated from each other into physically separate institutions. There are differences in curriculum as manifested by academic and nonacademic programs. However, movement between these courses of study is usually relatively simple and does not involve explicit selection procedures. There is nothing in the educational program which corresponds to the sharp distinctions between elite- and working-class curricula in a sponsorship system of education.

Within the school itself the lack of significant structural cleavages that would provide different socializing experiences would make it difficult for those who are bound for elite status to acquire a unique cultural background in which other students do not share. Under sponsorship, the most conspicuous cultural attributes of elite status are values and norms that can only be learned—such as abstract verbal ability, specific accent, rules of personal deportment, or a taste for high culture. Under contest, the elite are differentiated from the masses according to the exemplification of values that everyone is capable of emulating, especially extrinsic sorts of values—money or success. This would seem to imply a greater levelling of value systems under contest and the prevalence of a dominant value system.

Such a dominant system of values probably exists only at the ideological level, however. The notion that the elite are separated from oneself only by their emphasis on extrinsic values such as money or success does much to perpetuate the illusion that elite status is accessible to everyone. The reader will recall the distinction we made in Chapter 1 between general values and the instrumental norms. One example of such a distinction involves class differences in concrete translations of important extrinsic values. All classes endorse the generalized value of success, but the middle classes are most likely to endorse education as a means or a symbol. When the lower classes restrict themselves to material definitions of success, they are handicapped in terms of the values favored by the selective process.

Cultural differentiation is important in a contest system of education, but the social process supporting it is somewhat different in character. Since there are no formal structural differences to support the internalization of divergent values, socialization occurs through more informal social mechanisms and social interactions. These are not necessarily less effective. The school system and its educational program are designed in part so as not to discriminate between superior and inferior students. This does mean, however, that there is no differentiation between them. Under contest, the school teacher is, in fact, much more constrained to make relative evaluations of his students. First of all, because they do not constitute an homogeneous ability grouping as judged by previous intellectual performance. Secondly, because the norms of fair treatment under contest demand that achievement be differentiated on a competitive basis. These kinds of evaluations do not, it is true, have any direct impact on mobility career of the student, but they do affect the socialization of individuals to the values appropriate to their ultimate status.

Intellectual ability is generally not evaluated in terms of basic individual capacities alone but in terms of achievements or performances. These in turn involve allegiance to specific values. Thus intellectual attainments involve in the first instance some basic capacity. The vehicles of their expression, however, such little trials as the regular completion of school assignments in particular formats; the formation of an authority relationship to the teacher; the proper deportment for a classroom situation—all involve allegiance to specific values such as deferred gratification, self-control, and so forth. The moral and intellectual differentiation of students frequently go hand in hand. Those students who fit the behavioral image of a good student are more likely, according to current schemes of evaluation, to have ability imputed to them. Those individuals who remain in the educational process long enough to have their aspirations translated into permanent status are likely to favor the normal values inculcated by the school.

As we have already emphasized, the secondary school does not differentiate students according to their future class destination in any explicit or formal way. Therefore, other mobility agents may act to promote an individual's mobility and help him internalize the requisite attitudes. Parental socialization can be quite important if the values of parents diverge from those of their own social class. Internal cleavages based on peer groups can also be quite important in providing models for specific values. Anticipatory socialization breaks down, however, as we have previously commented, when the level of aspiration or mobility orientation is high relative to class background. If a contest system were characterized, as we have suggested, by a high rate of mobility, then future orientation as a mechanism of socialization would probably be more compatible.

The contest pattern encourages differentiation of aspirations between students on a competitive basis. The tension between achievement and fulfillment or between origin and destination are much greater under a contest system. Therefore, it seems highly likely that individuals who pursue different levels of achievement or who have different aspirations for success should seek each other out for social support. From this standpoint, individuals with similar aspirations are more likely to form bonds of friendship, or clique relationships. The values predominant in these groups are more likely to be aligned with the individual's class of destination than with his class of origin. Rather than having to break old bonds of friendship or group affiliation based on class of origin, therefore, the individual first establishes such bonds according to his class of destination. The learning of values appropriate to his class of destination proceeds in a similar fashion: rather than having to renounce the values he has initially learned, the individual first learns them in the context of the social group that sets his level of aspiration. The models for these values are most likely to be those favored within the context of the educational process.

Neither anticipatory socialization nor future orientation are likely to be relevant in a sponsored system, however. Since the choice of future class destination has already been made, differentiation of aspirations between students is not likely to function as an axis of group formation. Since students have been removed, to some extent, from their class peers and placed together according to destination, friendships are less likely to form according to background. Friendship choice and clique formation are probably more closely related to certain aspects of youth culture under a sponsored system.

Now let us return briefly to the question of the operational confirmation of patterns of socialization in this study. Socialization, like selection, will be inferred from a multivariate pattern of relationships. In our description of institutional socialization under sponsorship we have made certain key assumptions. If these are correct we should expect a certain series of results. The most important finding that we anticipate, if sponsorship patterns of socialization are affecting our students, is the stratification of value orientations by school level, independent of all other factors. Personal mobility orientations may well have a moderate effect on values, but the major proportion of the variance should be explained by the type of secondary school which the student attends. Class background may also exert a minimal direct impact on values. In accordance with the structure of sponsored selection, however, the major proportion of its influence should be indirect: that is, mediated by its prior determination of the student's school level.

The validity of this inferential pattern, however, depends upon simultaneous confirmation of a system of selection via the interaction between the three independent variables (class background, school, aspirations) that can determine value orientations. If, for example, we found that values were stratified by school, as anticipated, but that school in turn had no impact on mobility aspirations, then we might have to assume there is either something defective in the design of this study, or in our assumptions regarding social selection in the Netherlands. If this were the case, it might be that the values measured were either not central to mobility, or, at this stage in the student's life cycle, not yet sufficiently crystallized with the student's perception of his future status.

It may also be that our central hypothesis affirming the existence of a sponsored system of selection is in error. One purpose in describing in the previous section our anticipated findings under contest was to leave open the option that our null hypothesis might receive more support. Even more important, however, was our anticipation that not all values would be affected by sponsorship or by any single agent of socialization. Some values can be successfully imparted only in the context of family of origin and via primary socialization. An example would be the values of an aristocratic or traditional social elite. Those from the traditional elite may go through the same educational process as the upwardly mobile while retaining their own distinctive values and norms of social interaction. Social acceptance into the old elite might be impossible or accessible only via anticipatory socialization. On the other hand, some values may be relevant only in a context of competitive ambition. That the base for competition is somewhat narrowed does not mean that they will lose this identification. All the various contingencies affecting value orientations will receive fuller treatment in Chapter 5.

In describing the impact of the sponsored and contest systems on socialization, we have purposely overstated our case. We have been dealing exclusively with ideal type descriptions of these two systems, although in reality such pure types are hardly ever encountered. Many examples of sponsorship processes could undoubtedly be found in school systems characterized by contest and vice versa. For example, we have made it seem as though the aspirations of the individual are largely, irrelevant, because his class destination is determined almost totally by his school level. This is far from being completely true. Although the sponsorship system places distinct limitations on the level of the individual's aspiration, there is still considerable range of opportunity within each educational stratum. Within a group of individuals who possess a specific set of educational prerequisites, there may still be considerable competitive aspiration for particular jobs.

3

Some Methodological Notes

The Sample

The subjects chosen for this study consisted of 519 males from the third and fourth years of public secondary school in the city of Amsterdam. The schools from which these subjects were drawn represent the three major types of secondary schools in the Netherlands: the technical, clerical, and grammar schools.

The sampling strategy adopted in this study was to specify as clearly as possible, in advance, the social contexts that could be conceivable sources of variation in our dependent variables. The sample was then stratified so as to exclude, where feasible, those exogenous variables whose effects could be confounded with those of interest to this researcher. This approach is the converse of randomization procedures, whose aim is to control all possible *unmeasured* or *unspecified* sources of variation.

Those theoretical considerations having implications for the stratification of the sample are discussed under the headings below.

Educational Structure

One of the major foci of this study is influence of educational structure on aspirations and values. As a consequence, a major goal of the sampling design was to select schools or other subunits in such a manner that the most salient features of the Dutch school system could be laid bare in the subsequent analysis. The high degree of standardization and centralization of the Dutch school system gave us both special advantages and difficulties in solving this problem.

As already discussed, the most important axes of structural differentiation in the Dutch school system are the hierarchical grading of school types according to ability and vocational preparation and the pillarization of schools by confessional group. Unlike the United States, however, the individual school is not internally differentiated (e.g., into college preparatory and vocational arts curricula). Each step in the graded hierarchy is reflected by a physically and structurally separate school. These distinctions are further replicated in every confessional bloc. Thus, as it turned out, the most expedient method of stratifying students with respect to these divisions was to sample entire schools.

The schools sampled belonged to each of the three major types of secondary institutions, already referred to as technical, clerical, and grammar schools. Each of these, as we have already indicated, represents a distinct step in the graded hierarchy of secondary education. The choice of these three school types represents the outcome of a conscious selection by the researcher from a broader population. There are at least twenty to thirty additional (or supplementary) kinds of secondary school in the Netherlands and, therefore, the full range of structural types is not represented in the sample schools. Moreover, the restriction of the sample to these types was not based on economic considerations. For a number of reasons it was felt that the choice of these three school types would best illustrate the dynamics of the Dutch school system: Since the majority (65%) of the students attend one of these three types of schools, the general public possesses a clear notion of their function, the quality of preparation they offer, and the social destination of their students. Most Dutchmen are aware of the vast number of specific types of vocational education obtainable on the secondary level, but not even an experienced educator could begin to catalog them or describe them in their entirety. Furthermore, it is apparent that these schools play a somewhat different role in the educational structure. Should the student decide that he wants to enter one of the more specific types of vocational schools, he must first attend one of the three types of *primaire* institution (lower technical, clerical, or grammar) for a period of two years before he can apply. Moreover, the level of general secondary school attended previous to his application determines the level of specific vocational training for which he qualifies. Thus it is entirely likely that such further education is the evolution of an occupational choice already conditioned by his previous schooling and an early expression and channeling of occupational objectives. In general, this researcher feels that the same processes of selection and socialization characterize these types of supplementary education and that little bias is introduced by excluding them. On the other hand, had they been included in the sample numerous problems might have resulted: That these schools train for specific careers would have compressed the range of occupational and educational aspirations and limited the scale of the very attitudes whose variation we are most interested in examining.

The Confessional Bloc

The most important limitation on the representativeness of this sample is its restriction to public schools. As we have already pointed out, the pillarization of Dutch society into confessional segments extends to the school system, and parallel facilities are provided for all three major groups. It is difficult to assess the amount of sampling bias introduced by this restriction because of the paucity of previous research on the attitudes of confessional subgroups. Much of the data we do have, however, suggest that the school system affects the different subgroups in very similar ways by standardizing and legitimizing the avenues of occupational training. The Catholic segment, for example, has improved its relative socioeconomic position considerably since the institution of confessional schools, until it is now on a par with the other groups. There is also evidence to suggest that the social segregation associated with the pillars has declined drastically over the last fifteen years. This process of disintegration has proceeded to the point that many parents ignore confessional distinctions and simply send their child to the closest school which meets his needs. Nevertheless, despite the presence of forces tending to weaken the pillarization process, we must conclude that the choice of public schools represents an explicit limitation on the generalizability of our results.

The Selection of an Age Cohort

The selection of an appropriate age cohort was the most difficult sampling problem faced by the investigator. This problem stemmed from the fact that in any society objective and subjective age roles do not always coincide.

In the previous chapter it was emphasized that the relationships between mobility and values can only be examined in the context of a developmental sequence. It was felt that one of the most fruitful stages to analyze the interrelationship between these variables is the period of adolescence. It is at this period that the major impact of mobility determinants—school, family, ability, aspirations—are not yet disentangled from each other. Furthermore, it is quite evident that at this stage the individual must manifest the attributes that will make him mobile and make the crucial decisions that determine his future career.

But the term "adolescence" does not refer to an homogeneous category of individuals. It denotes both an age grouping and a position in the career or life cycle of an individual. In many ways a youth who has left school and entered the work force can no longer be considered an adolescent. His attitudes and aspirations are no longer uncongealed, they represent either a commitment or rationalization of a course already taken: In our society the term "adolescent" almost always refers to someone who is at an intermediate stage in the educational process and is as yet uncommitted to any adult role.

This definition of "adolescence" circumscribed our sampling frame. We had to strike a balance between choosing students who were in the last stage of the educational process, when large numbers of their fellows were already dispersed in the occupation structure, and choosing them at such young age that they would not have had a chance to crystallize those attitudes or decisions in which we were interested. It was felt that the best way of attaining this objective would be to select a group of students who were in the last year of compulsory schooling. In this way we would be most likely to obtain a cross-section of a group the majority of whom were still involved in the educational process but who would soon be making decisions regarding their future careers.

The structural diversity of the Dutch school system, however, rendered it difficult to select such a group of students. The three major types of secondary schools chosen for this study all take different periods of time to complete. The lower technical schools graduate the major proportion of their students in their third year and a smaller proportion of their students in the fourth year. On the other hand, the clerical schools graduate the major portion of their students in the fourth year, and a smaller group following less-advanced curricula in the third. The grammar schools, by contrast, take anywhere from three to six years to complete depending upon the school type.

Thus, it was impossible to choose a group of students who were both at the same stage in the educational process and the same age. It was decided that the choice of homogeneous age groups was the more important of the two objectives. With this aim in mind, grade cohorts were chosen from the third and fourth years of technical and clerical schools and from the fourth year of grammar schools.

Nevertheless, subsequent analysis showed that the sample selected was not very homogeneous with respect to age. This is due mostly to the phenomenon of *doubleren*, the repeating of grades. If a student does poorly at a particular level, he is not, as in American high schools, given poor grades and automatically promoted to the next grade. As a matter of general educational practice it is felt better to keep him at the same level until he measures up. No student is promoted automatically and as many as 25 percent are made to repeat grades until they master the subject matter. This is especially common in the last year of schooling. Thus the age distribution of a given grade cohort within our sample is never very homogeneous. Dutch educational statistics indicate that a spread of four years is not uncommon (such a spread is, indeed, found in our sample). The practice of *doubleren* is most frequent in the grammar schools and, as a consequence, in our sample these students are, on the average, almost a year older than those selected from the clerical and technical schools.

The lack of homogeneity of the grade cohorts creates special problems for the interpretation of our results. Age is an important feature of social structure and is capable of producing significant variance in the phenomena under investigation. One means of overcoming such a problem is the use of selective subsamples or "control groups." In this study another expedient was adopted. The major portion of the data analysis presented in this study involves the use of multiple regression techniques. Therefore, it was decided that in each case where age could possibly confound the relationships between important variables, it would be included as an independent variable in the regression model. This technique for eliminating correlated bias is very similar in its effect to the use of control groups but possesses a decided advantage in that it involves no reduction in cases.

The Social Composition of the Sample

Time and access pressures made it impossible to insure, by means of prior procedures, that we would be able to acquire a representative distribution of all socioeconomic levels in our sample. Although the Dutch school system is highly centralized, the individual headmaster of each school retains considerable autonomy in the matter of apportioning schooltime. Obtaining the cooperation of any particular school was always a topic for negotiation between the researcher and school officials. Thus it was necessary to exclude several potentially suitable schools because of conflicts in examination schedules or difficulty in obtaining access at the desired time. In addition there was little current information on the socioeconomic composition of the individual schools, which would have provided a reference point for selection.

In those instances where we did have a choice, schools were selected on the basis of existing information concerning the social rank of school neighborhoods, which have been assembled by the Amsterdam Census Bureau.[1] The procedure adopted involved eliminating both extremes of socioeconomic residential segregation from our sample. Initially thirteen schools agreed to cooperate. Four of these were rejected because they were in a preponderantly lower- or higher-status area and one school, while not in a residentially segregated area, was used only for the pretest. This method, although statistically unrefined, at least insured that our sample would not be skewed at the upper and lower ends of the socioeconomic spectrum.

We have some confirmatory evidence that the above procedures, while rough, did yield the desired results. To evaluate the distribution of socioeconomic characteristics in our sample a family class-background index was constructed, which, like the measure of social rank (used in determining the initial selection of schools), had education and occupation as its two components. This class-background index was computed by assigning weights to each category of father's occupation and education and combining them additively into a single score. In Table 3-1 the results of a comparison between sample socioeconomic status (SES) in each school and the social rank of the school neighborhood are presented. As we can see, the rank order of school neighborhood SES and school SES are identical within school types. The social rank index itself runs from 1 to 66, the larger numbers indicating the lowest social rank. The greatest extremes in residential segregation were to be found in neighborhoods ranked 1-10 and 50-66. With the exception of two schools these extremes were successfully eliminated from the sample.

In Chapter 2 it was emphasized that the lower-socioeconomic groups in the Netherlands availed themselves much less frequently of university and university preparatory training. As one ascends the graded hierarchy of secondary schools the lower-socioeconomic groups are more and more underrepresented. This pattern repeats itself in our sample. Returning to Table 3-1 we can see a clear relationship between SES and the grade of secondary school. The schools are

Table 3-1

Mean Background Index of Sample Schools Stratified by School Type and Social Rank of School Neighborhoods

Sample Schools (Stratified by Type)	Social Rank of School Neighborhood	Mean Background Index
Technical		
A	11	4.46
B	62	3.87
Clerical		
C	9	4.98
D	29	4.88
E	34	5.00
Grammar		
F	14	6.81
G	27	6.64
H	39	6.15

designated by letter only, in order to preserve confidentiality. When we compare between school types, the social rank of the neighborhood does not retain any significant influence, for the average spread of the mean background index within school types is smaller than the spread between school types. Furthermore the mean background index rises consistently as one ascends the graded hierarchy from technical to grammar schools, with no overlap between levels.

In Table 3-2 the relationship between father's occupational background and school type is presented. Again we can see a similar pattern. As one moves from the technical to the grammar schools the higher strata are better represented than the lower ones.

As in Chapter 1 we must insert some cautionary remarks about the interpretation of these figures. As with the national census data already presented, it is obvious the lower classes are underrepresented with respect to the relative size of student enrollment. This does not imply, however, that with respect to the occupational structure, the schools do not facilitate considerable mobility. The technical schools train for a range of occupations held by almost 65 percent of the work force in the Netherlands. The clerical and grammar schools train for a range of occupations held by 30 percent and 5 percent of the work force, respectively. In competition for the small number of elite stations, the lower strata do achieve a considerable degree of success, despite initial handicaps. In our sample (see Table 3-2) for example, the lower class is not underrepresented in the clerical schools, the completion of which already represents a distinct step upwards to a white-collar job. In the grammar schools,

Table 3-2

Distribution of Father's Occupation for Sample Schools Classified by Census Categories

Occupational Category	School Type		
	Technical	Clerical	Grammar
1. Managerial and professional	6.0%	6.6%	34.7%
2. Middle managerial, semiprofessional, and self-employed	16.4	46.8	43.3
3. Skilled manual labor and lower clerical	77.6	46.6	22.0
Total	100.0%	100.0%	100.0%
Total number	164	124	202
No answer	12	3	14

which are a prerequisite for managerial and professional positions, almost 65 percent of the students are not from managerial or professional families.

That there is considerable variance of socioeconomic status within school types is of the greatest importance for this study. A major portion of the data analysis following this chapter devotes itself to demonstrating the independence of family background, as measured by the classical stratification variables, from the influence of the school environment.

To further evaluate the representativeness of our sample, data were obtained on the distribution of socioeconomic characteristics in the general population of Amsterdam. Table 3-3 presents a comparison of the occupational distribution of fathers in the sample and for employed males in the city of Amsterdam. The sample contains a slightly larger proportion of professional occupations and a significantly higher proportion of middle-level occupations than the city does in general. Manual and clerical occupations, by contrast, are significantly under-represented. In Table 3-4 another comparison is made between the distribution of father's education in the sample and the educational level of employed males in the city of Amsterdam. There is considerable discrepancy between these distributions, and on the whole, the education attainment of the sample fathers is much higher than that of the general populace.

Neither of these two comparisons is really fair, however. First of all there is no real equivalence between the census categories and those used in this study. The collapsing process used in the tables no doubt results in considerable distortion. More important, however, the census population includes many categories of individuals who could never be the parents of the students sampled, for example, employed males 14-25, the unmarried, and senior citizens. It is

Table 3-3

Occupational Dsitribution of Sample and 1960 Dutch Census

Occupational Category	Distribution of Father's Occupation for Sample	Dutch Census: Occupational Level of Employed Males	
		City of Amsterdam	Netherlands
1. Managerial and professional	10.1%	8.9%	5.4%
2. Middle managerial, semiprofessional, and self-employed	40.9	33.6	29.3
3. Skilled manual labor and lower clerical	49.0	57.5	55.3
Total	100.0%	100.0%	100.0%
Total number	504		
No answer	15		

Table 3-4

Educational Level of Sample and 1960 Amsterdam Census Population

Educational Level	Distribution of Father's Education for Sample	1960 Amsterdam Census: Educational Level of Employed Males
1. Primary	22.0%	51.8%
2. Lower secondary	49.9	35.3
3. Higher secondary, higher vocational, and university	28.1	12.9
Total	100.0%	100.0%
Total number	493	
No answer	26	

entirely likely that the parents of the youths in our study have considerably higher proportion of higher-status jobs because of the general increase in the proportion of white-collar or tertiary sector jobs in the last forty years. The educational distribution of the parents must also be interpreted in the light of the enormous expansion of the Dutch secondary school in the 1920s and 1930s and rise in compulsory schooling age. Since the older cohorts received much less schooling, it would indeed by surprising if the parents of our student sample did not have a much higher average level of educational attainment than the general populace, which includes a large proportion of people who grew up in the early part of the century and who no longer have children in school.

The above-mentioned difficulties render it impossible to make any sure assessment of the representativeness of our sample with respect to the distribution of socioeconomic characteristics. It is assumed, however, given the constraints already described, that the composition of the sample is fairly representative and this assumption will be maintained throughout the research report in establishing limitations on the generalizability of the data.

The Indicator of Social Class
Employed in This Study

In cross-national studies, one of the most critical problems is the development of indices for stratification variables that measure roughly the same thing in all the countries under investigation. The design of such indices was one of the primary methodological problems which had to be solved before this study went into the field. In deciding upon the final set of questionnaire items and coding categories, the investigator relied heavily upon the advice of Dutch colleagues and took very seriously the examples set by previous studies and publications on the subject. Many decisions, however, had no specific precedent, and are unique to this study. These are defended below on their own merits.

The major indicator of class background used in this study was occupation. Before deciding upon an appropriate occupational classification for use in this study the most prominent and frequently used Dutch schemes were reviewed and evaluated. Only two were felt to be worthy of attention. The first of these was a scheme of occupational classification developed by J.J.M. Van Tulder.[2] It consists of six categories and is based almost exclusively on prestige ratings of occupations derived from previous research. Another frequently employed classification was developed by the Dutch Census Bureau. It is trichotomous and also based upon prestige rankings.

Neither of these two classifications was employed directly in this study. Instead another classification was developed to distinguish subcultural differences. The inspiration for its use came from the previous work of Ralph Turner, and the actual classification represents a conscious adaption of the scheme he describes in *The Social Context of Ambition.*[3]

There were two reasons that a subcultural scheme was used in opposition to extant ones. First was the consideration of comparability. Since this study is most readily comparable in its design and theoretical focus to Turner's, a number of distinct advantages accrue from using his classification. Secondly, since this study is concerned with evaluating the subcultural differences between socioeconomic levels such a scheme might provide more sensitive measurement of such distinctions.

Another, perhaps largely unanticipated, benefit came from the use of a subcultural scheme. The exercise of creating such a subcultural classification led to a conscious awareness and operationalization of those cultural differences which affected the classification of an occupation in the Netherlands.

Methodologically the appropriate categories of a subcultural classification can only be developed on the basis of "insider" type knowledge regarding the way various cultural characteristics cluster to form occupational subgroups. There are many ways of locating such groups. Frequently inferences can be made from historical trends, since a subculture tends to develop its identity and make its presence felt over a long period of time. Probably the best way of isolating such subcultures, however, is in terms of stereotypes, which are readily available to us in both popular and scholarly literature.

The present researcher used the technique of searching Dutch literature in order to determine what kinds of occupational categories were distinguished as stereotypes by sociologists and popular writers. The results of this investigation yielded a classification parallel to Turner's in some respects and different in others. The categories chosen were externally similar to the American ones in terms of the types of occupations assigned to them and the way that they were ranked. But, the criteria by which occupations were stratified leads to a somewhat different interpretation of the meaning of the overall occupational classification. The most important contrast is the overwhelming weight that was given to the educational criterion in the classification of occupations. In Turner's classification, for example, a clearcut distinction was made between a category of occupations termed "semiprofessional" and between another one termed "business agents and managers."[4] Such a separation could not be justified in the Netherlands, however. The first problems arose when, in the pretest, a sophisticated group of coders were unable to differentiate between the occupations that were supposed to fill these categories. It was thought perhaps that this might be a clue to the fact that other types of criteria operated to distinguish occupational subcultures in the Netherlands. Subsequently, an intensive investigation of the Dutch sociological literature on the occupational structure was made. This investigation suggested that educational differences between occupational groups might be more important in the Netherlands than the author had previously thought. Numerous examples could be found in Dutch field studies which bore out this conclusion. In one study, for example, conducted by H.M. In 't Veld-Langeveld, groups of respondents were asked to describe the background or qualities which they felt were most important in acquiring a semiprofessional or managerial position.[5] They responded almost invariably that education or "intelligence" were perceived by them to be the primary prerequisite for obtaining such jobs. A brief review of other authors also suggested that managerial positions were not—to the degree that one might find in the United States—the product of climbing up through the ranks. Rather, employers seem to depend more heavily on initial educational qualifications in promoting individuals.

The preeminence of the educational credential could also be seen in the types of distinctions made between blue-collar occupations. Skilled and unskilled manual labor encompass the same categories of occupations as in the United States. In the Netherlands, however, the distinction usually made between these two types of work is based upon educational qualifications. The transition from an unskilled to skilled occupation cannot generally be made on the basis of experience, for all employers must recognize the national system of credentials, which imposes a minimum of three years technical school as a requirement for entrance. It is no accident, therefore, that blue-collar occupations are referred to as either "schooled" or "unschooled," depending upon whether a trade-school diploma is a strict prerequisite.

At the upper end of the occupational spectrum, education is an even more important differentiator. A university education, by virtue of its exclusiveness, sets a man apart and makes him a member of an educated elite, the *academici*. A university degree, irrespective of the area of specialization, is considered a general credential for admission to high-ranking jobs, and many government agencies will place advertisements in professional journals for positions of a broad administrative nature. Possession of a university education will also, frequently, differentiate individuals employed in the same occupational situs. For example, in all Dutch schemes of occupational classification (including prestige rankings) secondary school teachers at the lower technical and clerical school level are classified far below teachers of grammar schools. There is, of course, little functional difference between these positions. A grammar school teacher, however, must have a certain number of years of university preparation, and this provides a major increment in his "social credit."

4 Mobility Aspirations and Sponsorship

The substantiation of the character and extent of mobility aspiration is crucial to the demonstration that sponsored patterns are operating to focus individual mobility among our students. Such evidence is also of relevance to the validation of subcultural differences later in this study. A high degree of mobility aspiration relative to social origins would lead us to look for value differences along the lines of mobility destination, whereas a low degree of mobility aspiration would lead us to a search for subcultural cleavages along the lines of class background.

Most crucial, perhaps, to the substantiation of a sponsored pattern of mobility is evidence regarding the way in which aspirations are channeled. In a sponsored pattern, structural cleavages within the school system are very influential in determining the student's ultimate class of destination, despite his original class background. Thus, the most important evidence that students are orienting themselves subjectively to such a system would be that a large proportion of their mobility aspirations are determined by their school level. If we cannot find such structural determination of aspirations, then we may safely say that sponsorship is not operating at this stage in the student's life cycle to focus his career goals.

If structural determination of mobility aspirations through the school system does occur, then the role of personal aspirations in determining or indicating potential mobility must be diminished. Ultimately, therefore, we must also consider that more than one social force may be operating to produce potential subcultural variation in the student's class of destination. Thus, our findings will lay a background for a later analysis, in which the combined effects of all important stratification variables on the value constellations of all students will be evaluated.

Aspirations and Realism

In recent years there has been a great proliferation of studies dealing with the mobility aspirations of adolescents. Most of these studies have been concerned with demonstrating the extent to which aspirations are determined, or constrained, by class background. The results have generally been positive. That is to say, aspiration is almost always moderately correlated with social class, in the greatest number of cases. In their haste to show the impact of social class, however, researchers have frequently overlooked the significance of the absolute levels of aspiration. Little note is taken of the fact that the aspirations expressed by youths, although statistically related to background, are frequently unrealistic, and out of proportion to opportunities either contemporary or projected. Almost all studies of youthful mobility orientation have reported unrealistic levels of aspiration. And, in the majority of cases, the goals expressed by students are too high for eventual realization.

The consistency of high-aspiration levels reported by various studies suggests incorporation of a few cautions into our own thinking about the measurement of mobility attitudes. First of all, we must be aware that many of the mobility goals expressed by students are, in fact, fantasy choices—in that they are not faced with the realistic constraints of those cast upon the labor market. A few researchers have recognized this fact and have attempted to tap a dimension of realistic choice, by purposely asking students to indicate their minimum expectations, as well as their aspirations. The results have indicated that students do revise their choices downward when asked about their minimum expectations.

Secondly, we should be aware that high aspiration, by itself, constitutes an important datum. For even in those studies which measured realistic choices, aspiration levels were still unrealistically high when compared with potential opportunities. The accumulated evidence seems to suggest that high aspiration may be the rule. As we have already speculated, this finding may be a reflection of American mobility ideology, or of indigenous American cultural patterns. And, since most of the studies of aspiration referred to above have been done in America we must consider the implications of such findings for the comparative aspect of this study. We have already asserted (see Chapter 2) that realism in aspirations is more consistent with a sponsored pattern of mobility. Therefore, an empirical examination of realism will be useful in testing at least one important hypothesis that we have advanced.

Realism was operationalized in this study by using two different types of questions to measure educational and occupational aspirations. One type of question was phrased in order to elicit the fantasy aspirations of the student with respect to occupational or educational goals; the other was phrased to elicit realistic aspirations, or plans. Responses to these two types of questions were compared in order to ascertain the degree of realism or fantasy expressed in the aspirations of our subjects. It was not deemed important to separate fantasy and realistic responses for other varieties of aspiration measured in this study, since we rely upon occupational and educational goals, throughout the study, as the principal measures of aspiration. Furthermore, the paucity of previous research and theoretical speculation about other varieties of aspiration would make the meaning of such additional distinctions rather unclear.

Occupational Aspirations

The end-product of mobility is most frequently symbolized by higher-occupational position. Therefore, the occupational aspirations of our students must be regarded as a kind of primary measure of mobility aspiration, and should be given a central role in our evaluation of the extent of mobility orientation.

The occupational aspirations of our male students were tapped by asking two questions, one intended to elicit fantasy goals, the other intended to elicit reality goals. These were phrased as follows:

What kind of job would you most like to have 10 to 20 years from now? (If you can't name a specific occupation, please write the name of the kind of occupation you would most like to have 10 to 20 years from now.)

What kind of job do you really expect to have 10 to 20 years from now? (If you can't name a specific occupation, please write the name of the type of occupation you really expect to have 10 to 20 years from now.)

These questions followed each other in the above order on the questionnaire. We required some labels for convenience. Therefore, the first, or fantasy, question will be referred to henceforth as the "desired" occupational choice and the second, or reality, question will be referred to as the "expected" choice.

The responses are classified into nine categories according to sector of employment and the status of the occupation. One of the categories, that of middle-managerial occupations, makes little sense for our respondents; a fact we have already discussed (see Chapter 3). It was included in the presentation of the results, anyway, in order to make them more comparable with those of Turner's study.

Table 4-1 presents the resulting distribution of students' occupational aspirations compared with that of their parents' occupations. An examination of these distributions reveals a profile of moderately high levels of fantasy aspiration (desired occupation). The professions and semiprofessions (Categories 6 and 8) are the overwhelming focus of high aspiration, receiving together over half of the choices. By contrast only one-fifth of the sample fathers are actually employed in such occupations. Next in order of importance comes skilled labor, receiving a quarter of the desired occupational choices. This level of choice almost exactly matches the proportion of fathers in the sample who are employed in such occupations. Together all three categories (skilled labor and the professions) account for four-fifths of all desired occupational choices.

The above pattern of preference is by no means a new finding. Despite the diversity in their methodologies, the majority of studies of occupational aspiration have encountered high rates of choice for the professions. There seems to be little question, in view of the consistency of such findings, that the

Table 4-1
Background and Occupational Aspirations*

Occupational Category	Background	Desired Occupation	Expected Occupation
1. Unskilled labor	2.8%	0.0%	0.5%
2. Semiskilled labor	8.3	0.9	0.2
3. Skilled labor	23.3	24.4	32.1
4. Clerical	15.0	3.0	7.4
5. Self-employed; owners of small- to medium-size businesses	6.3	5.0	2.9
6. Semiprofessional	12.8	27.8	20.7
7. Middle-level managerial	21.9	6.9	12.1
8. Professional	7.0	28.1	22.5
9. Executives; large-business owners	2.6	3.9	1.7
Total	100.0%	100.0%	100.0%
Total number	459	459	418
No answer	60	60	101

*The background and desired occupation columns were made comparable by removing nonresponses, including those who had failed to answer both questions.

professions are the primary focus of those expressing high-mobility aspirations, rather than the other highly placed occupations in business or officialdom.

The comparative significance of our findings must be interpreted, however, in terms of the ratio of aspiration to background categories. Our sample has a marked skew because it contains larger numbers of high-status families than the average for the Netherlands. Thus one would expect higher levels of aspiration as a matter of course (assuming a correlation between background and occupational aspiration). Consistently higher ratios of aspiration to background, however, would not be anticipated unless the level of aspiration were higher. The ratios between desired occupational and parental background for each aspiration category were compared with similar ratios derived from two American studies. Consistently higher or lower ratios are not found, although there are some differences in specific emphases. In R. Turner's study, for example, the ratio of professional aspiration (professional and semiprofessional choices combined) to background is much greater than for our respondents (4:1, vs. 3:1).[1] On the other hand, the ratio of manual labor choices to background is higher for the Dutch sample. It would appear that the Dutch students, on the whole, do not find the professions quite as important as a focus for upward mobility aspiration as the American students. It also seems as though the Dutch students feel less of a stigma against manual labor. In addition, menial clerical work is not popular for either American or Dutch students; however, the Dutch seem to have a greater aversion for it. In a very broad way the pattern of choice is similar for both American and Dutch students, in that glamorous white-collar occupations are consistently overchosen relative to background, whereas, nonglamorous white-collar jobs (e.g., clerical and middle-managerial positions) are consistently underchosen.

As in comparable American studies the desired occupations of students do not appear to be oriented to the realistic distribution of opportunities. The degree of overchoice of the professions relative to background and the degree of underchoice in other categories testify to a stereotypical distribution of aspirations. The overwhelming choice of the professional categories may be more a reflection of the attitudinal nature of occupational aspiration than a concrete aspiration preference. The information possessed by fifteen- and sixteen-year olds regarding the real range of available occupations is probably somewhat meager. And, it may be that the occupational stereotypes of the crafts and professions are more highly developed in the cultural environment of the adolescent.

It is also notable that the skilled crafts have not been underrepresented in aspiration choices despite the alleged cultural stigma on manual labor. However, we should note that the semiskilled and unskilled labor categories received almost no choice by our respondents. We could conclude, therefore, that the college-educated professions seem to occupy the aspiration ceiling for those interested in advancement and willing to tolerate the insecurity of the climb, whereas the skilled crafts occupy the aspiration floor and provide a focus for those who are at least partially interested in security. The unionized position of the skilled crafts in the Netherlands, as well as in the United States, provides the members of these occupational groups with job security as well as an assured, though moderate, income. The two adjacent categories above and the two adjacent categories below lack either assured income, sufficient job security, or both. Although clerical occupations can lead to higher status, they are insecure and low paid compared to the skilled crafts. It would appear that those who feel themselves destined for higher-status occupations would prefer to aspire to one immediately rather than settle for a long and tenuous climb. Self-employment in business is highly insecure although it may promise high financial reward. Unskilled labor, however, is clearly in the worst position since it can offer neither promise of security nor financial reward to compensate for lower status.

The expected occupation column in Table 4-1 summarizes the distribution of responses to the question intended to tap the realistic job choices of our respondents. Two elements presumably worked together to force the student to consider reality factors: The way that the question was phrased and the fact that it came second in order after the fantasy question. The question compels the student to consider revision of his fondest wishes, and the distribution of responses should reflect this. Thus we would anticipate that the pattern of expected occupational structure, as reflected either by the distribution of father's occupation or as specified by our own knowledge of the emerging structure of the labor market.

Our findings bear out these predictions. In all but two cases the ratio of expected aspiration to background more nearly approaches 1:1 than for similar ratios computed with desired occupation. It is assumed that these closer ratios reflect some of the possible constraint of background on aspiration. The two exceptions to this pattern are quite revealing. Self-employment declines as a choice relative to its distribution among parental occupations. This may reflect the knowledge of students that entrepreneurial occupations involve risk-taking, and are, therefore, quite insecure. Skilled labor, on the other hand, receives 50 percent more choices as an expected occupation relative to its distribution among parental occupations. This may reflect, as we have already noted, the fact that skilled labor is viewed as an acceptable occupation for which to settle if one is interested in security.

The marked increase in choice of clerical and managerial occupations implies that these too are perceived by students as jobs they may "end up in," although they would prefer not to. In general, however, the overall picture does not reveal complete realism with regard to the opportunity structure. We know, for example, that the proportion of clerical and middle-managerial occupations is increasing very rapidly in the Netherlands. Yet these categories are underchosen by students. On the other hand, the proportion of professional occupations increases very slowly, as it has throughout the century. And yet, the professions are overchosen by a ratio of 3:1. Furthermore, the relative position of the professions is only diminished by approximately 25 percent between the desired and expected columns. This finding would seem to indicate that students do not perceive such an aspiration as particularly unrealistic.

Educational Aspirations

The early limitation and channeling of career patterns under sponsorship should influence educational aspirations even more strongly than other career goals such as choice of occupation. The school structure has a more direct and immediate impact on educational choices because, unlike the job market, it is a reality factor that is already impinging on the consciousness of the student. The operation of a sponsored system of mobility may be even more dependent upon channeling of educational opportunities than are other types of controls, for under sponsorship one's ultimate occupational position is more heavily dependent upon his level of credentialization. We anticipated, therefore, that the educational aspirations of students would be more restrained in extent and more realistic in orientation than their occupational aspirations.

In order to tap the level of educational aspiration, two questions were asked of each student regarding his educational plans. And, as with occupational aspirations, one was phrased to elicit fantasy responses, and another, which directly followed it in sequence on the questionnaire, was phrased to elicit reality responses. Following each question the student was presented with a checklist of rank-ordered levels of education from which to choose. The names of these levels, or the specific references to type of education made at each level, were derived from examples used in a previous study of college-student educational aspirations in the Netherlands. One addition was made to the response format used in this study: students were advised that if any of the eight forced-choice categories did not accurately express their specific aspirations they could simply write down the name of the kind of school they wanted to attend. Ten percent of the responses fell into this write-in category. These were coded and rank-ordered according to an extant classification of school levels developed by the central bureau of statistics. The phrasing of the two questions is reproduced below.

What type of education would you most like to have?

What type of education do you really expect to get?

Table 4-2 summarizes a comparison of the distribution of educational aspirations with the level of parental educational attainment. The general level of desired education is fairly high relative to background: 73 percent of all student

Table 4-2
Educational Background and Aspirations

Educational Level of Father	Background	Desired Education	Expected Education
1. Primary	20.7%	0.1%	0.4%
2. Lower technical	25.0	10.3	20.7
3. Clerical or middle-technical	22.0	14.5	22.6
4. Some grammar	4.9	2.1	3.5
5. Grammar or equivalent	14.4	16.2	17.5
6. Higher-vocational or teacher training	7.5	24.6	15.5
7. Some university	1.4	4.5	7.6
8. University	4.9	27.7	12.2
Total	100.0%	100.0%	100.0%
Total number	492	512	507
No answer	27	6	6

aspire to the top four school levels, whereas only 28 percent of their parents have had this much education. Especially notable is that a little over half (56.8%) the students would like to have an education beyond grammar school, which is the highest level at which any of them are currently enrolled. Thus, the average student expresses a considerable desire for upward mobility in terms of educational attainment.

The modal category for desired education is training at some type of university. As in the United States, a university education is an important avenue to high status. Yet, the moderate degree of fantasy aspiration directed towards a college education (only 32.2%), compared to that expressed by respondents in American studies, would seem to indicate that it is not perceived as so generally available. In a contest system, the prevailing ideology disseminates the belief that there is equal access for all to a higher education, although the prevailing opportunity structure limits their chances. In a sponsored system, equal opportunity is neither institutionalized nor regarded as desirable. Therefore, students are not likely to aspire to a level of elite education from which they are explicitly excluded (which is the case with technical and clerical school pupils in our sample) despite the fact that they recognize its value. It is notable that almost as many respondents have chosen higher-vocational education (24.8%) as the upward limit of their fantasy goals as have chosen technical and clerical educations (24.6%). Under a sponsorship system, this makes sense because the higher vocational level is more easily accessible to those who have missed out in the sorting process at age eleven or twelve: vocational school is a natural choice for those who feel constrained by the lack of access to grammar school. Later on we shall substantiate this conclusion by cross-tabulation of educational aspirations within school type. Finally, we must note that a little over two-fifths (43.1%) of our students aspire only as far as secondary school (categories 2-5) although many of them would qualify upon graduation for some type of higher-ranked educational institution.

When we move to the expected-education column, the same general trend seems to be evident as with desired education; levels of expected education still express considerable mobility aspiration relative to parental attainment. It is also clear, however, that considerable revision takes place when students are asked about their expectations. Such revision is comparable in extent to the already discussed revision in occupational aspirations, and is predominantly downwards. In particular, university training shows a most pronounced decline in choice. This result may be a manifestation of the general perception among students of university education as an exclusive and elite commodity. Therefore, very few of the sample students realistically expect to receive a college degree. More of the expected choices are focused on higher-vocational education, which is more generally accessible. Most notable of all, however, is the fact that the majority (64%) of students realistically expect to achieve no better than one of the 4 levels (categories 2-5) of secondary school training.

As with occupational aspiration, the question arises: How realistic is the distribution of aspiration in our sample relative to actual opportunities? The realism of the overall distribution of educational aspirations for our students can be evaluated in three ways. The first method of evaluation is to note the degree to which educational aspirations conform or harmonize with occupational choices. A lack of articulation between the two would tend to indicate less realism, for it would imply less knowledge of job requirements. Such conformity between these two types of aspiration should be even more evident in a sponsored system, for our respondents should know more clearly that the most important avenue of mobility or occupational advancement is a specific degree of educational attainment. This should be especially true for elite occupations, to which access is impossible for the nonuniversity educated. A comparison of the distribution of the desired levels of aspiration yields a pattern of close harmony between occupational and educational choices. Thus, 28.1 percent desire a full professional occupation (access to which is somewhat limited by university education) and a corresponding 27.7 percent also desire a university education. With regard to the semiprofessions the pattern is similar: 27.8 percent desire a semiprofessional occupation compared with 24.6 percent who desire a higher-vocational education. Since higher-vocational training is the most important avenue to the semiprofessions, the above results indicate a close concordance between the two types of aspiration.

When we move to a comparison of expected levels of occupation and education it would appear at first that there is less articulation between the two distributions. Because of the exclusiveness of a university education in the context of a sponsored system, one might conclude that academic plans would be profoundly affected by reality considerations—sooner perhaps than occupational plans because the constraints on educational progress come earlier in the student's career and are felt more directly. Thus, within our data we would anticipate that educational plans would suffer the most drastic decline when students are asked about their expectations. This is, in fact, the case; 22.5 percent expect professional careers as opposed to 12.2 percent who expect a university education, although the proportion desiring educations or occupations at this level were nearly equal. However, we need not interpret these results as evidence of low articulation between educational and occupational plans. For at least 30 percent of the occupations classified as professional, a university education is not strictly requisite, although the competitive advantage of those with college degrees is very great. Dutch national statistics indicate that many in specific professional occupations possess a number of years of college without a diploma or with only higher-vocational training.[2] The best example of this is the occupation of secondary school instructor. Although classified as professionals, a large proportion of grammar school teachers have only partial college or extended teacher training. That proportion of students aspiring to only a few years of college (7.6%) might indeed be anticipating such an occupation. The same seems to be true for the relation between credentials and various varieties of middle-managerial and semiprofessional jobs. In many cases an employer would prefer a higher-vocational background for a semiprofessional position. The demand, however, exceeds the supply, so a grammar school diploma is regarded as a good credential for this level of employment when supplemented with on the job training. Middle-managerial positions also compete for those who have higher education, but a grammar school diploma is all that is formally required for most positions.

In summary of the first method of evaluation, it must be emphasized that the degree to which occupational and educational goals are realistically articulated with each other cannot be told from the hypothetical relationships between the content of an educational program and the requirements of broad categories of jobs; the relationship between these two things in job market must be known. In our case students may simply be revising their educational aspirations downward to the minimum possible level for entrance to the occupations they anticipate obtaining.

The second way of evaluating the realism of educational aspirations is to examine the opportunity structure in which such goals are involved. If we judge by parental attainment, then educational aspirations are somewhat unrealistic. But we know that in every major industrial country the educational system has undergone moderate to great degrees of expansion, thus making parental levels a poor guide to the current distribution of educational opportunities. This is especially true in the Netherlands. Just since 1940 (few of the parents in our sample could have been born after this date) lower-technical education expanded threefold, grammar schools fourfold, and universities fourfold. Within the city of Amsterdam itself, expansion has been more moderate, but average expansion, controlling for population growth, has more than doubled the proportion enrolled in secondary and higher education since 1940.[3] There is no way go gauge with accuracy how the continuing expansion of the educational system affects the student's perception of his opportunity structure, but we made some rough evaluations based on available data. First, the distribution of aspirations was compared to the actual proportion of students completing a specific school level in the city of Amsterdam.[4] Desired levels of aspiration far exceeded expectations based on the proportion enrolled in institutions higher than secondary schools. Expected-education levels came closer to the actual proportion of enrollments. On the basis of expected levels students overaspired for university by 9 percent, yielding a 2:1 ratio of aspiration to enrollments. On the other hand, aspiration for higher-vocational education almost exactly matched the proportion enrolled. On the basis of these figures one could conclude that with respect to the current opportunity structure educational aspirations are moderately unrealistic in regard to their level of choice for university; whereas aspirations for higher-vocational education are completely in line with opportunities.

There may be yet a third way of evaluating realism. We must give some allowance in interpreting our results to the problem of sampling error. We have purposely oversampled three specific types of secondary schools, eliminating a significant proportion of students in other schools (25%) who conceivably might have different aspirations. We have also undersampled dropouts and student transfers; although absolute school dropout is low in the Netherlands, there is still some question as to whether those who transfer to other schools for academic reasons are not, in fact, less ambitious. Ideally, an evaluation of the realism of educational aspirations should be based on data concerning the actual proportion of students who go on to various types of higher education from those specific school types included in our sample. Such data were only available for grammar school students. Dutch national statistics indicated that for 1966, 63 percent of all male grammar school students went on to university.[5] Since grammar school students comprise 40 percent of our sample, if 60 percent of them aspired to university, a minimum of 24 percent would anticipate this level of education. Since only 19.8 percent anticipate going, we might conclude that the university was underchosen with respect to the opportunities open to a portion of our respondents. Later we will look at the educational aspirations of grammar school students separately to see if this conclusion can be further supported.

Mobility Orientation as the Relation Between Class and Aspiration

The data already presented bear witness to the fact that our respondents are moderately mobility-oriented. As a group they express fantasy choices that would indicate considerable desire to move upward on the status ladder. And, at the very least, when asked about their most realistic expectations for future status, they do not anticipate any downward mobility.

We cannot make any valid inference about the extent of mobility aspiration, however, unless we look at the relationship of a respondent's aspirations to his class background.

Mobility itself is a relative phenomenon; for an individual is only mobile if he changes his status to a level different from that of his parents. Mobility is, therefore, the difference between two variables: the positions of a generation of parents, and the positions of a generation of offspring. The sum of such differences, their direction, and their extent gives us a measure of the amount of collective mobility which takes place.

It follows, therefore, that mobility aspiration must also be measured in a relative fashion. An individual, for example, has high-mobility aspirations only if he expresses an intention to improve his status from that of his parents. Thus, in this study we are not concerned with the absolute level of aspiration of a respondent, but rather with the difference between his aspirations and his parent's status. The overall extent of mobility aspiration, for example, will be evaluated by looking at the degree to which class background determines our general aspiration indices, and at the more specific types of aspiration operationalized in this study. Throughout this study, relationships between various types of aspiration and other variables are examined. But only the impact of relative aspiration (that variance in aspiration which is left after its determination by class background has been removed) is considered in our analyses when we are, in fact, concerned with mobility aspiration.

The reason for our emphasis on relative aspiration rates is that sociological thinking and research has frequently overlooked the analytical distinction between relative and total movement. The tendency to ignore relative rates of aspiration stems from a similar tendency in macroscopic mobility studies.

Sociologists have frequently been more concerned with examining absolute mobility rates than with the consideration of mobility as a relative or circulative phenomenon. Thus, one frequently hears arguments such as the following: Mobility is low because only 10 percent of the lower class reach elite positions, or 20 percent of the lower class reach middle-class positions. The statement of rates in such a manner does not take into account the relative size of the different strata and the total potential mobility which could take place. Nor do such statements take into account the relative distance moved by individuals within the status hierarchy. Such simplistic rates are usually arrived at by simple twofold or threefold divisions of the status hierarchy and by the calculation of the percentage of a specific class group who change their status upward. When presented in this way, the data generally support high inheritance of parental position and stability in the class structure. If the same rates are calculated in a relative fashion, a completely different picture emerges. Thus, because the lower class, according to a tripartite division of the class structure, constitutes 66 percent of the population, a contribution of 10 percent of their membership (or 6.6 percent of the total population) to the elite, which in turn constitutes only 5 percent of the population, would actually be impossible without expansion of the elite stratum, because, in this case, the absolute contribution of the lower class to elite membership would exceed potential mobility of any stratum to the elite. Manipulated in this way, then, the data show high mobility, not in absolute terms, but in the relative or circulative sense.

Our use of the adjective "circulative" requires a little explanation. The calculation of relative rates, illustrated above, might be criticized on the grounds that they are merely an artifact of improper categorization of status levels. If we divided the class structure up in a hierarchical fashion, but in such a manner that each step in the status ladder contained an approximately equal number of incumbents, the mobility of those in the lower strata to the higher ones might still be rather low. A set of statistics compiled by Otis Duncan on American mobility patterns, in which he divides the status ladder into seventeen levels, gives us an opportunity to test this assertion.[6]

If we consider the movement between the highest and lowest categories, Duncan's data would appear to support the picture of low mobility. This is shown by the fact that farm laborers who occupied the bottom of the status hierarchy contributed only 22,000 individuals to a total professional population of 4,638,000. However, if one peruses Duncan's data a little further, it becomes apparent that while the contribution of farm laborers to the professional group is low, so is that of all other categories, including that of those from professional backgrounds. The highest contribution of any category was only 8 percent (proprietors). Thus, Duncan's study, although it attempts to categorize as many status distinctions as possible, supports a picture of low inheritance and high circulation. Circulation is illustrated by the fact that the recruitment of most occupational categories (both high and low) draws not just from adjacent categories but from a wide variety of groups; thus, upward mobility is almost evenly matched by downward mobility in Duncan's data. It may be convenient to refer to the sum of upward and downward moves as vertical circulation. Whether one cuts the class structure into a large or small number of categories, it is apparent that such vertical circulation is high. Throughout most industrial countries the amount of vertical circulation or mobility is fairly substantial. Most national mobility studies report a product moment coefficient of .4 to .5 between the status of fathers and sons.[7] Thus, at best, inheritance as a mechanism of stability in the class structure accounts for only 25 percent of the variance in social status.

The attempt to demonstrate low-mobility rates and blockages of opportunity emanates from that sociological tradition (see Chapter 1 for a fuller discussion) which associates class barriers and inequality with high inheritance of status privileges. That the data do not fit an inferential structure supporting such a picture of the class structure has been carefully ignored. The distributive concept of inequality proposed in Chapter 1 has received little support. Equality is seen as maintained in an absolute rather than a distributive fashion by most theorists.

The preference of sociologists for a picture of the class structure as characterized by high inheritance has also affected their interpretation of data on mobility aspirations. Most studies of educational or occupational aspiration limit themselves to the measurement of absolute differences in aspiration rates between classes. One of the most consistent and highly replicated findings in the entire sociological literature is that the middle and upper classes have higher absolute mobility aspirations than the lower or working class. Such evidence is frequently cited as a phenomenon due to inheritance within the class structure. The interpretation usually advanced is that as a group the middle and upper classes are more motivated to succeed than the lower class. Hollingshead states, for example,

Lower class youngsters have limited their horizons to the class horizon, and in the process they have unconsciously placed themselves in such a position that they will occupy the same levels as their parents.[8]

Such conclusions are based on an incomplete inference. Researchers fail to consider certain relativities inherent in the class structure. Aspirations are reported in terms of hierarchical levels, but the class groups of the aspirants are somehow seen as being on the same plane, although they are, in fact, the hierarchically ordered objects of mobility aspiration. Furthermore, the distance aspired is computed from the same starting point for all aspirants; yet differential levels of aspiration are accounted for, strangely enough, as in the quote from Hollingshead above, in terms of different starting points.

The failure to consider relativities in the class structure based on differential starting points has resulted in an incorrect assessment of the extent of mobility aspiration. The consistent finding of absolute differences between strata in the level of occupational aspiration between strata does not necessarily support the conclusion that the class structure is characterized by high inheritance of parental position. High transmission of parental class position would only be indicated if aspirations were totally limited to the class horizon. The data would have to demonstrate that the average level of aspiration was very close to the level of parental status. Instead, in almost all studies of aspiration there is considerable evidence that in terms of relative standing the lower classes frequently aspire as far or further on the status ladder than those who are from higher social origins. The author has personally computed ratios of aspiration for other studies and found this to be the case.

The first deliberate empirical attempt to measure relative occupational aspirations was made by L. Empey in a study of Washington state high school seniors.[9] He calculated relative ratios of aspiration by taking the difference between the mean aspiration score for each class group and its ordinal position in the class hierarchy. Such a method takes into account that the aspirations of an individual who aspires from a semiskilled background to a clerical position are equally high as those of the individual who aspired to a professional position from a small business or semiprofessional background. Similarly, the individual of semiprofessional background who aspires downward to a skilled craft occupation would receive the same aspiration weight as the individual from a skilled craft background who aspires no further. Employing this type of measure, Empey's findings were that the relative aspirations of lower-class individuals were, in fact, higher than those from the middle and upper classes.

The use of a relative measure also makes it easier to assess the proportional impact of inheritance and mobility on the aspirations of individuals. The range of values on the ordinal scales of background and aspiration can be used to interpret the relative influence of each. Thus, the closer the mean aspiration for a particular status category to the value of the ordinal position of that category, the greater the impact of inheritance on mobility aspiration, and the lower the extent of relative aspiration. On the other hand, the further the mean aspiration for a particular status category from its ordinal position, the greater the relative mobility aspiration, and the lesser the impact of inheritance.

A relative measure of mobility aspirations also allows one to conduct analyses of mobility patterns. The interpretation of the extent of mobility aspirations depends, to some degree, upon what kind of mobility configuration the researcher is looking for. That interpretation will differ, therefore, according to whether he is looking at upward mobility, downward mobility, or vertical circulation as his focal point.

We have argued that in analyses of actual mobility rates the predominant pattern, when the data are correctly interpreted, is that of vertical circulation, with upward mobility being nearly matched by downward mobility, except insofar as structural elimination of categories alters the extremes of the continuum.

In determining whether the aspiration pattern approximates a vertical circulation model, one must take into account the interaction between upward and downward mobility, and the limitations at the upper and lower ends of the status continuum. Thus, if mobility aspirations express perfectly the empirical finding of vertical circulation, the results would have to look something like this: The incumbents of the lower strata would aspire upward toward the median status category, with the increment of relative aspiration in each case being just the difference between the ordinal position of that category and the median category; those in the median category would have a relative aspiration score of zero, since their upward mobility would be exactly matched by their downward mobility; thence, upward the relative aspiration score would become negative, expressing again in each case the exact difference between the ordinal position of each category and the median category.

If the reader has thought carefully, he will already have concluded that if the specifications of the above model were perfectly met, the absolute aspiration score for each status category would be the same as the value expressed by the median category. Empirically such a perfect pattern is probably rare, for although the weight of current evidence implies vertical circulation, the impact of inheritance is still notable in all industrial societies and would probably influence aspiration patterns. The specification of an ideal pattern, however, does serve the purpose of providing a standard of comparison for empirical data.

There is a second reason for the specification of the "perfect" vertical circulation pattern of aspiration. The pattern of mobility can vary from that of vertical circulation without any change in the impact of inheritance. In Ralph Turner's[10] study of mobility aspiration he posited two ideal patterns of *upward mobility* aspiration, one of which incorporates high inheritance, the other of which incorporates low inheritance. The first pattern he terms the "race model" and the second the "ladder model." The race model pattern expresses a general desire of all respondents for mobility to the extreme upward end of the status continuum. The pattern would be reflected in ever-increasing aspiration score increments as one moves from the top category to the bottom, expressing in each case the proportional distance of each category from the highest one. The ladder model expresses a general desire of all respondents for the same degree of mobility relative to their position on the continuum. Such a pattern would be reflected by equal aspiration increments from every status category. Except at the top, where one could aspire no higher, the correlation coefficient between class background and aspiration for a ladder pattern of mobility would be high, and the coefficient for a race pattern would be moderately low, limited from further decline only by our ability to predict the aspirations of high status respondents.

If one assumes a different set of patterns from that of upward mobility, however, the correlation coefficient no longer reveals the degree of inheritance. Patterns of downward mobility and vertical circulation, when either strong or weak, can be expressed in similar correlation coefficients, although only perfect vertical circulation would yield a correlation coefficient of zero.

Thus, the determination of the pattern of mobility aspiration must proceed independently of the evaluation of its extent. In most cases we rely upon correlation, and multiple regression coefficients for an evaluation of the extent of relative mobility aspiration; however, in the analysis below, we interpret both the pattern and extent of mobility aspiration by using the mean as a descriptive statistic.

Before we proceed with the data analysis, one further point must be discussed regarding our students' mobility aspirations, which will perhaps clarify the purpose of all of the foregoing distinctions between patterns of mobility aspiration. In a contest system, as we have argued, one of the primary mechanisms of social selection, as well as of social control, involves high-mobility aspiration. Since the major institutions of status selection are more voluntaristically oriented, selection occurs to some extent according to level of aspiration, and students must be differentiated more competitively. The norm will be for higher mobility aspiration, since the ideology perpetrates the belief that sufficiently high aspirations are, to some degree, all that is necessary for the achievement of high status. Furthermore, adolescents, of the age group in our sample, will not be differentiated according to ultimate occupational status until after they leave secondary school. Consequently, under a contest system, aspirations are more likely to be at fantasy levels, reflecting a general desire for upward mobility. Therefore, the race and ladder models, which describe possible patterns of upward mobility aspirations, are more likely to be appropriate to a contest.

In a sponsored system, students are already to some degree by adolescence differentiated according to future occupational status. If their destination is downwardly mobile from their origin, according to their school level, they are more likely to express the downward mobility aspiration which reflects what will happen. Since upward mobility aspirations yield little mileage in a sponsored school system, there is no competitive pressure to help them. Consequently, in a sponsored school system, upward mobility aspiration should be matched to a greater degree by downward mobility aspirations, reflecting greater realism with respect to knowledge of destination. This should be true whether the relationship between aspiration and background as measured by correlation expresses high or low inheritance of parental status.

Desired and Expected Occupation
and Background

The correlation between class background and desired occupation is .42; the correlation between class background and expected occupation is .48. The low levels of these two coefficients indicate that inheritance is only moderately important in explaining the aspirations of students. The value of r^2 for the highest correlation is approximately .25, leaving 75 percent of the variance in occupational aspiration unexplained.

Because of the moderate size of the coefficients between occupational aspiration and background, we can tell nothing about the pattern of relationships between the two variables without using other descriptive statistics. In order to accomplish this end, a cross-tabulation of father's occupational background and the two occupational aspiration measures was made for our sample. The mean occupational aspiration was computed for each of the nine parental background groups and subtracted from the hypothetical midpoint of each background category. The resulting relative aspiration scores are arrayed against the absolute aspiration scores and ordered by background in Table 4-3. The results fall closely in line with a vertical circulation model of aspiration. The distribution of relative aspiration scores (background-desired occupation) for desired occupation shows that upward and downward mobility aspiration are almost matched. As one proceeds up or down from the median category each step away in either direction shows an almost equivalent decline or climb in aspiration score. One may remove the bottom and top categories as possible sources of sampling and measurement distortion; however, if one does this the picture is not altered. The distribution of aspiration scores for expected occupation shows a similar pattern, with a higher tendency towards downward mobility from the upper-status categories.

The above findings show an interesting contrast with the two American studies conducted by R. Turner[11] and L. Empey,[12] in which similar analyses of occupational aspiration data are presented. Both of these show distributions of relative aspiration which approximate most closely to the "race" model. Therefore, without making allowance for sampling error, it would seem that our hypotheses concerning the patterns of aspiration in sponsored and contest school systems would be corroborated. Both the American studies and the present one, nonetheless, show similar correlations between class background and aspiration.

Table 4-3
Mean Occupational Background and Aspirations

Occupational Category	Mean			Difference	
	Desired Occupation	Expected Occupation	Desired-Expected	Background-Desired Occupation	Background-Expected Occupation
1. Unskilled labor	4.23	3.16	1.07	+2.73	+1.66
2. Semiskilled labor	4.65	4.27	.38	+2.05	+1.67
3. Skilled labor	4.67	4.31	.36	+1.67	+1.31
4. Clerical	5.47	4.92	.55	+ .97	+ .42
5. Self-employed; owners of small- to medium-size businesses	6.10	5.93	.17	+ .60	+ .43
6. Semiprofessional	5.84	5.69	.15	− .66	− .81
7. Middle-level managerial	5.91	5.48	.43	−1.59	−2.03
8. Professional	6.43	6.50	− .07	−2.07	−2.00
9. Executives; large-business owners	7.25	6.45	.80	−2.25	−3.25

School and Mobility Aspiration

Under a sponsored system of mobility the impact of school on aspiration should be even more profound than that of social origin. The social class origin of the students' parents determines to a moderate extent what kind of school they attend. But after the initial sorting and sifting, the level of secondary school in which they are enrolled is the primary determinant of their mobility chances, and undoubtedly overrides their class origin in importance. Thus, whatever the initial impact of social class on aspiration, this effect is almost totally mediated by the influence of the school environment and by the relationship of the school to future class position. The level of aspirations instilled in him by his parents before he entered the secondary school must frequently be changed. The evidence indicates that the parents in team with the school teacher cooperate in the "cooling-out" process accompanying reduction of aspirations and in the adjustment process accompanying the improvement of his mobility chances.

Ideally, under a contest system, personal aspirations play a very important part in determining the future destination of the student. Under such a system the secondary school is not structurally differentiated with regard to either the abilities or mobility paths of its students; the major mechanism of selection for future status is the competitive differentiation of aspirations. Although many have argued that certain ascribed factors, such as class background, intelligence, or race, are responsible for recruitment in the American system, the fact remains that such advantages must be manifested in a certain level of aspiration or they go unrewarded. Therefore, since persistence of the aspirant is the most problematic aspect of selection, the primary emphasis is placed on maintaining a generalized "ambitious" or competitive stance that will give the student sufficient drive to proceed further. The main drive for an educationally ambitious individual under contest norms is to "go to college" rather than to achieve at the specific level that will allow him to come favorably through the selective process. Under sponsorship, however, it is not aspiration but rather the right type of secondary schooling which will determine whether he goes to college. Consequently the ambitious parent or student must concentrate their efforts on seeing that he attends the appropriate school at an earlier age.

Under a contest system, the status dimension of an individual's future occupation is dependent upon the level of education he achieves relative to his peers. Thus, a college education will yield him a more prestigious job than a high school education. However, under a sponsored system, the impact of the educational system on occupational allocation is almost entirely determined by the type of school the student attends. It is true, of course, that those who receive college preparatory training must attend school longer. However, since this level is not accessible to students in other school types, there is no particular competition for it once the initial selection of educational destination has been made.

Because such a large proportion of the status dimension of the student's occupation is determined structurally by a sponsored system of secondary education, personal aspirations at variance with the range of jobs for which he is destined would tend to be either constrained or discouraged. The major lines of cleavage in aspirations should be found in the structural distinctions made within the school system, whereby schools are graded by the ability of the student and his occupational destination. The socialization of students to the appropriate goals is probably considerably strengthened by institutional segregation of the promising from the less than promising. The curriculum the student receives and the expectations of both teachers and peers are all geared to attainment at a specific level. Consequently divergent aspirations are likely neither to be inspired or to receive social support. Because of the institutional isolation of the different school types, it is entirely likely that a distinctive student-teacher subculture develops which even further focuses aspirations by limiting the student's knowledge and comprehension of alternative careers.

Within the Dutch system each level of secondary school trains for a specific range of occupational opportunities. Within the constraints set by this range, there is probably, however, still a good deal of competitive aspiration. The credential structure of the Dutch school system places the severest constraints upon the occupational career of the technical school student, who is restricted to skilled manual-labor occupations. The clerical and grammar school students may compete for an overlapping range of jobs in the middle-status categories, although the grammar school student has both a sharp competitive advantage for higher-status positions, and the only claim to jobs at the upper end of the status continuum, which require elite education.

Since the sponsored system operates by restricting the educational opportunities of students at an early age, its impact on educational aspirations is even more profound than on occupational goals. The student may retain some familial socialization as regards an appropriate or desirable occupational goal, because he has not had to face the harsh realities of the job market. But he is directly involved in school structure, and, whether or not the restrictions on his occupational destination are transparent to him, he is acutely aware of the credential structure whereby his educational opportunities are restricted. One of the tasks of the secondary school curriculum is to make the student familiar with his credential structure and align his goals accordingly. At each level of secondary school the student may aspire further to some type of higher education, but at the technical school the handicaps on his progress are more extreme than at the grammar school.

If a sponsored system does inculcate relatively realistic aspirations, the primary evidence for this would be that the student's school level has a strong impact on his goals. Since the school determines the ultimate mobility of the student, the alignment of his aspirations with those most appropriate for his school level would be indicative of realism. One way of determining the realism of aspiration levels would be to compare them with the projected opportunities for students at each school level. If aspiration is an attitudinal variable as we suspect, then the most important evidence for realism in aspirations is simply the presence of sharp cleavages in aspiration levels between schools. Students may not be capable of making truly realistic decisions regarding their destination because of insufficient knowledge, but they would acknowledge the constraints upon their futures by expressing markedly different levels of aspiration at each school level.

**School Type and Occupational
Aspiration**

Tables 4-4 and 4-5 present the distribution of desired and expected occupation by school type. Simple inspection reveals that the level of aspiration increases in substantial steps for both varieties of aspiration as we move from technical to grammar schools. In addition, the choice of higher-status occupations declines as one moves from desired to expected occupation, at all school levels. In general the results seem to indicate that students acknowledge the constraints upon their occupational futures placed upon them by the school system. While there is some overlap in choice of specific occupational categories between schools, the average student is most likely to align his aspirations with the norm for his school.

Table 4-4
School Type and Desired Occupation

Occupational Level Desired	School Type		
	Technical	Clerical	Grammar
1. Unskilled labor	0.0%	0.0%	0.0%
2. Semiskilled labor	2.3	0.0	0.0
3. Skilled labor	57.8	14.3	1.0
4. Clerical	4.6	3.8	1.0
5. Self-employed; owners of small- to medium-size businesses	4.6	6.7	4.6
6. Semiprofessional	16.7	45.6	27.6
7. Middle-level managerial	5.3	13.4	5.1
8. Professional	4.6	16.2	55.1
9. Executives; large-business owners	4.0	0.0	5.6
Total	100.0%	100.0%	100.0%
Total number	173	105	196
No answer	3	22	20
No answers as a percentage of respondents per school type	1.7%	17.3%	9.2%

Gamma = .752
Chi-square 260.2; $p < 0.001$

In terms of the gross pattern, therefore, students seem to be making realistic evaluations of their mobility opportunities. A more refined analysis of realism can be conducted, however, by considering the variations within school levels. Cleavages in aspiration levels probably come about in *two* different ways: Primarily, the system operates to restrict the magnitude of aspiration levels for those in the lower plateaus of the educational hierarchy by distributing their aspirations according to the actual opportunities which await them in the job market; in addition, however, the structure of sponsorship also acts to restrict the *range* of the student's choice. Because of the structure of educational credentialization certain aspirations become implausible rather than merely less likely. For example, the choice of an academic profession is not just unrealistic for the technical school student, it is clearly illogical, because he cannot even enter competition for such a career. The appropriate mobility channel is simply closed for him. On the other hand, the choice of corporation president as an aspiration may be unrealistic, but it is not illogical, for he could theoretically reach this level without credentialization. Therefore, within the logical "range" (the range of possibilities, however remote) of goals available to a student the

Table 4-5
School Type and Expected Occupation

Occupational Level Expected	School Type		
	Technical	Clerical	Grammar
1. Unskilled labor	1.3%	0.0%	0.0%
2. Semiskilled labor	0.7	0.0	0.0
3. Skilled labor	77.5	12.3	2.3
4. Clerical	1.3	13.5	9.6
5. Self-employed; owners of small- to medium-size businesses	1.3	6.7	3.4
6. Semiprofessional	13.3	48.4	26.4
7. Middle-level managerial	2.6	13.5	6.1
8. Professional	2.0	5.6	48.3
9. Executives; large-business owners	0.0	0.0	3.9
Total	100.0%	100.0%	100.0%
Total number	151	89	178
No answer	25	38	38
No answers as a percentage of respondents per school type	14.2%	29.8%	17.5%

Gamma = .829
Chi-square 320.6; $p < 0.001$

pattern of aspiration could conceivably reflect a contest. Students may simply select the most highly valued goal available to them, even if it is highly improbable. It follows, therefore, that in evaluating the realism of the student's choices, we need to consider separately whether the student's aspirations are (1) logical, given the structure of the educational system, or (2) excessively high or low, given the structure of opportunities.

Let us turn first to the occupational goals of technical school students. Their horizons are clearly the most restricted. The majority (57.8%) do not desire an occupation other than that of skilled labor. Enough individuals express desired choices above this level to indicate that they are probably aware of the desirability of higher-status occupations. When we move to expected occupations, however, such higher-status choices have largely disappeared. Only the semiprofessions receive a substantial number of expected choices (13.3%).

Even this level of choice for the semiprofessions may be somewhat unrealistic, for the Dutch national statistics indicate that very few technical school students will acquire enough supplementary education (2%) to lead them to such an occupation. The reason that technical school students focus their higher aspirations on the semiprofessions may be related to the structure of the school system. The only available mobility channel for lower-technical school students is the higher-technical school which leads directly to semiprofessional employment, as a technician. Few students make this move because the scholastic standards imposed by higher-technical schools are as high or higher than the grammar school. But the path is theoretically open to them, whereas others are closed. Thus technical school students may be focusing the majority of their higher aspirations on this category because it is the only mobility avenue open to them.

A different set of constraints is operative in the clerical school. Clerical school students may not enter a university without first transferring to a grammar school and completing another course of study. In practice, only 13 percent of Dutch students make this transfer. Therefore, since clerical school students have a low likelihood of obtaining the requisite education, we would anticipate a low rate of aspiration for the professions. This prediction is supported by our data. A moderate number (16.2%) desire a professional occupation, but only a very few (5.6%) actually anticipate entering one. By contrast, the rate of aspiration for the semiprofessions and middle-managerial positions is high and somewhat optimistic. Almost half of all clerical school students anticipate entering a semiprofession. If aspiration reflected actual employment opportunity, however, the skilled labor and clerical work categories would have to receive more choice than the semiprofessions. It would seem that, within certain constraints the clerical school students are aspiring to the upward limit of the range of occupations available to them. This pattern of results is entirely plausible. For a student would tend to know more about his potential than his realistic chances. The route to an academic profession is indirect and difficult of access, whereas the route to the semiprofessions via supplementary education is direct and considered a logical next step.

We can see the same picture in the aspirations of grammar school students. Almost half anticipate entering professional occupations. This finding cannot be simply interpreted as a desire for higher status or as a desire for a glamorous job, although both of these factors probably enter into the level of aspiration. For if prestige were the only concern, we would anticipate higher levels of aspiration for the two adjacent status categories. The mechanism influencing grammar students towards higher professional aspiration may be simply that they perceive the professions as the upward limit of their potential mobility via the school system. All grammar school students have the option of proceeding on to the university, they need do nothing but exercise it. This path is already ascribed for them by the educational system and is a natural route to a professional position. But students may perceive selection for middle-managerial, or higher managerial status to be more achievement-oriented, and this would act as a barrier to aspirations. Or perhaps, students may simply understand more clearly the route to higher status via a college education, whereas they might have little knowledge concerning promotion in organizational hierarchies.

School Type and Educational Aspirations

In examining the influence of school type on educational aspirations we can employ the same mode of analysis as with our exploration of its relation to occupational aspirations. Again, the most important indicator of realism would be the presence of sharp cleavages in aspiration levels by school type. Inevitably, however, there would also be overlap between schools in choice of educational goals because secondary school level does not completely determine access to further education. Because of these overlaps the full extent of realism can only be ascertained by determining whether such concurrences in goals would be logical given the structure of the Dutch school system. Thus, for example, it would be reasonable to expect some overlap in choice between school types for the higher-vocational level of education, since this level is accessible to students from all secondary schools even if not with equal ease. Although the particular level of choice observed may not be realistic from the standpoint of opportunities available we cannot discount it as unrealistic from the student's knowledge of mobility channels available within the system. On the other hand, we would not anticipate any overlap between school types in terms of aspiration for university, since this level is theoretically open only to those who have completed grammar school or its equivalent. Whatever their frequency aspirations for university by other than grammar school students would have to be counted as unrealistic, since the school structure makes no provision for the regular transfer of these students to a college preparatory curriculum.

Table 4-6 illustrates the distribution of desired education by school type. The responses reveal that, in terms of fantasy aspirations, a majority of the students in all school types anticipate obtaining some further education; between a quarter to a third within each school type contemplate going no further than secondary school. The overall level of aspiration rises as one ascends the graded hierarchy of secondary school types, but there are still considerable overlaps. The highest level of aspiration for university is registered by grammar school students. However, enough token aspiration for university is expressed by clerical and technical school students to indicate that they are probably aware of the superior prestige associated with this level of education. Even more notable, however, is the fact that the dominant focus for higher educational aspiration among clerical and technical school students is the level of higher vocational education. Since students in both these types of schools are severely handicapped in terms of access to a university education, it is not surprising that they concentrate their highest aspirations on the next available level.

Table 4-6
School Type and Desired Education

Educational Level Desired	School Type		
	Technical	Clerical	Grammar
1. Primary	0.6%	0.0%	0.0%
2. Lower technical	29.3	1.6	0.0
3. Clerical or middle-technical	22.4	27.6	0.0
4. Some grammar	1.7	3.9	1.4
5. Grammar or equivalent	4.6	20.5	23.1
6. Higher-vocational or teachers training	29.3	35.4	14.2
7. Some university	0.6	1.6	9.4
8. University	11.5	9.4	51.9
Total	100.0%	100.0%	100.0%
Total number	174	127	212
No answer	2	0	4

Gamma = .592
Chi-square .285.7; p <0.001

When we compare the distribution of expected education (illustrated in Table 4-7) with that of desired education the first thing we should encounter is a reduction of illogical aspirations—those which the school structure inhibits, irrespective of the degree of individual initiative. This is clearly the case with our students. The choice of university drops to an insignificant percentage for clerical and technical school students, which would be expected since it is far beyond their reach. A higher-vocational education, although theoretically available to technical school students, would be extremely difficult for them to acquire from the academic standpoint. Because of their diluted academic curriculum they could not compete with clerical and grammar school students for this level. Therefore, it is not surprising that there is drastic decline in choice of higher-vocational education at the expected level for technical school students. The same process of revision can be observed with respect to the clerical school student's aspiration for grammar school. Although 20.5 percent of clerical school students express desired choices for grammar school, statistically only 8 percent of all clerical school students ever attend this level, because of the handicaps faced by the student in making such a transfer.[13] The expected level of choice for grammar school (8.7 percent), corresponds, therefore, very closely to actual opportunity.

On the basis of the above analysis we can conclude that given the structure of the Dutch school system, our male students do not consistently make illogical choices. Their aspirations might still be unrealistic, however, from the standpoint

Table 4-7
School Type and Expected Education

Educational Level Expected	School Type		
	Technical	Clerical	Grammar
1. Primary	0.6%	0.8%	0.0%
2. Lower technical	60.2	1.6	0.0
3. Clerical or middle-technical	26.9	54.8	0.0
4. Some grammar	1.2	5.6	4.2
5. Grammar or equivalent	1.2	8.7	35.8
6. Higher-vocational or teachers training	9.4	27.8	13.2
7. Some university	0.0	0.8	17.9
8. University	0.6	0.0	28.8
Total	100.0%	100.0%	100.0%
Total number	171	126	212
No answer	5	1	4

Gamma = .825
Chi-square 530.5; $p < 0.001$

of the levels of choice expressed. To test for this possibility we compared the expected educational levels with actual opportunities, as gauged by national statistics on school transfers.[14] The outflow of students to different types of higher education from the three school types was used as an index of current opportunity. In general, it was found that the educational aspirations of our students, on the basis of expected levels, were unduly pessimistic. In particular the aspirations of grammar and clerical school students were considerably lower than opportunities. According to the national average, almost 63 percent of grammar school students attended college in recent years, but only 46.7 percent of those in our sample anticipate going. Most remarkable is the fact that 54.8 percent of clerical school students and 35.8 percent of grammar school students do not anticipate going any further than their current level of education, for the statistics indicate only a very small percentage of male students in either school actually do not pursue some higher level of schooling. Only the aspirations of technical school students match actual opportunities. The percentage of technical school students actually completing various levels of education is very close to the proportion aspiring to that level in our sample.

The overall impression that the above data convey is that the educational aspirations of our students are realistically oriented, both in terms of the student's knowledge of the workings of the system and in terms of his awareness of his competitive chances. Educational aspirations, when compared with actual opportunities, are far more realistic than occupational ambitions; they are even somewhat pessimistic. The cleavages in aspiration levels by school type indicate that the student is aware of the constraints that the sponsored system places on him, and the absence of illogical choices further reinforces such a conclusion. These data are most consistent with the proposition that the sponsored system works primarily by constraining educational goals and that its impact on occupational selection comes later and, indirectly, through credentialization.

The Indices of Preferred and Anticipated Status

Numerous studies rely upon only one indicator of aspiration, such as occupational or educational plans. In this study a more general measure was employed; it attempts to tap mobility aspirations in a more comprehensive fashion. Two indices were constructed, of which one was designed to summarize fantasy aspirations, and the other to measure realistic expectations. An index of fantasy aspiration was constructed by assigning ordinal weights to levels of desired education and occupation; the weights were then combined into a new variable termed "the index of preferred status." The same procedure was followed in combining expected education and occupation to form a measure of realistic expectations termed "the index of anticipated status. In order to reduce sampling bias, the weights given for each level of a specific variable were based on the number of prominent modes in its distribution. Following this procedure, the distributions of desired- and expected-educational aspiration were collapsed into four categories, which received values of one to four, and the distribution of desired- and expected-occupational aspirations were collapsed into three categories, which received values from one to three.

A Causal Model of the Determinants of Mobility Aspiration

The recently popularized method of path analysis was used in this study as a multivariate technique for analyzing the relative effects of different variables. Path analysis is basically a technique for the application and interpretation of multiple regression coefficients used in testing complex causal models. The most extensive description and rationale for sociological applications of path analysis has been given by O.D. Duncan in a recent article on the subject.[15] Duncan's use of path analysis contains many refinements such as the calculation of residuals and of path equations; the former are not used in this study since they are not essential and provide surplus information which is of dubious value here. For a description of the computational methods the reader is referred to Duncan's article.

Path analysis is a means of evaluating complex causal models that contain more than one variable. The object is to establish a set of equations which predicts how much any one variable in a causal system affects another. Before one can do this he must be explicit about the theoretical assumptions around which his model is constructed. These will be reflected in two procedural steps: (1) the specification of networks or paths of causation between the variables and (2) the specification of the quantitative contribution of each path or causal process. The organizing assumptions of the model must be validated theoretically since it is clearly possible to specify absurd causal linkages. Once this has been done, the application of path analysis to a set of variables enables one to evaluate the quantitative parameters. The specification of the expected quantitative effects prior to the construction of the model is not absolutely essential. These may be arrived at inductively and the causal parameters described in an ex post facto fashion; however, the specification of causal processes and the inclusion of appropriate variables must be done in advance. And, if feasible, possible omissions of exogenous variables should be noted beforehand. In particular, assumptions regarding the causal ordering of specific variables in the model must be made explicit and graphic.

The determination of causal priorities is a complex methodological issue and in the social sciences, especially, there are few clearcut criteria for their determination. One of the few basic rules available to us is a guideline developed earlier by natural scientists, that is, nevertheless, not always reliable. This rule of thumb can be stated as follows:

When events which one can otherwise presume to be connected follow one another in sequence, the earlier events may have caused the later events; and at any rate it is logically difficult to imagine that a later event caused an earlier one.

Temporal ordering has been used frequently by sociologists to uncover causal sequences, although such a procedure is not without its problems. It is difficult, for example, to support the notion that events are always discrete and do not extend into the past or future.

In this study the causal model employed to examine the determination of mobility aspirations was also organized according to temporal assumptions. The model used is illustrated graphically in Figure 4-1. Following the precedent of other studies it was assumed that the causal influence of class background is temporally prior to that of other variables influencing aspirations. The usual rationale for this assumption would be that the major impact of familial socialization comes early in the life-cycle of the adolescent. However, we placed this variable first in temporal order because of our knowledge of the dynamics of the sponsored school system. We assumed that the impact of class background would be totally exhausted at the age of eleven or twelve, the time when background characteristics and parental initiative exert a moderate influence on

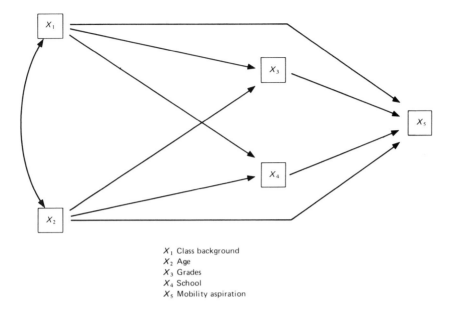

X_1 Class background
X_2 Age
X_3 Grades
X_4 School
X_5 Mobility aspiration

Figure 4-1. Path Diagram of the Effects of Class Background, School, Age, and Grades on Mobility Aspiration.

school choice. (It was assumed that the school would exert a major influence on the mobility chances and aspirations of an adolescent after this time in his life.) The school, in turn, could be assumed to be a causally prior influence on aspirations (rather than aspirations on school), because our knowledge of the social psychology of adolescence leads us to believe that solid aspirations are not formed until about age fifteen or sixteen, and then only in conjunction with approaching entry into the labor market. There are many other reasons, which we have already spelled out in our previous discussion, why school should have a major causal impact on mobility aspirations; however, the temporal priority of the school's influence is a separate assumption. The students have already been enrolled in school for three to four years, but, of course, the causal relation between school and aspirations could be simultaneous.

Two other variables were included in the model: age and grade-point average Age was included primarily as a control for sampling bias, since our group was not homogeneous with respect to this variable, which in time of adolescence can exert a strong independent influence. No assumptions were made about its causal priority; it is, therefore, placed first in order, as would be the case with any "background variable." Scholastic achievement has been found to be strongly associated with aspiration in American studies. Under a sponsorship system, however, we hypothesized, that after the sorting into school types a competitive standard of school achievement would have little place, since the primary differentiation of students by academic ability has already occurred. Thus the variable of student grade-point average was included in the model in order to test this assertion. It was assumed that the effect of academic achievement would be causally prior to mobility aspirations and collateral with that of the school. One could easily support the competing assumption that academic ability is causally dependent on mobility aspirations, but alternative models were not tested because the overall relationship of scholastic ability to other variables was extremely low.

The arrows drawn between the variables (see Figure 4-1) indicate the direct and indirect causal paths between variables. The indirect impact of age was of no interest because it bears no meaningful relationship with other intervening variables; we were primarily interested in its contamination of mobility aspirations. The indirect impact of background via school was the causal path most crucial in supporting our basic hypothesis in that it would illustrate the mediation of class background through school level. The indirect path connecting class background, grade-point average, and aspiration and the other indirect paths connecting age and aspiration were included merely for completeness.

The evaluation of this model can proceed according to two criteria. The first criterion would be the specification of important causal processes. This could be observed by the extent to which one is able to improve the explanatory power of a series of bivariate correlations, by reducing these into separate components that circumscribe different causal processes. The second criterion would be the overall efficiency of the model in explaining variance as revealed by a multiple correlation coefficient. The lower the total explained variance, the more likely it is that other exogenous causal processes have been left out of the picture.

The Relative Effects of Class Background
and School on Mobility Aspirations

The first step in the evaluation of our causal model is the examination of the correlational relationships between those variables which are of theoretical importance to us. If the variables involved in the model were not significantly correlated, at least in part, there would be little use in trying to determine their relative contribution to the overall dependent variable. In fact, the use of multiple regression makes the most sense when several variables are highly correlated, because it permits one to dissect the independent effects of different factors from their mutual correlation.

The correlations between all the variables incorporated in the path model are illustrated in Table 4-8. Of greatest importance to us are the relationships between the independent variables in the model (class background, age, grades, school level) and six measures of mobility aspiration: the indices of preferred

Table 4-8

Zero Order Correlation Matrix of Stratification Variables, Aspiration Variables, and Other Control Variables

Variable*	X_2	X_3	X_4	X_5	X_6	X_7	X_8	X_9	X_{10}	X_{11}	X_{12}	X_{13}
X_1	−.02	.45	.46	.36	.42	.65	.67	.48	.74	.49	.63	.78
X_2		·03	−.04	.00	−.05	.06	.05	.10	.09	.04	.10	.08
X_3			.25	.15	.21	.31	.27	.31	.31	.25	.35	.32
X_4				.44	.60	.40	.45	.32	.42	.83	.39	.48
X_5					.50	.31	.32	.24	.34	.53	.32	.37
X_6						.34	.39	.30	.38	.94	.36	.43
X_7							.74	.50	.63	.42	.82	.73
X_8								.45	.66	.48	.66	.87
X_9									.65	.35	.90	.62
X_{10}										.45	.73	.94
X_{11}											.43	.51
X_{12}												.77
X_{13}												

*X_1 = School X_6 = Father's education X_{10} = Expected education
X_2 = Grades X_7 = Desired occupation X_{11} = Background index
X_3 = Age X_8 = Expected occupation X_{12} = Index of preferred status
X_4 = Father's occupation X_9 = Desired education X_{13} = Index of anticipated status
X_5 = Mother's education

and anticipated status and their components, desired and expected occupation, and desired and expected education. Age, class background, and school are significantly correlated with all measures of mobility aspiration (whereas grades are not). This gives a basis for exploring their causal impact. We must also take note of the fact, however, that the independent variables are all intercorrelated to some degree. Thus, without decomposing the mutual correlation between them we cannot make any accurate assumptions regarding their separate influence. We may note, for example, that the highest correlations with aspiration measures are obtained with school, the second highest with class background, and the lowest with age. To render any conclusions regarding these results would be premature, however, for this rank-order might disappear when we control for spurious effects due to intercorrelation.

To control for dependencies between the hypothesized causal variables a multivariate analysis of independent effects was carried out according to the technique we have already referred to as path analysis. This procedure involved two steps: (1) the computation of "direct effects" (without any assumption of causal priority) through a single-stage multiple regression analysis; (2) the computation of "indirect effects" through a nesting of several regression analyses, utilizing an explicit causal model wherein some independent variables were assumed to be causally dependent on others.

The results of the single-stage multiple regression analysis are presented in Table 4-9. If it is true that social-class origin is the primary "stratifier" of aspirations, then these data should reveal that class has a considerable effect independent of the level of school the student attends. If the opposite is true, then school should have a considerable effect independent of social-class background.

It is the latter proposition which is clearly supported by the data. The effect of being in the appropriate level of school far overrides that of class background in determining the level of an individual student's aspiration. Although mobility aspirations and social class are moderately correlated, the direct effects of social class, controlling for other variables, are small. This is true whether one looks at the summary measures of aspiration (preferred and anticipated status) or at their components (desired and expected education and occupation). The effect coefficients range from nonstatistically significant values to marginally significant ones. By contrast, the independent effects of school stand in even clearer relief, far outweighing those of social class. For the summary measures of preferred and anticipated status, the effect coefficients for school are .52 and .72, respectively, versus .16 and .17 for class. The increase in relative impact of school as we move from preferred to anticipated status indicates, in addition, that school is the primary axis for the revision of mobility aspirations. Most of the school's impact on revision is probably via educational expectations, where the increase in its relative effect from desired to expected levels is the greatest.

As the reader will recall, age and grade-point average were included in the regression model primarily for the sake of completeness. Age is a control for sampling bias, and the nature of its effect is not of interest to us theoretically. If its effects had been large, however, we would have had to conclude that our sample was inadequate with respect to stratification by age. Grade-point average was also of minor importance. It is interesting to note, however, that its effects are exactly as hypothesized: either very small or statistically insignificant.

Table 4-9
Direct Effects of Four Variables on Aspiration

	Dependent Variables (X_5)					
	Occupation		Education		Status	
Independent Variables	Desired	Expected	Desired	Expected	Desired	Anticipated
X_1 Class Background	.13*	.20*	.15*	.12*	.16*	.17*
X_2 Age	.00	.05	.10	−.04	.06	−.05
X_3 Grades	.07	.07	.11*	.11*	.12*	.11*
X_4 School	.55*	.59*	.35*	.70*	.52*	.72*

*$p < 0.05$

On the basis of the analysis (of direct effects) we would normally assume that a good portion of the original correlation of class background with mobility aspirations was spuriously produced by its covariation with school level. The correlation however, between school level and social-class background is not a meaningless one which can be discarded as spurious. The relation is actually one of prior causation of school level attended by parental class background, with a consequent reduction of the variance in social class for each school type. Thus, part of the impact of social class on mobility aspirations is produced indirectly by the fact that higher-status parents tend to send their children to higher-ranked schools.

Path analysis was used to test for indirect effects of social class. Path coefficients, which were first computed in line with our causal model (see Figure 4-1), specify school as an intervening variable between class and aspiration. Duncan's method of taking the product of coefficients along particular indirect paths was used to estimate the amount of mediation which took place.[16] The results are reported in Table 4-10. It is apparent that the indirect path between class and aspirations via school is either equally important as or more important than the direct one. The indirect effect of class through school accounts for the following proportions of its total effect[a] on aspirations (indirect effects/total effects): preferred status, 56 percent; anticipated status, 63 percent; desired occupation, 62 percent; expected occupation, 54 percent; desired education, 50 percent; expected education, 70 percent. From these data we can conclude that the primary impact of social-class background on aspirations is mediated by oblique causation through school level.

The patterns of both direct and indirect effects support the same conclusions, although in a slightly different way. Our initial hypothesis was that a sponsored system would function to channel aspirations by educational streams rather than

Table 4-10
Indirect Effects of Class Background on Aspiration

Dependent Variables (X_5)	Indirect Effects of Class		Total Indirect Effects
	Via Grades (X_3)	Via School (X_4)	
Desired Occupation	.00	.22	.22
Expected Occupation	.00	.24	.24
Desired Education	.00	.14	.14
Expected Education	−.01	.28	.27
Preferred Status	.00	.21	.21
Anticipated Status	.00	.29	.29

[a]The correlation between class and aspiration was used as a measure of the total effects of class.

by social class. This is supported by the overwhelmingly greater direct impact of school on mobility aspirations. Being of higher social status than the norm for a particular school has little or no independent impact. For the two summary measures of aspiration, however, a significant portion of the impact of class comes about because higher-status parents send their children to correspondingly higher levels of secondary school. The partial coincidence of parental status and school level only underscores the impact of the school, for the higher status of the parent can only be said to have a causal relation to the formation of aspirations if this results in the placement of his child in the appropriate plateau of the school structure. Once he is so placed his aspirations resemble those of his schoolmates rather than of his class cohorts.

The above conclusions were based on an analysis of relative weights derived from multiple regression calculations. Such weights can only be interpreted in the context of a single equation or regression model. Several of the assertions we were interested in investigating do, though, involve comparisons of causal models in terms of the total explained variance and its component parts. Of great interest, for example, was a comparison of the relative importance of social class and school level as causal determinants of different types of mobility aspiration. In order to accomplish a uniform criterion of comparison between equations was necessary. The one most acceptable to this author seemed to be the contribution of independent variables to the explained variance in the ultimate dependent variable.

The computational scheme used to partition the variance in each equation was borrowed from a method suggested by O.D. Duncan in a recent work.[17] His procedure, as illustrated in Table 4-11 (see heading Computational Procedure), extracts the unique contribution of each variable, working backward from effect to more remote causes through a formula for the manipulation of coefficients of multiple determination. This method obscures the indirect effects of variables. Thus we must keep in mind, as we compare the impact of variables between equations, that we have further knowledge regarding the nature of their causal influence.

The major object of this analysis was a determination of the relative importance of social inheritance in stratifying student mobility aspirations—as opposed to the importance of other social processes, known or unknown, which sort the individual by destination. Within the context of this study the major agent of sorting by destination is the school, whereas the major agent of social inheritance is parental status.

For our subjects the data reveal that both processes play a significant role in the determination of aspirations; there is no clear pattern of either variable outweighing the other for all varieties of aspiration. Even if we wish to regard the two summary measures of preferred and anticipated status as the best indicators of mobility aspiration the picture still does not change. The impact of social class is slightly more pronounced for the preferred status index, but there is no clear domination by one or the other variable.

Table 4-11

A Partitioning of Variance for the Determinants of Mobility Aspiration

Components*	Computational Procedure†	Dependent Variables (X_5)					
		Occupation		Education		Status	
		Desired	Expected	Desired	Expected	Preferred	Anticipated
Total effect of X_1	$r^2(51)$	.151	.176	.116	.157	.199	.266
Increment for X_2	$r^2 5(12) - r^2(51)$	.041	.021	.053	.067	.034	.041
Increment for X_3	$r^2 5(123) - r^2 5(12)$	.002	.002	.010	.010	.006	.009
Increment for X_4	$r^2(1234) - r^2 5(123)$	.218	.202	.123	.330	.163	.334
Sum, total variance explained	$r^2 5(1234)$	.412	.401	.264	.554	.402	.650

*X_1 = Class background
X_2 = Age
X_3 = Grades
X_4 = School
X_5 = Aspiration variable (column variable above)

†From O.D. Duncan, *Socioeconomic Background and Occupational Achievement: Extensions of a Basic Model* (U.S. Department of Health, Education, and Welfare, May 1968).

There is, in fact, no consistent way to summarize the pattern of relative and absolute contributions of the two primary causal variables. Yet, a small set of segmental interpretations are relevant to our hypotheses. It can be observed that the greatest relative contributions of school level are registered for the discrete indices of occupational and educational aspirations, whereas the greatest relative contribution of social class is to the variance in the two summary indices of mobility. It seems, therefore, that a more comprehensive desire to raise one's social status is more strongly determined by his class background; owing perhaps to the fact that middle- and upper-class individuals are more aware of the connection between education and mobility. Segmental mobility aspirations, on the other hand, seem to be more influenced by school level.

The differences between the fantasy and reality components of each of the varieties of aspiration are also noteworthy. The absolute impact of social class increases as we move from fantasy to reality measures for each of the three aspiration types. The tendency is very slight for occupational aspiration; the coefficient for desired choices is .151 and that for expected choices is .176. For the educational and summary measures of aspiration this propensity increases, and is accompanied by a corresponding rise in the absolute contribution of school level. There is also a sharp increase in explained variance as we move from fantasy to reality questions for both the summary measure and educational aspirations. These trends indicate that for both types of mobility aspiration the constraints of class and school level are felt most acutely when students are asked to give their most realistic preferences. On the other hand, students are most likely to disregard such constraints when asked about their fondest wishes.

Chapter Summary

The major purpose of this chapter is to determine the degree to which a sponsored system of selection is operating to channel the mobility careers of our students. Since our subjects were all adolescents, the only way of gauging the impact of social selection was to examine its consequences for their mobility aspirations. To evaluate the impact of sponsored selection, we formulated two general hypotheses.

First, we hypothesized that certain features of sponsorship, such as early selection for sharply differentiated educational paths, would be reflected in more realistic and stable aspiration levels than those reported by similar American studies. Secondly, we hypothesized that, as a result of the same factors, the school level of the student, when all other variables are controlled, would be the primary determinant of his mobility aspirations.

Insofar as the absolute levels of aspiration are concerned, the first hypothesis receives only weak confirmation. Our subjects are strongly mobility-oriented. Most students express higher levels of occupational and educational aspiration than those which their parents achieved. As in comparable American studies, these overall levels of aspiration far exceed the actual distribution of opportunities; while slightly more realistic, they do not seem to be aligned with reality. These findings are further underscored by the fact that we attempted to measure both the fantasy and the reality extremes of aspiration through the inclusion of separate stimulus questions.

Occupational aspirations are more consistently out of line with opportunities than are educational aspirations. Even the fantasy levels of educational aspiration are plausible considering the recent expansion of Dutch secondary and higher education.

Another finding consistently reported by earlier American studies and repeated among our Dutch subjects is a relatively stereotypical distribution of occupational aspirations. Rather than choosing from the entire range of low- and high-status occupations available to them, students select occupations primarily from one of three categories: the professions, the semiprofessions, and skilled labor. Taken together, these three categories account for four-fifths of all desired occupational choices made by our subjects. We speculated, however, that the adolescent's relative ignorance of the job market and specialized occupational titles was, to some degree, responsible for such a pattern and that it might be more useful to consider their occupational aspirations as relative positions on an attitude.

The data we have accumulated on absolute levels of aspiration, while they are suggestive, do not permit us to make any really valid inferences regarding the extent of mobility orientation. This can only be gauged by noting the degree of relative aspiration: that variance in aspiration which is left after its determination by class background has been removed. The extent of relative aspiration among our subjects, as indicated by the coefficient between background and occupational aspiration, is fairly similar to that reported in comparable studies conducted in the United States. The correlation coefficient, however, can disguise many different patterns of relation between background and aspiration. In American studies of adolescent mobility orientation, the predominant pattern uncovered can be described in terms of a race model in which incumbents of every class level express a similar desire for mobility into high-status occupations.

The pattern uncovered in this study, though, is closer to a "vertical circulation" model in which downward and upward mobility aspirations are almost equally matched. This is consistent with the early sorting and sifting of students into different mobility routes which characterize a sponsored system. The race model, on the other hand, is more consistent with the logic of a contest.

A sponsored system of selection does not appear to reduce the overall level of aspiration. This may, as further research accumulates, turn out to be a constant for societies at a certain stage of development—perhaps the subjective reflection of already observed constant rates of mass mobility in industrial nations. It follows, therefore, that the crucial test of the impact of sponsorship on aspirations lies not with the absolute levels of choice but rather in the way aspirations are stratified.

This conclusion is more consistent with the overall pattern of results presented in this chapter. Our second hypothesis (that school level determines the mobility aspirations of the student) receives a broad pattern of support from the data. Under a sponsored educational system as it operates in the Netherlands, the structurally differentiated school levels produce profound cleavages in the pattern of adolescent aspirations.

The pattern of educational and occupational aspirations among the three different school types can be summarized as follows. The level of aspiration increases in sizable steps for both varieties of aspiration as we move from technical to grammar school. Furthermore, in all three school types, the choice of higher educational and occupational levels declines as we move from fantasy to reality questions.

In general, these results indicate that the students acknowledge the realistic constraints upon their occupational and educational futures, placed upon them by a sponsored school system. The interpretation of these findings as evidence of realism would seem to be contradicted by the unrealistic overall levels of aspiration in our sample. To reconcile these two sets of data we must consider the mechanism whereby a sponsored educational system actually stratifies aspirations. Occupational aspirations within school types actually reflect a contest pattern because choices for specific occupational categories far exceed available opportunities. It is the range of aspiration which varies between school types and which actually produces the observed differences in levels. Sponsorship acts primarily to restrict the scope of choices which are considered logical careers. Within each school type, students choose the highest-ranked goals available to them but not those for which mobility routes are lacking. Thus, clerical school students choose the semiprofessions at a rate grossly out of proportion with opportunities, but very few choose occupations that require a university education. Educational aspirations are more in line with opportunities available to those within each school type. Again, as with occupational aspirations, there is an absence of illogical choices. Aspiration for educational routes that are not available to them is almost nonexistent.

The most important evidence confirming the impact of a sponsored system of selection on aspirations is the pattern of causal influences exerted by social class and school level. Our data indicate that parental class position exerts a similar overall impact on mobility aspiration as that uncovered in American studies.

Nevertheless, the social process whereby this impact occurs is completely different under sponsorship. Our multiple regression analysis indicates that the direct influence of school level greatly exceeds that of background when the latter is controlled. Furthermore, the computation of indirect effects via path analysis reveals that the major proportion of the effect of social class is actually indirect and accounted for by prior determination of school level. These results are fully consistent with the logic of sponsored selection. They testify to the fact that the impact of social class is largely exhausted after its initial impact on selection for a specific school type.

Only those high-status students, for example, who are selected for elite schooling are likely to have high aspirations. Conversely, those students whose school level is high relative to their class background are likely to have aspirations that conform to the mean for their school level. The same set of generalizations hold true, of course, for downward mobility.

5 Social Selection and Value Orientations

In this chapter we attend to the major goal of our study: an examination of the impact of sponsored succession on value orientations. The theory of social selection holds that the differences referred to as class culture are produced by an overarching set of social institutions and norms which arrange the sorting and sifting of individuals for different statuses in a society. In Dutch society, we have argued, educational institutions play the key role in this process. In the Dutch educational system, the selection and segregation of students at an early age produces a profound restriction of mobility channels. In this process, students are differentiated in terms not only of their future class destinations but also of their opportunities to acquire the attitudes and values appropriate to membership in a specific stratum. Because the school dominates the facilities for socialization in this manner the entire process is referred to as institutional socialization.

First we provide a brief review of earlier research on the relationship between social stratification and values, a rationale for the selection of values investigated in this study, and their research geneology. This material facilitates our effort to incorporate the results for this study in a cross-national comparison, and helps us to bring our findings into a broader context.

The second half of the chapter is an investigation of institutional socialization through observation of its competition with other agents and mechanisms as reflected by patterns of relationships between our variables. The inferential structure we employ in making this evaluation is fully laid out in the course of the presentation of our data.

Previous Comparative Research on Value Differentiation

Comparative research on the relation between stratification and values is, save for a few prominent examples, almost nonexistent. To some extent the absence of research interest in this area can be related to the history of social science. Since their inception both sociology and anthropology have tended to regard societies as relatively homogeneous cultural entities and have assumed that the really important differences in values are to be found between societies. As a consequence systematic empirical or theoretical treatment of cultural variation has been severely limited. This is because the study of cultural differentiation, while representing a considerable body of literature, has most frequently been focused on differences between whole societies rather than on cultural variation per se, of any order. The favored approach is to regard value systems as a field for endless qualitative variation between societies, giving them their unique character. The investigation of endogenous variations due to structural cleavages within societies (such as those produced by social stratification) has received relatively little attention.

From time to time isolated attacks have been leveled against the assumption of intrasocietal homogeneity (e.g., from the standpoint of metatheories developed in the sociology of deviant behavior), but on the whole this precept has remained unchallenged.

Perhaps the only thoroughgoing analysis of our deficiencies in the knowledge of cultural variation has been put forth by Florence Kluckholn.[1] She outlines the basic problems as follows:

Even the very broad concepts ... ["unconscious system of meaning," "core culture," "culture themes," and others] are empirical generalizations, not analytical constructs. In both formulation and application they have been too particularized to single cultures to permit systematic comparisons between cultures, and at the same time, too grossly generalized to allow for the analysis of variations within cultures. All too frequently those who have demonstrated a uniqueness in the value systems of different societies have ignored the fundamental fact of the universality of some human problems and its correlate that human societies have found for some problems approximately the same answers. Also, in most of the analyses of the common value element in culture patterning, the dominant values of peoples have been overstressed and the variant values largely ignored.[2]

Kluckholn's critique introduces three empirical possibilities which have been largely neglected by social scientists in their treatment of value systems. These are as follows: (1) Cultural variability may have certain ultimate metes and bounds rather than being infinite; (2) cultural differences within societies may, in many instances, be more profound than those between them; (3) given certain limits to cultural variability it may be that cultural differentiation takes place on a more systematic basis then had previously been assumed. That is to say, it may be that all types of value orientations are present to a certain degree in every society but that they exist in "balance" with dominant systems of cultural patterning.

In the same work in which she presents the above critique (*Variations in Value Orientations*) Kluckholn advances a classificatory scheme for the analysis of value orientation which is based on five "crucial problems common to all human groups."[3] The combinations and permutations of this typology are intended to yield a comprehensive range of the possibilities for value differentiation oth between and within societies. She conducted a field study utilizing this scheme to support her original thesis. Unfortunately the aim of investigating the entire range of intersocietal and intrasocietal value variability proved to be too broad a goal for a single piece of empirical research. Her results were too general, and frequently too confusing, to be of much use to social scientists. In what was regarded as a modest attempt she was forced to employ a series of variables with approximately 243 combinations (3 to the fifth power). Faced with the analysis of data of such magnitude Kluckholn was not even able to present a full descriptive analysis of her results.

Nevertheless, Kluckholn's work was very suggestive, and one would anticipate that a fair number of "middle-range attempts" might have followed her lead. Research focusing on the area of the relationship between social stratification and values would seem to be ideally suited for evaluating Kluckholn's theoretical assumptions regarding value variation. Since all societies have stratification this would provide a systematic basis for exploring intrasocietal value variation from a comparative perspective. Very few investigations have exploited this potential, however. The only comprehensive study with which the author is familiar is one conducted by Joseph Kahl in Mexico and Brazil and compared by him in a subsequent recent article with similar studies conducted by others.[4] His investigation was inspired by the work of Florence Kluckholn. Discarding her unwieldy typology, he chose a limited number of variables, easily worked with in the analysis of his data. He employed measures that corresponded roughly to some of the types in Kluckholn's classification scheme, but that had been previously tested in domestic research on the relationship between social class and values. The value dimension these scales referred to was termed by him as "achievement orientation." This general configuration of values is also employed in this study, and our own conception of it is presented in the following section.

Kahl's results were generally positive. With few deviations he found that the four value indexes he employed were all moderately associated with social class (the actual correlations ranged from .20 to .42). However, from our standpoint, a great deficiency of Kahl's study, which he shares with others who have investigated the relation between stratification and values, is his failure to consider the impact of mobility on the class position of his subjects.

There is very little domestic research, however, on the relation of mobility to values which can serve as an alternative model. A few studies have been concerned with this problem, such as those of Hyman,[5] Strodtbeck,[6] and Rosen.[7] Only two studies, to the author's knowledge, have considered the relative impact of both mobility and inheritance on value orientations: those of Turner[8] and Rehberg.[9] Both of these studies, like this one, dealt with adolescent social origins, mobility expectations, and values. They will be compared with the results for our Dutch students. However, the reader should be constantly aware that such a base for comparison is extremely narrow. The validity and reliability of this study, from a comparative viewpoint, has been improved by the inclusion of items similar to those used both by Turner and Rehberg. The inclusion of the Turner items was by design. The inclusion of the Rehberg items was a happy coincidence which arose from the simultaneous use of sources based on the previous research of Strodtbeck, Rosen, and Kahl.

The Selection of Value Orientations

The investigation of the entire range of human values and permutations is, as Kluckholn's study shows, a somewhat less than economical task. For this reason the range of values investigated in this study has been restricted to a more easily manageable research focus. Two broad considerations dictated our choice. First, it was felt that it would be desirable to investigate a dimension of values which had been a persistent object of theoretical attention by sociologists in explaining intrasocietal value differentiation. Secondly, and more important, it was thought best to select a constellation of values which research had previously indicated might be related to important dimensions of social stratification.

According to the above criteria, a group of values was chosen which were related to what Kahl has called "achievement orientation." This broad rubric covers many value orientations that were formerly described under other labels such as "mobility related values," "ambition," or "future orientation." As a global concept, achievement orientation has received extensive treatment in theoretical literature and empirical research, perhaps more so than any other aspect of value systems.

Sociological concern with achievement orientation dates back to the work of Max Weber, who made it the focal point for his explanation of the success of Western industrial capitalism. The religious doctrine and the social position of the Protestant entrepreneur, Weber argued, combined to produce a set of social values based on unlimited striving or achievement (this-worldly asceticism). Such achievement values were crucial factors in bringing about the type of entrepreneurial behavior characteristics of economic activity in the West, and were an important factor in the evolution of a commercial middle class.

More recently, theoretical concern with achievement orientation has shifted away from entrepreneurial behavior to class values. Many sociologists now argue that differential concern with achievement characterizes the middle and lower classes. As evidence for this assertion, the higher rates of mobility of the middle class are frequently cited. Furthermore, it is thought by many that those individuals who are upwardly mobile from the lower class move up only as a result of becoming socialized to middle-class values.

Until recently, however, evidence for the existence of class values has been incomplete. True, some mobility studies do support the contention of higher-middle-class mobility, and studies of occupational and educational aspirations do show differences between classes. But this evidence is far from conclusive. Comparative mobility studies show higher rates of blue-collar mobility in some countries and re-analysis of occupational and educational aspiration data seem to indicate that relative aspirations (i.e., relative to the class position of the respondent) do not differ from class to class.

What has clearly been needed to demonstrate the assertion of class differences in achievement values is direct empirical investigation of *abstract* achievement orientation through relatively standardized instruments. Efforts to construct such instruments have been relatively infrequent, but they have been encouraging. While the results obtained have often been contradictory, they have, nonetheless, led to further refinement of concepts.

The most systematic and extensive attempt to measure abstract achievement orientation is contained in the work of David C. McClelland and his associates.[10] Through them an intensive investigation has been made of a psychological dimension of personality which they have referred to as "subconscious need for achievement." They measured this characteristic by means of a projective test in which respondents were asked to respond to picture cards by writing stories. These stories were then coded by the investigators for achievement-related ideas. Since the projective test does not depend on the respondent's self-knowledge, McClelland has asserted that it measures a subconscious or "motivational" dimension of personality which may not and often does not have any relationship to the subject's overt beliefs and behavior.

Empirical investigations have revealed that need achievement is related to many types of accomplishment (for example, entrepreneurial behavior, school grades, performance in experimental situations, and so on). But despite McClelland's extravagant claims for it (in the *Achieving Society*), the measure has severe limitations. The available evidence points to the fact that it is a global or generalized measure which will predict desire for excellence in a wide variety of areas. On the other hand, it cannot predict to a large number of sociological variables such as mobility striving because it does not indicate the direction in which achievement will be expressed.

From this line of reasoning it follows that *achievement directiveness* may be a component of "self-conscious" values rather than an enduring psychological dimension of personality. Several recent studies give credence to this idea. Rosen (1955) employed both McClelland's measure of need-achievement and a measure of self-conscious achievement values (based on the work of Kluckholn) in a study of high school students.[11] He found that for his sample of respondents, need-achievement was highly related to school grades (which are presumably more indicative of a generalized achievement orientation), whereas his measure of values showed no relationship to them. On the other hand, his measure of values showed a stronger relationship to mobility aspirations (as measured by desire for higher education), whereas need-achievement showed no significant relationship to the same variable.

Another feature of McClelland's theoretical description of need-achievement is his assertion that achievement motivation is the outcome of a particular type of socialization experience during childhood. Specifically, he hypothesized that high warmth or nurture, high standards of achievement, and low authoritarianism in a child's relationship to his parents were related to the development of high need-achievement. Some research has suggested that this may indeed be the case. However, a recent study by Scanzoni (1967), utilizing value scales similar to Rosen's, has uncovered that child-rearing practices are completely unrelated to both achievement values and mobility aspirations.[12]

The research described above seems to indicate that the psychological and cultural aspects of achievement orientation should be kept conceptually isolated, for although they bear some relationship they can vary independently with respect to different types of achievement. In the same vein sociologists have frequently argued that presumably enduring components of personality are crystallized in childhood or adulthood, and that qualitatively different components of personality take form as the individual matures. Thus, self-conscious goals or values can be seen as the social modus operandi whereby motives or needs are translated into different kinds of culturally defined achievement—thereby explaining why (at least in American society) achievement values are more frequently associated with occupational achievement and social mobility.

The Selection of Specific Achievement Value Measures

Methodological Commentary

The set of items selected for inclusion in the questionnaire were the outcome of a long process of background research and field testing. The criteria which guided the author in selecting them were diverse and, in a few instances, the product of arbitrary choice. A few considerations figured prominently in his choice, however. Primarily, items were chosen which bore some relationship to the concept of "achievement orientation" referred to above. Secondarily, but not less important, items were chosen which, on the basis of previous research and theoretical speculation, could be related to social stratification. Finally, wherever possible, items were chosen which had previously been used in domestic or comparative research, with an emphasis on the latter. We had a fair degree of success in meeting this last requirement. Almost two-thirds of the items had been employed in other research, and 30-40 percent had been used in earlier comparative research or had been previously translated and employed by Dutch researchers doing replications of American studies. A smaller proportion of items were composed or adapted by the author and field tested in the Netherlands.

The resulting list of items was rather large as compared with previous studies. Not all of these were employed, however, and the data analysis reported in this chapter deals with only thirty-seven discrete value items. A variety of response formats were employed with these items in the questionnaire. Insofar as possible the items were kept in the format in which they were originally used. The reasoning was that, by changing the format, the comparability of the results of this study, with those obtained in previous ones, would be reduced. Most of them, including those composed by the investigator, are in Likert format. Those items taken from Turner's study (see questionnaire items 57 to 69) are composed as choices between two reciprocal-value alternatives. There is a strong theoretical argument for regarding values as choices or changes of emphasis between alternatives rather than as generalized endorsements of consensual norms. In addition to the consideration of comparability, however, there is no good methodological reason for changing the format. It has not been convincingly demonstrated by empirical studies that there is any difference between operationalizing values as positive or negative endorsements or as choices. On the contrary, the findings of the majority of researchers from whose investigations we have drawn the Likert scale items (Kahl,[13] Strodtbeck,[14] Rosen,[15] Cox,[16] and Sugarman[17]) agree with the findings of those who have used a choice format (Turner,[18] Kluckholn[19]).

Much of the previous research on achievement or class-related values has assumed that they constitute a global constellation. Frequently values have been measured in single scales, containing the diverse items, or in series of discrete items; either way a singular underlying dimension is held to account for their variation. In this study the more conservative assumption of multidimensionality was used to organize the study of values. Within the general rubric of achievement orientation, specific values were treated as independent of each other. Therefore, in addition to other considerations, items were selected to correspond to several broad categories that reflected those dimensions felt to be most important in studying the relationship of values to stratification. These categories are employed in analyzing and interpreting the data from this study. In a later phase of the analysis, groups of items within specific categories are combined into several value indices.

In classifying specific items into different value categories the researcher did not rely entirely on his own judgment. Because the item intercorrelations were frequently low it was difficult to employ them as a criterion of classification. So, in order to avoid biases in the investigator's perception the method of independent judges was employed. Statements of each value dimension, both positive and negative were composed or, in some cases, drawn from R. Turner's study. These were then read by three graduate students in sociology, each of whom was instructed to classify all questionnaire items employed in this study according to his own preference. Their classifications were compared with the investigator's own and whenever it was felt to be desirable changes were made; however, the final classification is not based on any single criterion. In several cases the investigator reserved his own judgment or employed evidence of intercorrelation between items.

The value categories and the items grouped under them are presented below. Some items belong to more than one category, and these are indicated by parentheses. Others, although classified, were felt to be ambiguous and are indicated as such. A number of items remain unclassified but are referred to discretely in the data analysis. The items are identified by a number keyed to the questionnaire to be found in the Appendix.

1. Deferred gratification
    (a) Postponement of reward: 16, 29, 36, 34.
    (b) Carpe diem: 20, 21, 31, 38.
    (c) Impulse control: 18.
    (d) Impulsivity: 25.
2. Success
    (a) Achievement gratification.
    (b) Secular success: 47e, 47d.
    (c) Existential gratification: 81, 82.
    (d) Self-expression: 47a, 47b.
    (e) Achievement vs. existential gratification: 59, 60.
    (f) Self-expression vs. secular success: 57.
    (g) Familism vs. secular success: 58.
3. Individualism
    (a) Self-reliance vs. mutual aid: 61, 67.
    (b) Individuality vs. fitting-in: 63, 65, 69.
    (c) Independence and freedom vs. authority & tradition: 68.
    (d) Individuality: 24.
    (e) Fitting-in: 19.
4. Familism
    (a) (Positive Expression): 75, 80, 87.
    (b) (Negative Expression): 89, 91.
5. Opportunism
    (a) Opportunism: 17, 23.
    (b) Interpersonal gratification: 47h.
    (c) Opportunism vs. rational mastery: 66.
    (d) Opportunism vs. interpersonal gratification: 62.
6. Mastery
    (a) Mastery: 35, 70, 76, 79.
    (b) Passivity: 26, 32, 74, 93.
7. Trust
    (a) Trust: 71, 73, 85, 95.
    (b) Distrust: 72, 84, 86, 88, 92, 94.
8. Miscellaneous and unclassified

Because the above classification was applied after the data collection had already taken place, it has some procrustean characteristics. Each cateogry is subsumed as a component under a larger dimension. Moreover, some categories are simply the reciprocal positive (e.g., rational mastery) and negative (e.g., passivism) expressions of a particular dimension or of a particular facet of that dimension. Other categories represent value alternatives that, while indicating the application of a particular dimension, are not necessarily the converse of each other. Thus, interpersonal gratification is presented as the opposing value to opportunism, but could just as easily oppose secular success or individuality. Another set of categories organizes those items which, drawn from Turner's study, represent choices between value alternatives (e.g., individuality vs. fitting-in). A few of these crosscut dimensions, however, then are simply placed arbitrarily under one heading.

To arrive at the final classification of items, the investigator and the three judges employed the definitions of the value alternatives as given below. These statements give the reader the option of judging for himself the validity of the particular groupings of items. The judges, it should be noted, were exposed only to these statements as presented individually and were not made aware of the broader headings. Those statements drawn from R. Turner's study are identified by Turner's name in parentheses.

An attempt was made to measure more than one facet of a single dimension of achievement values. Thus, some pairs of value alternatives are grouped together under a single rubric representing the dimension to which they refer. This is a particularly important feature of this study. The investigator felt that the better he could isolate the specific expression of a particular value serving to motivate individuals, the more useful his findings would be.

The Value Dimensions

1. Deferred Gratification

Postponement of reward

One should always act with the future in mind, treating the fleeting present in a calculating fashion for its contribution to the much longer future. The sacrifice of some immediate or momentary pleasure or gain when such sacrifice will help to secure a more worthwhile or pleasurable goal in the future is highly valued. The logic is that of thrift, in which one forgoes the pleasure he could have at the moment by spending his money as he gets it so that he can buy something more desirable later on, or invest the money and secure even greater returns. (Turner)

Carpe diem

One should always live in the present, treating the future as undependable, unpredictable, and often a mere illusion. One should never pass up an opportunity to enjoy the present to its fullest, for no one can anticipate whether such opportunities will come later. Thrift is an illusion because of the unpredictability of the future. Those who save are no wealthier in the future than those who spend, but they will have had less enjoyment along the way. (Turner)

Impulse control

The expression or satisfaction of impulses as they occur must be restricted when they afford a threat to future benefit. A word unwisely spoken or a careless action may follow one for years. Since the long-range consequences of any action or word are not usually immediately apparent at the moment they occur, it is generally better to control impulses rather than express them, or at least to delay their expression until a reasonable time has been allowed to explore their possible effects. (Turner)

Impulsivity

The best time to satisfy an impulse is at the moment when it occurs. The satisfaction is fuller because it is spontaneous. Those who practice impulse control never fully enjoy anything because even when they do decide to act they are likely to feel ambivalent, to have lingering doubts as to the wisdom of expressing the impulse. (Turner)

2. Success

Achievement gratification

The individual who possesses this orientation is happy only when working hard. He is characteristically a doer and not a dreamer. He has a perpetual sense of the unattained. He feels that there is always someplace to go but no defined point at which to stop. He is generally oblivious to risk and considers failure only one of many obstacles to be overcome.

Secular success

The individual who values secular success is in many ways very similar to one who is characterized by achievement gratification. However, he differs in terms of the object of his aspirations. For this type of individual the only things worth striving for are in the realm of material possessions, power, prestige, and status.

Existential gratification

Happiness is achieved in the long run by being satisfied with what life has to offer you. The important thing is to tailor your desires to what is realistically available.

The individual who possesses this life orientation is characterized above all by a moderate assessment of his abilities and a distinct lack of ambition. Either through objective circumstances or personal conviction he has renounced the value of striving or getting ahead. There is not much sense in working hard to get somewhere, he rationalizes, when there is really no place to go.

Self-expression

Work and life activity are generally viewed as ends in themselves and as opportunities for expressing the talents and creative potential of the individual.

Consequently, since self-expression is the essence of artistic work, cultural and intellectual development are generally preferred to material or "worldly" accomplishments.

3. Individualism

Self-reliance

The most worthwhile accomplishments are those we achieve by ourselves, depending entirely on our own resources. The strong person struggles through difficult tasks on his own, while the weak person calls on others for help. A man can take real pride in what he knows is entirely his own achievement in a way that he cannot when the achievement is that of several persons. The competent person gives more to the group than he receives. (Turner)

Mutual aid

The principal value in accomplishment lies in working co-operatively with others. The finest persons are those who are equally ready both to give and to receive aid from others. An effective system of mutual aid, of pooling knowledge, skills, and resources is the best way of getting the most out of everyone. (Turner)

Individuality

The discovery and development of one's personal uniqueness is a prime satisfaction, and having some individuality is a point of pride. To be just like the common run of men is to be nothing. The effect of the group on the superior member is a leveling one. But whether one is superior or not, he should have some uniqueness to which he can point. (Turner)

Fitting-in

Excessive uniqueness is an obstacle to an effectively working system of mutual aid. The person who stands out too much from others, even because of his superiority, often creates friction. A person gets a more worthwhile sense of satisfaction from feeling that he has a great deal in common with his fellows than he does from feeling superior to them. (Turner)

Independence and freedom

An important goal in life is to free oneself from restraints upon behavior imposed by friends or associates or society. To feel completely free to make up one's own mind whether to do something or not to do it is the greatest satisfaction man can have. Working under the supervision of others is stultifying. Tradition is merely the tyranny of the past. Freedom is more important than accomplishment. (Turner)

Authority and tradition

A man gains most by accepting the supervision of those who are more experienced or better qualified, and by following the wisdom of the ages as it is incorporated in tradition. One should have more sense than to set his opinions against those of authorities in a field. The ability to accept supervision constructively and make good use of authorities, and to understand and use the time-tested recipes for behavior is the mark of a mature person. (Turner)

4. Familism

For the familistically oriented individual the family is an inclusive social world. The basic mores of society are centered on the family and the basic code governing relationships is family solidarity. Consequently everyone outside the family is regarded with suspicion and there is a strong feeling that the family should stay close together—physically close together. Authority is centered in the age and kinship criteria that differentiate members of the family: filial obedience and parental authority override loyalty to larger collectivities or groups of unrelated peers.

5. Opportunism

Opportunism

The individual characterized by this life orientation believes that success in most endeavors is to be achieved by any means, fair or foul. He regards the world as a "tough" competitive place in which the highest rewards generally go to the unscrupulous. He believes that contacts or inside dealings are of prime importance in getting ahead—ability is irrelevant: it's "who you know not what you know" that counts.

Interpersonal gratification

The individual characterized by this life orientation tends to have a strong need or desire for affective ties to others. For this type of person relationships with others are ends in themselves and not a means to other extrinsic goals. Consequently he is not interested in dominating or manipulating people: relationships are cultivated only for the intrinsic gratifications involved such as warmth or sympathy. This type of person may choose occupations, for example, which allow him to "work with people" in a cooperative or assisting manner.

6. Mastery

Rational mastery

The world is essentially an orderly place and amenable to rational control. Therefore a person can and should make plans which will control his destiny. The external world may sometimes be hostile, but it is by nature solvable or understandable. Luck and chance are specifically discounted; in the long run, hard work and careful planning yield the best results.

Passivity

Man is affected by forces larger than himself which he can neither master nor understand. Life's problems cannot be overcome by conscious effort or planning, for whatever a man does there is always the chance that fate will intervene.

A man may work all his life for something which destiny, in the end, may deny him. Therefore it is senseless to look ahead or to plan for the future.

7. Trust

Trust

The individual characterized by this life orientation has a firm belief in the goodness, honesty, generosity, and brotherliness of the mass of men. Consequently, he has a strong faith in the value and stability of interpersonal relations and he views human nature as essentially cooperative. He is inclined to be receptive to people; and, above all, he accepts everyone at face value, giving credence to what they say until they show him otherwise.

Distrust

The individual characterized by this life orientation has very little faith in the value or stability of human relationships. He has a general distrust for and contempt of people. He has, furthermore, a very cynical attitude towards human nature believing that the world is a jungle and that most people are likely to take advantage of you if they have a chance. Consequently he is abnormally wary and may interpret signs of friendliness as devices of manipulation.

Recapitulation of Theory and Hypotheses

In the previous chapter evidence was presented to show that a sponsored system of selection was operating to focus the mobility orientations of our student respondents. The impact of sponsorship on values is a separate question and, as we shall see, presents far greater problems of verification. Because of the explicit relationship between early selection and mobility in a sponsored system it would indeed be surprising if our respondents' mobility goals were not in concert with those facts determining their personal fate. Value orientations, however, unlike aspirations, are not restricted in their application to mobility; they can motivate or rationalize action in a wide variety of contexts. Every effort has been made to choose those values which have shown some relationship to social stratification. In almost each case, however, it is quite feasible that a particular value could be applied to a set of actions or situations having no direct bearing on social stratification or mobility.

In the course of the following data analysis, we deal with three separate questions bearing in some way or other on the relationship between social selection and values. The first issue, the relationship between socialization and social selection, receives the most attention as the central focus of this study. The other questions are of more tangential or subsidiary interest. Nevertheless, the same data and analytic manipulation are employed in evaluating all of them. Therefore, the issues are intertwined as themes in the interpretation and discussion of the results.

Social Selection and Socialization

Most empirical studies of the class values have treated the extent of cultural homogeneity within strata as the most important variable to be investigated. This issue is by no means completely neglected in this study; yet, our central concern is to throw light on the process of cross-generational maintenance of class cultures. The cross-generational maintenance of inequality requires that social stratification be conceived of dynamically as a process of social selection rather than as a static set of specified strata. In similar fashion class cultures are the outcome of specific features of the selective process which induce both the selection of individuals with appropriate values and differential access to institutional channels of socialization. This is in distinct contrast to conceptions which treat class cultures as self-perpetuating enclaves.

The overall process of social selection and socialization affecting the destinies and attitudes of Dutch students has been described in terms of sponsorship logic. The manner in which socialization is articulated with a sponsored system of selection deserves a brief recapitulation. Under sponsorship, individuals are selected in early adolescence for the positions in the class hierarchy they will occupy as adults. In the Netherlands this is implemented by selecting students at the age of eleven or twelve for one of three educational strata which prepare them for different occupational destinations. In this process individuals are sharply differentiated not only in terms of mobility opportunities, but also in terms of the facilities and experiences made available to them for internalizing important values. Students enrolled in elite programs receive education that goes beyond instrumental considerations and is oriented towards fashioning him into a specific cultural mold. The education of students in nonelite programs is much more instrumental in character and directed toward vocational preparation. Because the primary facilities for validating important values are invested in the school, socialization under sponsorship has been termed "institutional socialization." As in most systems of selection the social origin of the individual is important, but under sponsorship the influence of parental background operates primarily to produce a moderate class bias in initial selection for elite schooling. Once this selection process is over, the impact of competing agents of socialization, including parental influence, should be relatively minor.

The operational confirmation of institutional socialization via multivariate analysis is by no means an unambiguous problem. In sociological analyses, interaction between variables is a routine expectation and instances of unequivocal causation are rare. In the data under examination here it would not be plausible to expect that school will account for a completely dominant proportion of the variation. If, for example, this were the case, then those values would have little meaning in terms of a continuous class culture, for the implication would be that the school was socializing the current generation to a completely different set of values than those adhered to by the students' parents. The more plausible expectation is that the school socializes lower-class background students who are selected for mobility to the values of students from higher backgrounds, and vice versa. Thus, it would be anticipated that the primary direct impact of any variable on values should be made by the school; however, the social-class background of the student should have a considerable indirect effect via its prior determination of his school level. The same pattern would be anticipated for the already observed interaction between mobility aspirations and school level. It would not be plausible to assert that aspirations will be entirely unrelated to values in a sponsored educational system, because that system is not so restrictive of the student's class destination as to make aspirations completely irrelevant. On the other hand, we would definitely anticipate that the school would have a strong indirect effect on values via its prior determination of the level of aspiration.

We also do not anticipate the complete negation of anticipatory socialization under sponsorship. On the contrary, with regard to certain types of values it may be the more plausible pattern. Some values, for example, related to elite status may be accessible only via anticipatory socialization because social acceptance into certain echelons of the elite is not guaranteed by education, and may involve endorsement of values antithetical to those internalized in the educational process. Because of the high degree of interaction among our variables, however, the pattern of anticipatory socialization may be difficult to demonstrate. The persistence of anticipatory socialization would receive the most support from a predominance of strong direct effects by background and aspiration irrespective of notable indirect effects of school level. The confirmation of the pattern we have referred to previously as "future orientation," or the complete alignment of values with aspiration, would require the presence of strong direct effects of aspiration alone when other variables are controlled.

Ideological Variation in Value Endorsement

The choice of specific questionnaire items was based upon the assumption that, in large part, similar sorts of values would turn out to be related to social stratification in the Netherlands as in other countries. A qualitative departure of the data from this assumption would be surprising. It would not be implausible, however, that the operation of sponsored norms of selection might produce different degrees of relationship between specific values and social stratification. The logic of a sponsorship system clearly implies that some values will be stressed above others.

Two dimensions of values employed in this study might receive less emphasis under a sponsored system: opportunism and deferred gratification. Contest norms condone and even favor opportunistic striving that bypasses normal mobility routes. Under sponsorship, however, early selection gives the individual an exclusive and noncompetitive claim to elite membership. Thus, opportunistic strategies are not as likely to be associated with mobility, and deferred gratification is likely to receive less emphasis since the level of achievement which secures confirmation of elite status is reached relatively early in life. Extraordinary sacrifices of time and energy are not rewarded in terms of improved mobility chances.

Subculture vs. Value Pluralism

The determination of the degree of association between social stratification and values is an overall goal of this study although not the central one. If we cannot demonstrate at least a moderate tendency towards value discrepancy between social strata, then our more important objective, that of determining the impact of various components of social selection on value orientations, will have little meaning. In addition the overall credibility of our hypotheses concerning sponsorship will also be enhanced if it can be shown that the addition of variables indicating the impact of social selection improves our ability to predict value orientations.

As a theoretical issue, the extent of association between social stratification and values has been stated in terms of the choice between a pluralistic and subcultural conception of class culture. Because it would be unlikely that at least a few values are not associated with stratification, the existence of value pluralism should not be difficult to demonstrate. The real issue will be the extent to which our data give support to a subcultural pattern. Methodologically speaking, definitive support from our data would involve (1) consistent association of stratification of a broad range of values and (2) an ability to explain at least 50 percent of the variance across this range of values. Because of the well-known difficulty in measuring abstract value orientations we might relax these two criteria somewhat. But we cannot go too far in this direction. Weak support from our data should lead us to a reconsideration of theory.

A Causal Model for the Determination of Adolescent Values in a Sponsored System of Education

The data analysis presented in this chapter is conducted exclusively with multivariate techniques. One reason for this is that the full description of bivariate relations between value items and the hypothesized causal variables is not an economical task. A more important consideration, however, is that all of our central hypotheses (that is, those concerning the relations between sponsorship and value orientations) were based on the logic and power of path analysis as a multivariate method.

As we argued in the preceding chapter, the construction of an explicit causal model is a singularly important step in conducting any path analysis. Such procedure forces a discipline on the researcher, compelling him to acknowledge his assumptions and preventing him from conveniently ignoring unanalyzed relationships that are part of an implied causal chain. The presentation of a model is a particularly important step in this study because of the large number of variables which were analyzed in evaluating our hypotheses. To avoid any confusion in the exhibition and discussion of the results it is necessary to lay out completely the structure of our paradigm and the status of our causal assumptions.

The model used to analyze value orientations is illustrated graphically in Figure 5-1. The reader will note that class, age, school, and mobility aspirations, all used in the causal model of mobility aspiration in the previous chapter, are employed here again as independent and intervening variables. Even the interrelationships between these variables have not changed. The only difference in the model is the addition of value orientation as the ultimate dependent variable.

The causal ordering of the first three antecedent variables in the model was relatively unproblematic. As before, the causal positions of class and school are based on the temporal sequence in which they affect the posterior variables. Class was placed first in the causal order because its primary impact on selection and attitudes comes earlier in the life cycle via familial socialization. School was assumed to be a causally prior influence on both aspirations and values. The rationale for its position was based on our central hypotheses regarding the operation of sponsorship and the temporal location of its influence. The supposition was that values or aspirations unfold and congeal later in adolescence at least partially in response to the socializing effect of the school itself.

The crucial problem in constructing the model was to determine the causal relation between values and aspirations. The temporal location of both variables is ambiguous, and equally plausible theoretical arguments can be assembled for two sets of causal assumptions: (1) that the antecedent variables (class background and school) affect values through their prior influence on aspirations or (2) that they affect aspirations primarily through their prior influence on values. Some writers have expressed the conviction that it is the learning of appropriate

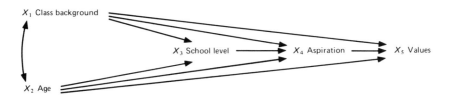

Figure 5-1. Causal Paradigm on Assumption That Aspirations Determine Values.

values which accounts for differential aspiration. Others have asserted that achievement values are learned subsequent to the formulation of personal goals. It is the latter assumption (that aspirations determine values) which was accepted by this investigator. The resultant causal paradigm is illustrated in Figure 5-1. This scheme is employed in evaluating our various hypotheses.

The Construction of Indices

Nine value indices were constructed as an aid to the final summary of our data. Seven of these were designed to tap some of those specific dimensions of value orientation that guided our initial selection of items. They were constructed by selecting highly intercorrelated items that had been classified under a specific value dimension and by summing the responses to a single score. The component items for each index are listed below, identified by a number keyed to the questionnaire (see Appendix).

Opportunism: 17, 23, 62, 66.
Familism: 80, 87.
Mastery: 26, 32, 35, 39.
Achievement gratification: 59, 60, 81, 82.
Individualism: 19, 24, 61, 63, 65.
Deferred gratification: 16, 21, 31, 34, 36, 38.
Trust: 71, 72, 73, 84, 85, 86, 88.

Another index was constructed with two items originally designed to measure the impact of sponsorship ideology on the folk norms of our respondents. Respondents were asked if, in their opinion, "drive and ambition are more important in getting ahead than the right education" (item #28) or if "the right education is somewhat more important in getting ahead than are drive and ambition" (item #33). The index was created by summing the responses for the two items so that the highest score would represent endorsement of education as a means of getting ahead. Because this measure deals with the respondent's idealized conception of routes to social advancement in his society, it was termed the "mobility paths index."

In addition to the above, another index was designed as a general measure of achievement value orientation, and is referred to as the "composite value index." This measure has two purposes. First, since only a minority of the item correlations with stratification were high, it was thought desirable to have an index which explained the maximum possible variance in our respondent's value orientations. By analyzing the portion of the value spectrum which appears to be most strongly related to stratification, we might gain a better understanding of causal mechanisms, and our findings would have broader applicability. It was also felt that an index which crosscut value dimensions would tap a qualitatively different dimension of attitudes. The respondent's willingness to endorse a comprehensive set of achievement values, rather than one or two discrete values, probably reflects more complete socialization, as well as a more consistent and reliable response pattern.

The composite index was constructed by selecting those items which had the highest average correlations with class background, school, and the two aspiration measures. The nine items which met this criterion were as follows (referenced to numbers used in the questionnaire): 19, 24, 26, 59, 64, 78, 79, 80, 81. Because not all the value dimensions are represented (e.g., familism and deferred gratification are excluded), comprehensiveness is sacrificed somewhat for predictive ability. Because of these and other limitations the composite index is not used to make a final assessment of our hypotheses. In actual fact, it only covers the same kind of ground as the separate indices from a different perspective. Therefore, the investigator felt that the more prudent course would be to weigh the results for this index with those for the discrete measures (taken together) in making final evaluations.

The Structure of Determination for Value Orientations

Correlations between the hypothesized causal variables and the value indices are presented in Table 5-1. The number of significant correlations is high, implying that every independent variable is somehow causally involved in the determina-

Table 5-1
Correlation of Value Indices with Age, School, Background Index, and Aspiration Indices

Value Indices	Background Index	School	Age	Index of Preferred Status	Index of Anticipated Status
Mobility paths	−.06	−.15*	−.12*	−.09*	−.12*
Opportunism	−.00	−.14*	−.04	−.12*	−.09*
Familism	−.14*	−.21*	−.11*	−.23*	−.23*
Mastery	.06	.13*	.04	.16*	.11*
Achievement gratification	.20*	.27*	.18*	.25*	.31*
Individualism	.27*	.30	.21*	.29*	.34*
Deferred gratification	−.08	−.10*	−.09*	−.00	−.02
Trust	−.03	−.02	−.10*	.00	.00
Composite value index	.42*	.50*	.27*	.41*	.49*

*$p < 0.01$

tion of values. The actual structure of causal effects is still obscured, however, since the correlations summarize not only the unique contributions of each variable but also those proportions of the variance produced by antecedent variables, and mediated by posterior variables in the system that we have specified.

The first step in decomposing these correlations is the computation of partial regression coefficients for the direct paths in our causal model (see Figure 5-1). The results of our computations are illustrated in Table 5-2. Note that two indices of aspiration have been included as independent variables: the preferred status index and the anticipated status index. Initially the multiple regression effects were calculated with each of these variables incorporated in a different model. When both aspiration measures were included jointly, however, it was found that they behaved differently both with respect to each other and with respect to other variables. We concluded that the combined effect of these two measures represented a better specification of the process whereby aspirations determined values. In the analysis which follows, the "effect" of aspiration always refers to the sum of the effects for both of these variables (negative and positive effects are subtracted).

Based on the paradigm of socialization that we elaborated for a sponsored system of education, the following series of results were anticipated. We assumed that, because of the preeminence of institutional socialization, school would have the primary direct effect on value orientations when the effects of all other variables were controlled. Secondly, we assumed that class background should have a moderate but smaller effect, based on the persistence of socialization in the class context. Finally, we assumed that the smallest direct effect would be registered by mobility aspirations, since these are so strongly determined by school level that they are but an indirect manifestation of its influence.

Table 5-2
Direct Effects of Five Variables on the Value Indices

Dependent Variables	X_1 Class Background	X_2 Age	X_3 School	X_4 Preferred Status	X_5 Anticipated Status
Mobility paths	.01	−.08	−.09	−.03	−.06
Opportunism	.09*	.04	−.22*	−.13*	.12
Familism	−.01	−.01	−.05	−.12*	−.07
Mastery	−.02	−.03	.11	.19*	−.09
Achievement gratification	.04	.09	.00	−.01	.26*
Individualism	.12*	.08	.01	.03	.20*
Deferred gratification	.07	−.05	−.16*	−.06	.10
Trust	−.03	−.12*	.00	.04	.02
Composite value index	.19*	.05	.22*	.03	.17*

*$p \geqslant 0.05$

For our subjects the data do not confirm these propositions in the manner that we had anticipated. School does have greater direct effect on values than class background; however, its relative impact is not overwhelming. School shows significant effects on three of the value indices, in each case stronger than that of background, but class background exerts a significant impact on individualism, while school does not. Furthermore, the effect of class background on the composite value index is fairly substantial relative to school. The importance of this latter finding must be underscored because the composite index is given equal weight with the discrete ones in assessing support for our hypotheses. The most striking contrast with our predictions, however, is the fact that four of the value indices (familism, mastery, achievement gratification, and individualism) are exclusively affected by one of the two aspiration measures. In addition, there is also a substantial effect by anticipated status on the composite value index.

These findings indicate a heterogenous pattern of causation. The case for institutional socialization is not as strong as we had projected. Although the direct effects do not control for prior causation (as opposed to simultaneous causation), they are extremely important in this study as evidence of the socializing impact of the school. The direct effect of school on values indicates the extent to which individuals divergent in social origin from the *mean for their school* are being socialized to institutional values. A strong indirect effect of class (which makes the school less heterogeneous with regard to social origins) would tend to support this inference as long as that effect was not so strong as to render it impossible to distinguish the separate effect of school. However, a substantial direct effect by class indicates that a portion of those divergent in class background from the mean for their school level are retaining the values of their origin. Our finding that school level and social class both have substantial direct effects is most consistent with the interpretation that both institutional socialization and socialization in the class context are of equal importance in stratifying the values of students.

The finding that the mobility aspirations of students also exert a significant independent effect on their values does not completely contradict the proposition of institutional socialization. This result does suggest, however, that we have misperceived the process whereby school effects values under a sponsored system. We know that school has a considerable direct effect on aspirations; therefore, it may easily be that the major impact of school level on values is indirect, via its prior determination of mobility goals. Within certain limitations, an active stance towards mobility may be just as important under sponsorship as under contest. It is plausible that the individual who actually perceives his school level as a step to mobility is the one, in fact, most likely to internalize the modal values that he finds in the institutional environment.

To assess the quantitative impact of such indirect effects we employed the method suggested by Duncan.[20] The actual coefficients for the direct and indirect paths between the variables in our causal model are illustrated in Figure

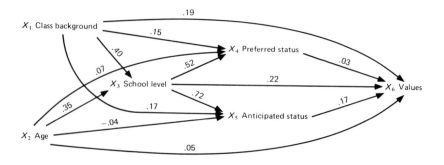

Figure 5-2. Path Diagram of the Effects of Class Background, School, Age, Preferred Status, Anticipated Status on the Composite Value Index.

5-2 for the index of composite values. The results of our computation of indirect effects are presented for each value index in Tables 5-3 and 5-4. The actual structure of both direct and oblique causation is illustrated in terms of the causal diagram, with the numerical coefficients for each path included. To present diagrams for every index would be redundant however. Therefore, we have included only the one diagram, Figure 5-2, to illustrate the pattern of causation for the composite value index. The coefficients for the indirect paths would be identical for the other indices; the reader need only fill in the direct paths from Table 5-2 to obtain a mental picture.

Table 5-3
The Indirect Effects of Class Background on the Value Indices

	Indirect Effects*					
Dependent Variables	Via X_3	Via X_3X_4	Via X_3X_5	Via X_4	Via X_5	Total Indirect Effects
Mobility paths	−.04	.00	−.02	.00	−.01	−.07
Opportunism	−.09	−.03	.03	−.02	.02	−.09
Familism	−.05	−.03	−.02	−.02	−.01	−.13
Mastery	.04	.04	.03	.03	.02	.16
Achievement gratification	.00	.00	.08	.00	.04	.12
Individualism	.00	.00	.06	.00	.00	.03
Deferred gratification	−.06	−.01	.03	−.01	.01	−.04
Trust	.00	.00	.00	.00	.00	.00
Composite value index	.09	.00	.05	.00	.03	.17

*X_3 = Class background
X_4 = Preferred status
X_5 = Anticipated status

Table 5-4

The Indirect Effects of School Level on the Value Indices

	Indirect Effects*		
Dependent Variables	Via X_4	Via X_5	Total Indirect Effects
Mobility paths	.00	−.04	−.04
Opportunism	−.07	.09	.02
Familism	−.06	−.05	−.11
Mastery	.10	.06	.16
Achievement gratification	.00	.19	.19
Individualism	.00	.14	.14
Deferred gratification	−.03	.07	.04
Trust	.02	.01	.03
Composite value index	.00	.12	.12

*X_4 = Preferred status

X_5 = Anticipated status

The results for our subjects provide ample evidence of interaction between school level and personal aspiration. The direct effects of school are an inaccurate estimate of its total influence on values. The indirect effects of school are substantial and, with the exception of the composite value index, such indirect effects are greater than the direct influences. Because the ratio of indirect to direct effect is a function of the relative size of the direct effects, those values which show the strongest direct effects by aspiration also show the highest indirect effects by school. In the case of individualism and achievement gratification, the dependence of aspirations on school level explains nearly all of its effect on values. On the basis of these findings there seems little question that, for our subjects, aspiration is important as a vehicle whereby school effects values.

The indirect effects of class background are equally substantial. With the exception of the composite value index, opportunism, and deferred gratification, the indirect effects of parental class either equal or exceed its direct effects. In the case of the composite index, the ratio of indirect to direct effect is nearly equal. Thus a great proportion of the influence of class is channeled via school.

The meaning of these indirect effects from the standpoint of our original hypotheses is not as clear as it was for the direct effects. The direct effects were the most rigorous tests of our hypotheses. They indicated the extent to which the institutional learning of values overcomes discrepancies in origin, and thus the completeness of the socialization process. However, if one variable is a prior cause of another then that dissection of direct effects is not particularly meaningful, since it deals with only a minor part of the variance in each variable and only a minor part of the causal process. In such a case most of the effect of one variable is thoroughly inseparable from that of the other, and we can refer only to their joint effect. This, of course, is precisely the case with our data. An important portion of the contribution of both class and school level to the variance in values comes about because of the coincidence of status and school level. That is to say, for a number of our students the effect of being in a particular school level *combined* with that of being of a particular class background is stronger than that of either of these factors operating separately.

Another increment of indirect effect comes about because of the effect of class background on aspirations through school, and finally another increment because of the effect of class background on aspirations. To give a more concrete illustration let us take the case of mastery. The indirect effect of class background via school level on this value accounts for a larger portion of its total influence than its direct effect. What this means is that those students who are simultaneously of high status and of high school level are more likely to endorse mastery than those who are of either high school level and lower-class background or of high-class background and lower school level. In fact the latter of these two groups are more likely to render a negative endorsement of this value.

The indirect effects of school on mastery require a similar explication. In this case an important proportion of the effect of school on values comes about because of the coincidence of school level and aspirations. Let us illustrate again using the pattern of effects for mastery. The indirect effect of school level via aspiration, like that for class background via school level, is larger than its direct effect. This comes about because those students who are of higher school and who have, simultaneously, high aspirations are more likely to endorse mastery than those who are high on one variable to the exclusion of the other.

The data for direct effects were not sufficiently consistent for us to decide between hypotheses. The data for indirect effects do not give us much more help. What the indirect effects show, in fact, is not a relative ordering of variables but a structure of causal linkages. It is apparent that class background causes school level, which in turn has an effect on aspirations, which in turn has an effect on values, and so on for all conceivable causal patterns. From this sort of data we cannot evaluate the relative importance of a variable but only the conditions under which it affects another. Thus we may say that socialization in the family context has the most favorable effect on values when it determines school selection, which, in turn, affects socialization to values. Nevertheless, this does not permit us to assign greater importance to one process than to the other since they are interconnected. Similarly, we may say that institutional socialization has the most favorable effect on values when it determines aspirations, which, in turn, produce greater orientation to specific values; but this fact does not permit us to assign more importance to either institutional socialization or future orientation. In part, our inability to find definitive support for specific hypotheses may be based on the limitations of our methodology. Path analysis permits the determination of the relative impact of various variables and is useful for illustrating the structure of causal effects. Statistically, however, this is not the same as establishing the relative importance of variables (or causal connections) in terms of their contribution to the explained variance. The validation of a particular causal path between a set of variables does not imply anything regarding its *overall impact*. In an analogous fashion, the summation of indirect or direct effects does not tell us anything about the unique contribution of each variable to the explained variance, since these quantities are always relative to intercorrelations within the system. Our failure to discriminate between hypotheses was based on the fact that none of the theoretically relevant causal paths could be completely excluded; nevertheless, their contribution to the variance in values is a separate question.

Based on the foregoing reasoning it was decided that a supplementary statistical technique would be employed to determine the relative importance of our variables, even though it has the disadvantage of obscuring certain types of information regarding causal connections. The technique employed was borrowed from the work of Duncan and was introduced in the preceding chapter. This method (illustrated in Table 5-5) extracts the contribution of each variable, working backward from effect to more remote causes, by manipulating the coefficients of multiple determination. The partitioning of the variance which results from this operation provides a calculus for the relative importance of variables. However, the technique does not permit one to dissect either causal paths or indirect effects. The increment in variance attributed to each variable includes both direct and indirect effects, with the exception of the last variable, in the causal chain which cannot logically have any indirect influence. This method is superior to partial correlation when the researcher wishes to retain the anatomy of his causal system in establishing the relative importance of his variables.

The results of the partitioning of multiple correlations are illustrated in Table 5-5. It can be seen that the rank-ordering of variables differs somewhat from that produced by either the direct or the total effects computed as components of path analysis. The most striking contrast is indicated by the coefficients for the composite value index. Almost 60 percent of the variance in this index is explained by class background, another 21 percent is explained by school level, and a very small percentage of the variance can be attributed to aspirations. What this indicates is that the relative importance of both direct and indirect causal influences for class background far exceed those of school level. Although the increments do not distinguish between direct and indirect effects, we can assume, from our previous analysis of causal paths, that almost 50 percent of the contribution of class to the explained variance comes about because class background causes school level.

The pattern for the discrete indices is very mixed. We may disregard the

Table 5-5

A Partitioning of Variance for the Determinants of Value Orientation

Components*	Computational Procedure+	Dependent Variables (X_6)*								
		Mobility Path	Opportunism	Familism	Mastery	Achievement Gratification	Individualism	Deferred Gratification	Trust	Composite Index
Total effect of X_1	$r^2(61)$	.004	.000	.019	.003	.042	.077	.007	.001	.182
Increment for X_2	$r^2 6(12) - r^2 6(61)$	.013	.001	.007	.001	.019	.020	.005	.010	.030
Increment for X_3	$r^2 6(123) - r^2 6(12)$	.009	.026	.020	.013	.022	.021	.001	.001	.086
Increment for X_4	$r^2 6(1234) - r^2 6(123)$	.000	.000	.010	.000	.024	.019	.008	.001	.013
Increment for X_5	$r^2 6(12345) - r^2 6(1234)$	.000	.007	.006	.014	.000	.000	.001	.000	.000
Sum, total variance explained	$r^2 6(12345)$	.026	.034	.062	.031	.107	.137	.022	.013	.311

*X_1 = Class background
X_2 = Age
X_3 = School
X_4 = Preferred status
X_5 = Anticipated status
X_6 = Value index (column variable above)

+From O.D. Duncan, *Socioeconomic Background and Occupational Achievement: Extensions of a Basic Model* (U.S. Department of Health, Education, and Welfare, May 1968).

results for trust, since the increments would not be statistically significant. For the remaining seven value indices there is no pattern of predominant causation by any single variable, based on the relative proportion of variance explained. If we base our judgment on the absolute sizes of increments, our ability to discriminate increases. We might then cautiously assert that class background is the most important determinant of values, and that school level and mobility aspirations play a secondary but equal role. However, the discrepancies between indices are so great that it might be more useful to completely discard the attempt to determine the relative importance of different causal determinants across the entire range of students' values. The data illustrate that the different causal processes that we have hypothesized are either equally important for a portion of the value spectrum or relatively more important for some specific values; but no overall pattern of causation is indicated. The author feels thus it might be more interesting and more illuminating to analyze each type of value endorsement separately. In this way we can determine (1) which types of values seem to be exclusively affected by a specific process of socialization and (2) which types of values are affected by a combination of processes. The different relationships can then be explained in terms of the content of the value or of the nature of the value endorsement involved. Thus the last section of this chapter deals with each index separately as a final summary of our data.

Analysis by Value Dimensions

In the analysis of the separate value dimensions which follows only a single-stage multiple regression model is assumed and only the direct effects of the independent variables are employed in deciding between hypotheses. This is done because the path analysis failed to reveal a consistent pattern of causation. In light of these results it was felt that the better course would be to return to more conservative causal assumptions in presenting a final assessment of the data.

A multiple-stage path model assumes complete prior causation of each variable in the causal chain by the preceding variable. This is by no means a cautious assumption. Placing a variable in the first position of a causal sequence strongly increases the probability that it will exhibit substantial indirect effects. In fact, when all of the independent variables in a particular model are highly correlated, as they are in ours, one can manipulate the sizes of their indirect effects simply by changing the order. Hence if indirect effects are not to be regarded as spurious, the causal assumptions involved must be fully defensible. This is not the case with the causal model employed in our path analysis. It is entirely plausible, for example, that the impact of school level and mobility aspiration are coincident and not part of a causal chain in which one effects the other.

It can be seen that the assumption of prior causation implied by path analysis requires definitive theoretical and empirical support. Lacking this we turn to a more parsimonious causal principle, that of contemporaneous causation, as an aid to the interpretation of our results. Contemporaneous causation assumes that each independent variable effects the dependent variable without interaction with any other independent variables included in the model. Therefore, any mutual correlation is assumed to be spurious and has to be controlled for in the presentation of results. The appropriate data for evaluating this causal assumption are simply the direct effects of path analysis (the standardized multiple regression coefficients presented in Table 5-2). The causal model is identical to our previous one (see Figure 5-1), but only the direct paths between independent and dependent variables are considered.

Mobility Paths

The mobility paths index was included in order to obtain information about the extent to which sponsored norms might be reflected in differential endorsement of a specific value. It was hypothesized that the extent to which an individual might endorse the validity of the educational path to mobility would be contingent upon the degree to which he himself was committed to this avenue. Thus the individual whose school level is relatively higher than the mean for his group of origin would be most likely to feel that education was the best way to achieve success in his society, whereas the individual whose social origin was relatively high for his school level might endorse ambition, or personal striving, as the appropriate route.

Our results (see Table 5-2) indicate that endorsement of distinctive mobility paths is almost completely unrelated to the variables in our causal model. The effect coefficients are all statistically nonsignificant. It is interesting to note, however, that, while small, the effects for school level and aspiration are both in a negative direction. This, because of the way in which the index was scored, indicates that those in higher school levels and those with higher aspirations are more likely to favor personal ambition.

These results suggest that an active or ambitious posture towards mobility is not necessarily discouraged under sponsorship. This is consistent with the findings on aspiration reported in the previous chapter. As the reader will recall, it was demonstrated that sponsorship works primarily by segregating mobility routes, and not by depressing the overall level of aspiration.

Opportunism

The opportunistic manipulation of people as a value does not appear to be strongly related to social class. As Table 5-2 indicates, there is a small positive effect by social class which is statistically significant. However, this is out-weighed by a more substantial negative effect of school level.

Such a pattern is completely consistent both with institutional socialization and with other aspects of sponsored selection. The value of integrity in relations with people appears to be part of the cultural complex internalized by those in elite educational channels. As already pointed out, the idea that success can be won through shrewd manipulation of other people is part of the ideology of contest; and, therefore, in a society wherein such norms predominate, the upper classes are more likely to favor opportunistic mobility striving. However, sponsorship norms are opposed to bypassing normal mobility channels via individual manipulation. In addition the legitimacy of the elite and of the entire process of sponsored selection is based on a type of ethical rationale. Because the best interests of society are seen as protected by the sponsorship process, there is a positive ethical value attached to its norms. The restriction of competition, for example, has the express purpose of preserving the social and cultural authority of the elite and preventing the advancement of the unscrupu-lous and the incompetent.

Institutional socialization is not completely responsible for the position of our students on this value, however. Personal orientations towards the future appear to play a minor and more complicated role. Returning to the table we note that there are smaller effects attributable to the two measures of aspiration. Although only the effect for preferred status is statistically significant, the pattern of results is very suggestive. Since coefficients for preferred and anticipated status incorporate controls for their mutual impact, we can deduce that the former represents that component of aspiration which is fantasy-ori-ented (those instances where preferred aspirations are sharply revised to a more realistic level) and that the latter represents that component of aspiration which is reality-oriented (or those instances where anticipated choices are high relative to preferred choices). It can be seen that those whose fantasy choices are high are least likely to endorse opportunism, whereas those with relatively high-real-ity choices are most likely to endorse it.

Familism

The comparative studies of achievement orientation referred to previously have all included items measuring the respondent's willingness to become independent of family bonds. So far only class cleavages in familism have been confirmed. Our data, however, indicate considerable involvement of this value with mobility striving. Preferred status produces the only notable direct effect, and the indirect effects of other variables come about almost entirely by interaction with this. For our male subjects, negative endorsement of independence from the family is almost completely contingent upon their level of mobility aspiration.

The literature on consequences of social mobility has always stressed social isolation from the group of origin as a feature of social advancement. The relation of the mobile individual and his family is undoubtedly a major focus of this process. As commitments to the group of destination increase there is progressively greater discontinuity between the experiences, attitudes, and desires of parents and those of the mobility aspirant himself, until finally the familial bonds become a distinct impediment.

Our evidence suggests, however, that the need to reject familial bonds at this stage of adolescence is probably still minimal. Since mobility for males is positively evaluated, there is probably little familial resistance to selection for elite schooling, and the student is relatively unconscious of the growing differences between himself and his family. The lower-class child who sees his elite schooling as leading to only a moderate increment in his status is not likely to feel estranged from his family, since there would be mutual comprehension of the material advantages and no great discrepancy in life style. However, if the same child had self-conscious aspirations for university education and training as a lawyer, he might soon begin to feel that his family had little appreciation or understanding of the social world that he would enter. It follows, therefore, that those with self-conscious desires for high upward mobility are more likely to experience estrangement. That familism is primarily related to aspirations (or the joint effect of aspiration and other variables) in our data confirms the foregoing interpretation.

Mastery

The only variable that makes a significant direct impact on this value is preferred status; hence belief in the value of hard work and planning is most strongly influenced by fantasy aspirations. The lack of substantial relationship between mastery and school level may be a product of the operation of a sponsored system. The sorting of individuals into different mobility channels involved the exercise of collective rationality, and may, therefore, be antagonistic to rational planning based on the individual's assessments of his interests. That individuals are selected at an early age for qualities appropriate to future status means that personal planning for mobility is somewhat irrelevant. Thus, it appears that only those whose personal goals exceed the norms for their school level are likely to endorse the value of rational mastery.

Achievement Gratification

There is strong reason to believe that generalized achievement-orientation is a less important value in a sponsored system. Although contest emphasized personal achievement in whatever form, a sponsored system emphasizes the

more circumscribed notion of talent or cultural attainments. It is not achievement in itself which is important but recognizing one's capabilities and
employing them in the right direction. Thus, there is no particular need to
encourage the grammar school students to strive harder than those in technical
school.

The data for our students clearly confirm the low relevance of institutional
socialization to this value. As illustrated in Table 5-2, the only substantial impact
on achievement gratification is made by anticipated status. It is precisely that
mechanism of socialization which is most closely related to the logic of a
contest, the development of an active stance towards one's future status, which
is most important in determining the level of endorsement for Dutch students.

Individualism

The data for individualism point to a pattern of causation which is distinctly
different from that of the other indices (see Table 5-2). Both class background
and anticipated status have significant effects on individualism, but the impact
of the latter variable is greater. School level, however, shows no independent
influence.

Individualism is the only discrete index on which class background exerts an
independent and statistically significant influence. Thus, it may be useful to
consider whether there is something distinctive about this value which would
explain the continuing influence of the group of origin. The persistence of class
influence might be related to an aspect of familial socialization which is so
effective that it continues to compete with other agents even into the period of
adolescence. Individualism is a value expressed in a wide variety of situations,
not all of them having to do directly with achievement. This value might initially
be internalized in a particular type of family structure. Many writers on
socialization have emphasized that the type of discipline and the relatively
equalitarian power relations between members which characterize middle-class
families tend to produce more self-reliance in children. Although the school may
channel the expression of achievement-oriented behavior, the family retains
control over the extracurricular life and discipline of the child. In this manner it
may leave a profound influence on the regulation of individualistic behavior.

Another feature of the data peculiar to individualism is the coincident
influence of class and aspiration in the absence of a positive effect by school.
This might be best explained as an aspect of sponsored selection. It may be that
the overall impact of sponsorship is to depress individualism. In a sponsored
system, as we have already shown, the general level of mobility aspirations is
strongly determined by school level. Those who accept the appropriate goals
established for them by the selective process, at all school levels, are not likely to
be individualistic. But those whose aspirations exceed the norm for their school

level—i.e., those who have personal goals rather than those who merely conform to institutional expectations—are probably more likely to be individualistic in outlook. In addition, the probability of endorsing individualism is also increased by a higher-status family background. Another corollary explanation would be the predominance of anticipatory socialization. Since, at all school levels, those of higher-status background are more individualistic, they may be providing the cultural models for this value to more ambitious students.

Deferred Gratification

Earlier we speculated that deferred gratification would not be endorsed by mobile students in a sponsored system because acquisition of future status has already been confirmed to a large extent; therefore, personal sacrifices would be largely irrelevant to mobility. Our data indicate some differentiation in endorsement by school level, however. As Table 5-2 illustrates, school is the only variable which has a significant effect on this value, though the effect is in a negative direction. This indicates that students in higher school levels are actually less inclined to endorse deferred gratification. In addition, deferred gratification shows an interesting, although slight, relationship to aspirations. Preferred status shows a negative effect, while anticipated status shows a positive effect. This indicates that those who possess high realistic aspirations are a little more inclined to endorse deferral of gratification.

In a roundabout way the above data may actually be confirming our hypothesis. It is entirely possible that not only does the sponsorship process eliminate the need (and the ideological rationale) for deferred gratification but that it also reverses its relationship to mobility in a small degree. The grammar school student in the Netherlands is being prepared for a relatively long educational career; a university degree in the Netherlands takes seven years to complete, and, in addition, he must stay in school at least two years longer than the students in other levels must to complete his secondary diploma. Throughout this long academic career the student is discouraged from seeking outside employment, marrying, or assuming any of the more burdensome responsibilities of adulthood. While undergoing university training all students without means are supported by the government, and there are few restrictions as to how long this aid can last. The clerical and technical school students, on the other hand—at least those in our sample—are all on the verge of entering their occupational careers and adjusting to the responsibilities of assuming an adult role. Thus, for them the deferral of gratification may be much more relevant to the hard economic realities which they are just beginning to face and which are still a long way off for the grammar school student.

Trust

The finding that the lower class place less confidence in the stability of human relationships has been consistently reported in a number of comparative studies. Our data (see Table 5-2) do not confirm these findings, however. Trust shows almost no relationship to any of our stratification variables. In addition, the overall explained variance for the trust, as measured by multiple correlation, is very low.

The low explained variance should be considered the most important datum in evaluating our results. Most of the previous studies in which measures of this value were included were conducted with samples of adults. It is entirely likely that general distrust of human relationships is a value that begins to differentiate people only in later stages of their life. There have been studies of the relation between age and values which illustrate very strong tendencies for older people to become misanthropic. Yet, it seems that those of higher status are immune to this progressive change. From the foregoing evidence we might conclude that this value is not likely to differentiate among our subjects, who are adolescents.

The Composite Value Index

The composite index is distinguished from the discrete measures because it alone shows simultaneous causation by all three categories of stratification variables. The effects of class background, school level, and preferred aspiration are all statistically significant and approximately equal in size. For females, the same pattern is evident, but preferred status also has a significant effect, thereby increasing the relative contribution of aspiration.

That all the independent variables are linked to this measure is an important datum, for it implies that all three of our hypothesized mechanisms of socialization play an important role in forming our students' value orientations. The only reasonable explanation of such a finding is that each of these processes works in concert with the other, and that each is an important link in an entire chain, or shifting process, whereby the mobile individual acquires his values. Some individuals appear to retain the values they learned in the class context, others acquire their values through the institutional subculture, and for still another group, the formation of achievement values appears to be contingent on their personal level of mobility aspiration. The interaction terms, as represented by the indirect effects, only reinforce the foregoing conclusion. As we have already illustrated, the joint effects of all three independent variables are substantial and sometimes exceed their independent influence.

While we have demonstrated that institutional socialization is an important component of the interlocking causal process which determines values, we have not demonstrated that it plays a dominant role in supporting a sponsored system of selection. A fuller discussion of the implications of this finding is presented in our concluding chapter. A tentative interpretation, however, may be offered on the basis of the data at hand. We observed in the previous chapter that the impact of sponsorship on perceived mobility chances was indeed profound. This impact is reflected (in the data for this chapter) in the substantial interaction effects between school and aspiration. This pattern of causation, if projected over time, suggests a slightly different role for institutional socialization. If the primary *contemporary impact* of school is on mobility aspirations rather than on values, it may easily be that the impact of school is always indirect, that school level commits the student to a certain type of mobility career, and that over time this is the crucial factor in the student's value choices. That aspirations are already such an important stratifier of values, even though very little reality testing has occurred to give them substance, may mean that ultimately they are the mechanism whereby mobility commitments are translated into value choices.

The Degree of Association Between
Stratification and Values

This study has assembled fairly impressive evidence of the breadth of association between stratification and values. The extent of association, however, is only moderate (see Table 5-5). The highest explained variance is exhibited by the composite value index; approximately one-third of the variation in this measure was attributable to our causal system.

Unlike many previous studies, we have not neglected the cumulative impact of class of origin and class of destination on our students' value endorsements. We have taken into account the respondent's class background, his selection for future mobility via the school system, and his personal mobility aspirations. Yet even for the value index which shows the highest degree of association with stratification, almost two-thirds of the variance remains unexplained.

On the basis of this evidence we must tentatively reject the subculture hypothesis in favor of cultural pluralism. The most comprehensive value index considerably improved our predictive ability. It is possible, therefore, that future studies, working with more sophisticated measures than the one employed here, could conceivably uncover a true subcultural pattern. For our subjects, however, we must assume that the major portion of cultural variation is determined by factors not measured in this study.

The foregoing pattern of results is fairly consistent with those obtained in prior studies of stratification and values; the majority of which employed only class of origin as a causal variable. A review of such studies by the author revealed consistent findings of very low or moderate association. The addition of variables related to social mobility did increase our explained variance to a considerable extent, but not to such a degree that we were able to support a subcultural pattern. Only the results for the composite value index diverge significantly from patterns reported in previous research. The squared multiple correlation of .31 is twice as great as that reported in any other studies employing this type of scale. It is probably safer, though, to compare overall patterns than actual quantitative results (especially in comparative research). Such a finding would only be interesting if it were consistently replicated by future studies of Dutch adolescents.

Chapter Summary

Our primary purpose in this chapter has been to investigate the relationship between social selection and socialization. The previous data analysis has already established that a sponsored system of selection profoundly affects the student's perception of mobility channels and his opportunities for personal advancement. Our aim has been to determine whether the educational structure also affects abstract achievement values via the hypothesized mechanisms of institutional socialization. We also investigated two subsidiary questions:

1. the degree to which variation in mobility ideology affects value endorsement, and
2. the overall degree of association between social stratification and values.

Two types of causal assumptions were employed in constructing the data analysis. Our first step was to specify a multiple-stage model in which all the independent variables were conceived of as standing in a causally prior relationship to each other. The direct and indirect paths of causation which resulted from these assumptions were analyzed with the technique of path analysis. Our second step was to specify a more primitive causal model in which each independent variable was conceived as operating contemporaneously and without interaction with the others.

Any mutual correlation was assumed to represent spurious causation. Since the quantitative evidence for the second assumption was a component of the overall path analysis (i.e., the "direct effects") there was no need for a segregated computation of results.

The contemporaneous causation model was given more weight in the final evaluation of our results than the prior causation schema because the latter carries a heavier freight of suppositions which are not accessible to confirmation.

Nine value indices were constructed, to provide a more economical representation of the data and to permit the use of path analysis. Eight of these covered discrete value dimensions, such as individualism, which the individual items were originally intended to measure.

Another index (the composite value index) was designed to measure achievement orientation in a more generalized fashion. Both the composite index and the discrete indices taken together were given equal weight in evaluating our hypotheses.

Our data analysis involved the use of path analytic methods to dissect the pattern of causation for each of the nine indices. A heterogeneous pattern of determination was revealed. The analysis of direct effects indicates that no one independent variable has a consistently greater impact than any of the others. A slight edge can be given, however, to mobility aspirations as a causal determinant of values. That aspirations have a substantial effect does not necessarily contradict a sponsored pattern. It merely suggests that the primary impact of sponsorship may be indirect, via its prior determination of aspirations. Appropriate manipulation of path coefficients shows that the indirect effects of class background and of school level are profound, indicating that all our independent variables are inextricably linked in the causal determination of values.

To make an overall evaluation of our hypotheses employing the assumption of prior causation we used a technique of computing increments to the total explained variance in values (subtraction of multiple correlations). The results, which combine the direct and the indirect effects of each independent variable, reveal a different but equally heterogeneous pattern of causation as does our analysis of direct effects. It is apparent, however, that the assumption of prior causation significantly increases the influence of background through its very strong indirect effect on the composite index and on a few of the specific measures.

Because of the diversity of the findings, we discarded the attempt to make an overall assessment of hypotheses for the entire range of values. The data seem to indicate that the different mechanisms of socialization which we have hypothesized are either equally important for some values or relatively more important for others, but no overall pattern is indicated. Thus, a segregated analysis of each value index (in terms of its content) was judged to be more useful.

The more conservative assumption of contemporaneous causation was employed in assessing the results for each index. The discrepancies between the discrete indices were generally explained in terms of the dynamics of sponsorship.

Only two indices are exclusively related to institutional socialization; these are opportunism and deferred gratification. Of these two, only deferred gratification is central to the achievement value complex.

The relatively small number of achievement values related to institutional socialization can be interpreted as a consequence of the emphasis on achievement-oriented values in this study. Such values may be more securely anchored to a contest system than we had assumed. Those values most closely connected with the logic of contest—achievement gratification, mastery, and individualism—are not at all related to school level, but they are related to mobility aspirations.

The explanation for this finding may simply be that those values retain their identification with social processes that are central to contest, such as competitive aspiration, even under a sponsored system. The passive sorting and sifting of individuals characteristic of sponsorship is not likely to produce stratification of individuals by values which emphasize active orientations. It is entirely possible that our value scales by-passed those cultural emphases most characteristic of a sponsored system.

The value postures we found related to institutional socialization may provide a few clues in this regard. The negative emphasis on deferral of gratification and the negative endorsements of opportunism both suggest the cultivation of certain elite values which are alien to a contest.

A somewhat different explanation for the relatively weak impact of institutional socialization was offered on the basis of results for the composite value index. The substantial interaction between school and aspiration in their causal impact on this value index suggests a somewhat different role for institutional socialization.

We speculated that the impact of the school is predominantly indirect throughout the student's mobility career. On the basis of the evidence we have obtained, it seems likely that the most important impact of the school is its function in committing the student to a specific channel of mobility. It is this commitment, in turn, which may later be the crucial factor in the student's value choices. Naturally, we cannot validate this interpretation without longitudinal evidence; it is one of many which are consistent with cross-sectional data available to us.

The overall degree of association between social stratification and values, as measured by the average explained variance for the value indices, is not substantially greater than that reported in other studies. We are able to explain the most variance in the composite value index; almost one-third of the variance in this measure can be ascribed to the impact of the stratification variables. Even this does not come close to the degree of association required for the demonstration of a subcultural pattern. This hypothesis was, accordingly, rejected in favor of its alternative: the proposition of cultural pluralism.

6 Conclusion and Overview

Wherever possible, we have presented fully elaborated interpretations and summarizing comments. Thus, in this final chapter, we present only the broadest overview, emphasizing the pattern of support for our initial hypotheses rather than the discrete findings. Our major purpose is to present the implications of the major findings for general theory and research.

The Comparative Analysis of Social Selection

In our examination of the relationship between social stratification and culture, the central concept we employed was the notion of social selection. We defined it as that social process which sifts and sorts individuals to staff the various social positions in a system of stratification according to institutionalized criteria. This concept covers the same ground as social stratification. It differs, however, in laying emphasis on the problem of cross-generational staffing of positions in different levels of a social hierarchy. Stratification, on the other hand, emphasizes the description and specification of various strata insofar as the strata possess certain kinds of group properties or affect human behavior.

The concept of social selection was also of central importance in comparing the impact of status transmission in the Netherlands and in the United States. Two ideal type descriptions of social selection, based on the work of R. Turner, were composed as a framework for this analysis. Selection in Dutch society was described as a sponsored system, whereas selection in the United States was typified as a contest system. When social selection is characterized by sponsored norms it is analogous to selection for a private club. Candidates for elite positions are selected by an established elite for specific qualities deemed to be appropriate for that status. A contest system, on the other hand, is analogous to a sporting event. Aspirants for elite status engage in a competitive struggle and elite status is won, not by the display of superior ability, but through the exercise of greater effort than one's fellow competitors.

The sponsored-contest paradigm was employed on two levels, both as a description of institutional arrangements governing selection and as a set of ideological formulations which facilitate social control.

In exploring the impact of social selection on mobility careers and values, we focused primarily on the educational structure. The broadest justification for

167

this was the fact that educational institutions are central to status transmission in industrial societies. An even more important consideration, however, was the choice of an adolescent sample. Our students were still involved in the educational process and this facilitated an investigation of the direct impact of school structure on their attitudes.

Therefore, a specification of the relationship between Dutch school structure and social selection was the most important step in setting the stage for our study. The author's structural analysis of the Dutch school system revealed a definite "strain toward consistency" with sponsored norms. The Dutch school system is characterized by controlled selection. Students at the approximate age of eleven or twelve take exams that determine whether they will be permitted to partake of college preparatory education. Those who do not qualify are sent to one of several other secondary schools which offer academic preparation of relatively poorer quality and which emphasize specialized vocational training. Once this initial sorting and sifting is over, selection is presumed to be complete and rigorous competition or elimination is not practiced.

These structural features of the Dutch school system were deemed to be consistent with a sponsored logic of social selection. Under this type of school system, the major object of selection is the recruitment of a limited number of individuals with appropriate qualities and their passive induction into elite status.

Our major research goal was to obtain evidence of the impact of a sponsored system of education on cultural stratification. In our general discussion of social selection, we argued that cultural differences between classes are produced primarily by the operation of a dominant set of institutions that organize the sorting and sifting of individuals for different strata. In this process, values, or cultural criteria, play an extremely important role. For systems of selection function not only to stratify individuals according to their class destination, but they also regulate the acquisition or learning of cultural attributes that result in selection for elite status.

Thus, the allocative and socializing functions of systems of selection are closely intertwined. Nevertheless, in this study these two matters were dealt with separately both in the analysis of our data and in the reporting of the results. Because of the cross-sectional nature of our study, allowance was made for a degree of interdependence between these two aspects of social selection. Little is known regarding the timing and the intensity of various types of commitments during adolescence. The impact of agencies of selection on mobility and values could easily come at separate stages, one of which our stratification of students by age level may have missed. This is particularly plausible under sponsorship.

Explicit selection for different avenues of mobility comes so early in the students' careers and is so well institutionalized in the educational system that it seems highly unlikely that they would not be aware of such selection. However, value commitments, although they are implicit in each student's goals, may not emerge until more comprehensive reality testing has occurred. The educational sorting and sifting which occurs under sponsorship is largely a passive matter from the standpoint of the individual; whereas the formation of values may involve taking a more active stance regarding one's personal fate.

Social Selection and Aspiration

In terms of its impact on the projected mobility of our students, a sponsored system of selection is fully in evidence. The students' aspirations are not realistic in terms of the absolute levels recorded. Yet, the students' occupational and educational goals are so sharply stratified by their school level that the institutional separation of mobility channels must be regarded as fully confirmed. There is no comparable pattern of results in American studies of adolescent mobility aspiration.

American research has frequently employed classifications of secondary schools on the basis of academic quality, social-class background of students, race mixture, or even facilities and teacher quality.

However, no characteristics related to the structure of the school or its composition have shown such an overpowering relationship to mobility aspirations as that recorded in this study.

The presence of a sponsored pattern of selection was further illustrated by the pattern of causal relations between mobility aspirations, school level, and social class. The direct impact of school level, for both occupational and educational aspirations, far exceeded that of class background. Furthermore, the impact of social class is predominantly indirect via its prior determination of school level.

This pattern fully confirms the logic of sponsored selection. Under sponsorship, the primary impact of social class comes at the time when selection for different educational avenues takes place. At this time, parental mobility advocacy should be influential in determining the students' educational courses. Once this stage is over, class background no longer operates to differentiate the students' mobility careers.

The overall significance of our findings can only be assessed against the background of previous stratification theory and research. The consistency of certain observations regarding stratification systems in industrial societies is so pronounced that they have come to be accepted as sociological articles of faith subject to infinite repetition in all important texts. One of the most important of these articles is the generalization that all societies at a certain stage of industrialization tend to have high overall rates of mobility. Another and corollary generalization involves the role of educational systems as instruments of social testing and allocation. The increasing importance of educational credentials has frequently been emphasized as a major factor in increasing rates of mobility, because education emphasizes personal achievement over the advantages of birth.

We have qualified both of these generalizations extensively. We have not assumed, for example, that industrialized societies have higher rates of mobility than do nonindustrialized societies; nor have we assumed that educational credentials have resulted in the general application of "achievement" criteria for occupations. Nevertheless, to some extent, these two generalizations have provided the point of departure for this study.

In one crucial respect, however, we have deviated from previous thinking. The majority of writers on social stratification have taken high-mobility rates and the prevalence of educational allocation as evidence of overall convergence between stratification systems due to common requirements of industrialization.

We have assumed, on the other hand, that such similarities are superficial in character and that they leave room for fundamental variations in underlying structure. The emphasis on *mass mobility*, for example, has obscured fundamental differences in patterns of long- and short-distance movement.

In a recent comparative study of mobility patterns, for example, S.M. Miller found that there was no correlation between rates of elite mobility and other kinds of movement in the class structure; this finding suggests the possibility of profound differences in the relations between elites and masses. Educational allocation may be important in all industrialized societies; however, the structure of educational systems, the nature of their articulation with other institutions, and the consequences of both for the overall pattern of mobility may be subject to considerable cross-societal variation.

These objections to convergence theory have resulted in the formulation of the theoretical alternative employed in this study; the notion of social selection. Overemphasis on the external similarities between stratification systems, such as the extent of mobility, has led to a relative neglect of institutional variations between societies in the process of status acquisition.

In this study we have shown clearly that two societies, the United States and the Netherlands, in which researchers have found similar rates of mobility and similar correlations between mobility and educational achievement, nevertheless differ profoundly in terms of their structures of educational selection. In the Netherlands, students are segregated early in the educational process according to their prospective mobility destination.

The students in our sample clearly acknowledged the impact of such early sorting and sifting. Although they could not be closely acquainted with the realities of the job market, the majority of them chose occupations corresponding to the constraints placed upon them by sponsored selection. In the United States, on the other hand, all explicit selection is deferred and candidates for elite positions are distinguished not on the basis of the quality of their education but rather by means of its length; those who acquire a relatively higher level of education than their cohorts have a better chance to acquire an elite position via this channel of mobility.

The contest model of selection which is implied is clearly reflected in many American studies of mobility aspiration. A "race" model of mobility aspirations, uncovered by the majority of research, persists, whatever control variables are employed.

Such differences in selective processes are not unimportant. Much of contemporary thinking on social stratification has emphasized the outcomes of social selection as manifested by a certain level of social inequality or a specific rate of mobility. It is as equally important to understand the institutional structure which produces such outcomes as it is to merely record them.

In particular, we have emphasized the role of ideological superstructures. Education is one of the central institutions of industrial societies (some have asserted that it is the central institution) and is closely articulated with social stratification. Yet, it is clear that there is no overwhelming tendency toward convergence in systems of educational selection in modern society.

The conclusion is inescapable that ideologies of social selection and social values have an autonomous impact on those institutions which support social stratification. The most dramatic example of this is enormous expansion of American higher education since the 1930s. The consistent increase in the educational ceiling over these years must be seen as outcome of contest logic. Some have argued this development has been the result of increasing affluence of our economy and its ever-increasing skill requirements. If this were the case, however, then we should see a similar expansion of educational establishments in countries like Sweden, which has a high standard of living and a complex occupational structure. Yet, Sweden has only one-quarter the number of students enrolled in universities as has the United States.

In the more heavily industrialized Western European countries, such as the Netherlands, the rate of increase in economic affluence and in occupational specialization since World War II has been very rapid. Nevertheless, we see no tendency toward the adoption of contest modes of elite selection. University enrollment has remained proportionately low. In the Netherlands the only significant changes in the last few years have been to increase the effectiveness of selective process in order to ensure that meritocratic standards are applied. Although there is probably some relationship between industrialization, affluence, and the level of university enrollments, the variations between countries with sponsored and contest ideologies far exceed what could be regarded as minimum thresholds.

As the reader will recall from Chapter 4, the evidence regarding sponsorship is not completely unambiguous. Our original expectation was that school level would act primarily to stratify the extent of aspiration. Yet, although such cleavages in aspiration levels were clearly evident, the pattern of results strongly implies that the mechanism whereby sponsorship influences aspiration must be conceptualized differently. Aspiration levels within specific school types far exceeded available opportunities for some categories of occupation or education.

Yet, categories chosen heavily by students in one school type frequently received almost no choice in another. Thus, it appears that sponsorship works primarily to restrict the range of aspiration; in terms of extent, the pattern of choices within school types actually reflects a contest. The implication is that the school types correspond to specific steps in segregated mobility routes. To step over from one avenue to another has a kind of illegitimate status. Within the range of ascribed opportunities, however, there is no diminution of competitive aspiration; students appear to be choosing from the highest-ranked occupations available to them as plausible careers.

The frequency of choice for highly ranked categories within the range available to school type also results in a moderately high absolute level of mobility aspiration for the entire sample. From the standpoint of comparative research, one of the most interesting findings of this study has been the fact that the *overall level* of mobility aspirations was only moderately lower than that recorded in comparable studies conducted in the United States.

On the basis of our ideal type description of sponsorship, we had assumed that the Dutch school structure would be more likely than its American counterpart to induce realistic levels of aspiration. The ambiguous finding obtained in this study certainly suggests some revision in our thinking about the theoretical significance of mobility aspirations.

Several types of interpretations might be attached to the above findings.

In Chapter 4, we proposed that it might be better to consider aspirations as relative positions on an attitude rather than as virtual reflections of personal goals. In this case, a comparison of absolute levels between societies might be meaningless.

A more plausible interpretation emerges if we consider that both sponsorship and contest are variants of "democratic" ideology and, therefore, have certain components of this in common. Meritocratic tests are legitimate in both systems of selection, though they are more explicit under sponsorship.

Thus, the restriction of certain elite positions to the holders of university degrees is accepted under sponsorship as relatively egalitarian, but the restriction of *all* highly ranked positions to those with elite credentials might severely challenge the legitimacy of these arrangements. A society must leave some upward mobility routes open to everyone even though they are clearly difficult of access. The constraints imposed upon the technical school student, for example, under sponsorship, are broad constraints. He may not aspire to become a physician nor to any other university-trained occupation. Such an aspiration would be considered illogical as well as merely unrealistic. On the other hand he is not restricted explicitly from working toward a position as a highly skilled and highly paid technician, although his chances of success are poor. Thus, within the ascribed range of opportunities, the individual's aspirations may be high. The evidence regarding students' value orientations, which we are about to discuss, suggests that personally ambitious students at all school levels endorse generalized achievement values while they do not endorse values that emphasize opportunistic and irregular results to mobility. Thus, the similar emphasis on achievement values in both the United States and the Netherlands may produce equal degrees of mobility striving. But, in the Netherlands, such striving is contained and regulated by a different structure of selection.

Social Selection, Socialization, and Achievement Values

We hypothesized that the major impact of sponsorship on cultural stratification would occur via institutional socialization. By institutional socialization we meant that every school type constitutes a separate subculture, or frame of reference, for validating important values. Under sponsorship, the student is selected at an early age for one of three educational strata. In this process, students are segregated, as we have already shown, according to future class destination. They are also differentiated in terms of the opportunities and facilities available to them for acquiring the types of experiences, skills, and values appropriate to elite status.

Our data do not indicate overwhelming support for institutional socialization. Our findings are, in fact, so heterogeneous that any generalization made from them must be appended with a number of qualifications or cautions.

No one mechanism of socialization appears to be clearly dominant. Not only our central hypothesis but every one of the alternative hypotheses advanced in Chapter 2 appears to be equally plausible in terms of the results obtained. Some values appear to be influenced primarily by socialization in the class context, others by mechanisms such as future orientation or anticipatory socialization. In the case of the composite value index and a few of the discrete indices, all the hypothesized types of socialization appear to be simultaneously relevant.

Because of the diversity of our findings a segregated examination of each index in terms of its content was judged to be more useful than an overall examination of our hypotheses.

This analysis revealed that the core achievement values—individualism, mastery, and achievement gratification—were not consistently related to institutional socialization. On the other hand, each of these values was strongly related to mobility aspirations.

One possible interpretation of such results is simply that we may have overemphasized achievement values in selecting items for our questionnaire. Initially, these items were chosen in order to provide a basis for comparison with studies conducted in the United States. In doing this, however, we may have overselected for values which embody contest norms. Among our respondents, it is primarily those who take an active stance toward mobility who endorse achievement values. This suggests that achievement values are most strongly related to social processes that have the logic of a contest even when sponsorship is the general norm. This conclusion is further reinforced by the fact that those value endorsements which we did find related to institutional socialization were more consistent with a sponsorship logic.

The foregoing interpretation, while it may be corroborated by future research, is much too facile. We cannot dismiss our results this easily. Probably the safest conclusion we can make from our results is that our original conception of how sponsorship influences cultural stratification may be incorrect. We had assumed that institutional socialization would play a dominant role in forming the values of our respondents. At the very least, our data suggest that the picture may be far more complex. Although institutional socialization is clearly evident in our data, it is apparent that it must be conceived of as acting in concert, or in interaction, with other mechanisms or forces.

It is entirely possible that our respondents are still too young to have formed solid value commitments. At the time when we measured their attitudes, our respondents were involved in day-to-day interaction with their families; that their values would reflect class differences in parental attitudes and other pressures exerted on them in the home environment is entirely to be expected. The impact of institutional socialization via the school which they attend may actually be felt a little later in the life cycle.

The value commitments made by a student as part of his educational experience and its consequences for mobility may only be apparent when he leaves school and begins to articulate his technical and cultural skills with the opportunities available to him. In the Netherlands, for example, the grammar school student has a considerably better command of the Dutch language than has the technical or clerical school student. This capability, in turn, opens up to the mobile student certain avenues to employment and to social intercourse which his parents did not have. Until he actually begins to exploit such options, however, the implicit value commitments involved are not likely to be clear.

From a more macroscopic perspective, the coincidence of socialization in the class context and institutional socialization was fully anticipated. If institutional socialization were dominant, this would imply that new generations were being socialized to different values than those adhered to by their parents. The more plausible pattern would be the socialization of upwardly mobile students to a set of values similar to those already internalized by individuals of higher background. The data are generally consistent with the operation of such a process.

The most important deviation from our original hypotheses is the finding that mobility aspirations have a strong independent impact on value orientations. In our original formulation of socialization under sponsorship, we argued that personal aspirations were largely irrelevant to the learning of values. We asserted that the values appropriate to the student's future class level are completely institutionalized in the educational program and informal structure of the school type in which he is enrolled. Furthermore, since the student's class destination is largely determined by his school level, those attitudes which he acquires as a member of his specific educational milieu are more likely to be reflected in cultural stratification.

It is entirely possible that we have overestimated the passivity of socialization in a sponsorship program. To some extent, both sponsored and contest systems require an active response from the individual. Under contest, the individual is selected to some extent on the basis of his aspirations; therefore, his motivation can be taken for granted. Under sponsorship, the individual is selected for elite schooling on the basis of his academic ability; once he is selected, he has the potential to enter an elite occupational position, whereas his cohorts, less favored by the selective process, do not.

Nevertheless, this is no guarantee that he will actually utilize his potential and develop explicit aspirations for some elite position. The initial process of selection is so passive that his motivation cannot be assumed. The lower-class youth who enters a grammar school may be able to complete the academic program with little difficulty. However, his aspirations may remain at the same level as his contemporaries in clerical or technical schools. Thus, the selective advantage that he gains by completing grammar school will have little ultimate effect on his mobility unless his educational experience also motivates him to raise his aspirations. Thus, the formation of personal mobility goals may be more problematic in a sponsored system than we originally assumed. We have already demonstrated that competitive levels of aspiration are clearly in evidence among the students in our sample.

Sponsorship functions primarily to place a ceiling on a student's aspirations, rather than to restrict their absolute extent. The effect of sponsorship on levels of aspiration can be likened to a visual configuration formation consisting of plateaus and intermediate steps. The students are, basically, segregated into different plateaus, separated by explicit differences in credentialization; however, each plateau contains a number of intermediate steps, each of which a student is quite capable of climbing if he only exercises sufficient initiative.

If mobility aspirations are important in determining the student's fate under sponsorship, it follows that they may also be an independent axis of socialization. As we argued in Chapter 5, the individual who actually perceives his educational level as a steppingstone toward mobility may be the one who actually internalizes the value models that are expressed in the school environment. Because of the nature of our data, it was difficult to make precise inferences regarding this mode of socialization, but the coincident impact of both school level and aspirations on the composite value index was judged to be consistent with this process.

Appendixes

Appendix

Questionnaire

*Part One: Some Questions about
Yourself and Your Parents*

1. My name is (be sure to include your last name) _____
   _____

2. The name of my school is _____

3. My parents have __ children (including myself).

4. In my family I am
   ____(1) the oldest child
   ____(2) the second oldest child
   ____(3) the third oldest child
   ____(4) the fourth oldest child
   ____(5) the fifth oldest child
   ____(6) the sixth or older child

5. How old were you on you last birthday? _____

6. What is your sex?__ Male __ Female __

7. Are either you or your family affiliated with any religion? __yes __no

8. If so, which one? _____

9. What is your father's or stepfather's occupation? (Try if possible to give his exact occupational title.)
   _____

10. Give a very short description of the type of work your father does in his occupation.
    _____

11. My mother
    ____(1) is primarily a housewife
    ____(2) has a part-time job
    ____(3) has a full-time job

12. If your mother has a full-time job, please indicate below what occupation she has. (Try if possible to give her exact occupational title.)
    _____

13. How far did your mother go in school? (Check one.)
    ____(1) attended primary school
    ____(2) attended lower-technical school
    ____(3) attended clerical or middle-technical school
    ____(4) attended but did not complete grammar school
    ____(5) completed grammar school
    ____(6) completed an education at the general level of of teachers
       college, higher-technical school, KMA, or social work school

179

_____(7) attended but did not complete university

_____(8) completed university

_____(9) attended some other type of school not mentioned above. Please give the name of the school type. _____

14. How far did your father go in school? (Check one.)

    _____(1) attended primary school

    _____(2) attended lower-technical school

    _____(3) attended clerical or middle-technical school

    _____(4) attended but did not complete grammar school

    _____(5) completed grammar school

    _____(6) completed an education at the general level of teachers college, higher-technical school, KMA, or social work school

    _____(7) attended but did not complete university

    _____(8) completed university

    _____(9) attended some other type of school not mentioned above. Please give the name of the school type. _____

Part Two: Some Questions about the
Way You Look at Life

Directions: Read each one of the statements below and give your opinion by placing a check on the correct line. If you agree with the statement, check the line labelled "Agree." If you disagree with the statement, check the line labelled "Disagree." If you _absolutely don't know how to answer_, check the line with the "?" beside it.

15. It generally bothers me to give other people orders.

    _____ Agree   _____ Disagree   _____ ?

16. It's silly for a teenager to put money into a car when the money could be used to get started in business or for an education.

    _____ Agree   _____ Disagree   _____ ?

17. If you want to get ahead you have to be able to take advantage of a few people.

    _____ Agree   _____ Disagree   _____ ?

18. It's generally better to be tactful and diplomatic instead of saying just what you think.

    _____ Agree   _____ Disagree   _____ ?

19. I would prefer a job where you are part of a group, even if you don't get individual credit.

    _____ Agree   _____Disagree   _____ ?

20. Sometimes trying for the really good jobs does not seem worthwhile because you have to wait so long to get them.

    _____ Agree   _____ Disagree   _____ ?

21. It's better to spend your money on things you can enjoy now, rather than save for the future.

_____ Agree   _____ Disagree   _____ ?

22. It generally doesn't bother me to give other people orders, if I need to.

_____ Agree   _____ Disagree   _____ ?

23. If you want to get ahead, you can't be too squeamish about the means you use.

_____ Agree   _____ Disagree   _____ ?

24. I would prefer a job where you are given credit for your achievements, even if that meant that you had to work alone.

_____ Agree   _____ Disagree   _____ ?

25. If a man is insulted by another man for no real reason, he has a right to hit him.

_____ Agree   _____ Disagree   _____ ?

26. Planning only makes a person unhappy since your plans hardly ever work out anyhow.

_____ Agree   _____ Disagree   _____ ?

27. In our country it makes little difference whether you are rich or poor, everyone has the same chance to get ahead.

_____ Agree   _____ Disagree   _____ ?

28. In the long run, drive and ambition are more important in getting ahead than the right education.

_____ Agree   _____ Disagree   _____ ?

29. You should always try to get a really good job even if that means waiting a long time before it comes your way.

_____ Agree   _____ Disagree   _____ ?

30. Most of the time a person should look out for himself, even when it puts others at a disadvantage.

_____ Agree   _____ Disagree   _____ ?

31. There's no sense in worrying about the future so long as you are doing all right now.

_____ Agree   _____ Disagree   _____ ?

32. People who make careful plans are no better off in getting what they want than those who do little or no planning.

_____ Agree   _____ Disagree   _____ ?

33. In the long run, the right education is somewhat more important in getting ahead than are drive and ambition.

_____ Agree   _____ Disagree   _____ ?

34. It's intelligent to give up some things now so that you can be sure of the future.

_____ Agree   _____ Disagree   _____ ?

35. It's important to make plans for the future and not just wait for what might come.

_____ Agree   _____ Disagree   _____ ?

36. You have to give up having a good time now in order to do well later on.
              ____ Agree   ____ Disagree   ____ ?

37. Most of the time a person should look out for himself first, even when he may put himself at a disadvantage.
              ____ Agree   ____ Disagree   ____ ?

38. It is more important to live life to the fullest now than to sacrifice for things that may never come.
              ____ Agree   ____ Disagree   ____ ?

39. Nowadays, the world conditions the way they are, the wise person lives for today and lets tomorrow take care of itself.
              ____ Agree   ____ Disagree   ____ ?

Part Three: For Boys, Some Questions about Your Future Plans

Directions: The following questions are *only for boys*. Girls, please skip questions 40 through 49 and proceed to question 50.

40. What kind of job would you most like to have 10 to 20 years from now? (If you can't name a specific occupation, please write the name of the kind of occupation you would most like to have 10 to 20 years from now.)

_____

41. Describe briefly what kind of work you plan to do in the occupation you chose above.

_____

42. What kind of job do you *really* expect to have 10 to 20 years from now? (If you can't name a specific occupation, please write the name of the type of occupation you really expect to have 10 to 20 years from now.)

_____

43. Describe briefly what kind of work you plan to do in the occupation you chose above.

_____

44. Twenty years from now, when you are working in the job that you have chosen, do you think you will be self-employed or be employed by someone else?

_____ (1) I think that I will be self-employed.

_____ (2) I think that I will be employed by someone.

45. Would you be disappointed if, in your whole life, the best housing you could ever afford is

___ yes ___ no   (1) one room

___ yes ___ no   (2) two rooms

___yes ___ no   (3) a two-room apartment
___yes ___no   (4) a three-room apartment
___yes ___no   (5) a four-room apartment
___yes ___no   (6) a five-room apartment
___yes ___no   (7) a large luxurious apartment
___yes ___no   (8) a villa or very large house

46. Would you be disappointed if, in your whole life, you could never afford better transport than
    ___yes ___ no   (1) a bicycle
    ___yes ___ no   (2) a motorbike
    ___yes ___ no   (3) an old secondhand car
    ___yes ___ no   (4) a nearly new secondhand car
    ___yes ___ no   (5) a new low-priced car
    ___yes ___ no   (6) a new medium-priced car
    ___yes ___ no   (7) a new high-priced car
    ___yes ___ no   (8) a new highly luxurious car

47. Of these job characteristics, which ones are important to you? The ideal job for you would have to
    (1) provide an opportunity to use my special abilities or aptitudes.
       ___Very important___Somewhat important ___Not very important
    (2) permit me to be creative and original.
       ___Very important ___Somewhat important ___ Not very important
    (3) enable me to look forward to a stable, secure future.
       ___Very important ___Somewhat important ___Not very important
    (4) give me social status and prestige.
       ___Very important ___Somewhat important___Not very important
    (5) provide me with a chance to earn a good deal of money.
       ___Very important ___Somewhat important ___Not very important
    (6) leave me relatively free of supervision by others.
       ___Very important ___Somewhat important ___Not very important
    (7) give me a chance to exercise leadership.
       ___Very important ___ Somewhat important ___ Not very important
    (8) give me an opportunity to be helpful to others.
       ___Very important ___Somewhat important ___ Not very important
    (9) provide me with variety and excitement.
       ___Very important ___ Somewhat important ___ Not very important

48. Which of the above job characteristics do you regard as most important?

[Part Four of the questionnaire (questions 49-56) was administered to another sample of female students. Since the data for these students are not presented in this book, the questions are not reproduced.]

*Part Five: Some Questions about the
Kind of Person You Would Like To Be*

Directions: All of us have some ideas about the kind of person we would really like to be. In each of the following questions, we want you to tell us which kind of person you would rather be, the kind labelled "a" or the kind labelled "b." Indicate your opinion by putting a check in front of either "a" or "b" for each question.

57. Which kind of person would *you* rather be?
    _____ (a) Someone who enjoys art and music and likes to read books but just barely makes enough money to live on; *or*
    _____ (b) Someone who makes a very good living but doesn't enjoy art or music or reading books at all.
58. Which kind of person would *you* rather be?
    _____ (a) Someone who is a real success in business, but isn't much of a family man (or woman); *or*
    _____ (b) A real family man (or woman) who isn't very successful in business.
59. Which kind of person would *you* rather be?
    _____ (a) Someone who takes advantage of any good opportunity to get ahead, even when he has to take the chance of losing what he has; *or*
    _____ (b) Someone who would rather have a small but secure position than take a chance on losing what he has to get ahead.
60. Which kind of person would *you* rather be?
    _____ (a) Someone who tries always to be satisfied with what he has and never to want more; *or*
    _____ (b) Someone who is always looking for something better than he has.
61. Which kind of person would *you* rather be?
    _____ (a) Someone who prides himself on doing things on his own, without asking anyone else for advice or help; *or*
    _____ (b) Someone who likes to have help and advice from other people on anything he does and seldom does anything entirely on his own.
62. Which kind of person would *you* rather be?
    _____ (a) A "smooth operator" who comes out on top of every deal; *or*
    _____ (b) Someone who often loses out because he is too kind to take advantage of anybody who isn't as smart as he is.
63. Which kind of person would *you* rather be?
    _____ (a) Someone who is quick to go along with anything the group wants to do and never tries to get people to do things his way; *or*
    _____ (b) Someone who has lots of ideas about things he wants the group to do and is always trying to get the group to do things his way.

64. Which kind of person would *you* rather be?
    _____ (a) Someone who always has something interesting to say about popular music and sports, but doesn't know anything about foreign policy and political trends; *or*
    _____ (b) Someone who always has something interesting to say about foreign policy and political trends, but doesn't know anything about popular music and sports.

65. Which kind of person would *you* rather be?
    _____ (a) Someone who does better than his close friends in many things; *or*
    _____ (b) Someone who does most things just about as well as his close friends—no better and no worse.

66. Which kind of person would *you* rather be?
    _____ (a) Someone who watches for "breaks" and for contacts which will give him "pull" while he is working to get ahead; *or*
    _____ (b) Someone who works hard and carefully, and refuses to use luck or pull to get ahead.

67. Which kind of person would *you* rather be?
    _____ (a) Someone who is good at making decisions for other people; *or*
    _____ (b) Someone who thinks people should make their decisions by themselves and tries never to influence others.

68. Which kind of person would *you* rather be?
    _____ (a) Someone who doesn't mind taking orders from somebody else if he can get ahead that way; *or*
    _____ (b) Someone who would rather be his own boss than get ahead by taking orders from anyone else.

69. Which kind of person would *you* rather be?
    _____ (a) Someone who is good at smoothing over disagreements between people by getting them to talk about other things; *or*
    _____ (b) Someone who is good at pointing out the real issues in any disagreement so that people can argue more intelligently.

Part Six: Some More Questions about the Way You Look at Life

Directions: Read each one of the statements below and give your opinion by placing a check on the correct line. If you agree with the statement, check the line labelled "Agree." If you disagree with the statement, check the line labelled "Disagree." If you *absolutely don't know how to answer* check the line with the "?" beside it.

70. What happens to me is the result of my own effort.
    _____ Agree   _____ Disagree   _____ ?

71. Most people are fair and do not try to get away with something.
_____ Agree _____ Disagree _____ ?

72. Most people are only interested in their own advantage.
_____ Agree _____ Disagree _____ ?

73. Most people will help you when you are in trouble.
_____ Agree _____ Disagree _____ ?

74. When a man is born, the success he's going to have is already in the cards, so he might as well accept it and not fight against it.
_____ Agree _____ Disagree _____ ?

75. When looking for a job, a person ought to find a position in a place located near his parents, even if that means losing a good opportunity elsewhere.
_____ Agree _____ Disagree _____ ?

76. Success is usually achieved by working hard; luck has little or nothing to do with it.
_____ Agree _____ Disagree _____ ?

77. One should accept the job opportunities that come his way even if it means moving far away from his parents.
_____ Agree _____ Disagree _____ ?

78. It is important in life to achieve more than your parents did.
_____ Agree _____ Disagree _____ ?

79. There is no such thing as "luck"; everyone determines his own fate.
_____ Agree _____ Disagree _____ ?

80. When you are in trouble, only a relative can be depended upon to help you.
_____ Agree _____ Disagree _____ ?

81. All I want out of life in the way of a career is a secure, not too difficult job.
_____ Agree _____ Disagree _____ ?

82. The secret of happiness is not expecting too much out of life, and being content with what comes you way.
_____ Agree _____ Disagree _____ ?

83. You should always try to get ahead in life even if your parents stand against this.
_____ Agree _____ Disagree _____ ?

84. When you get right down to it, nobody really cares what happens to you.
_____ Agree _____ Disagree _____ ?

85. You can trust most people.
_____ Agree _____ Disagree _____ ?

86. You can't be too careful in your dealings with other people.
_____ Agree _____ Disagree _____ ?

87. Even when teenagers get married, their main loyalty still belongs to their mothers and fathers.
_____ Agree _____ Disagree _____ ?

88. People help persons who have helped them not so much because it is right but because it is good business.
_____ Agree _____ Disagree _____ ?

89. Nowadays you have to look out for yourself before helping your parents.

      ____ Agree   ____ Disagree   ____ ?

90. The only way to reach the top of the social ladder is to have parents who are either wealthy or influential.

      ____ Agree   ____ Disagree   ____ ?

91. People should choose themselves what they want to do in life and not rely too much on the adivce of their family.

      ____ Agree   ____ Disagree   ____ ?

92. It is not good to let your friends know everything about your life, for they might take advantage of you.

      ____ Agree   ____ Disagree   ____ ?

93. What happens to me is mostly the result of chance or luck.

      ____ Agree   ____ Disagree   ____ ?

94. If you don't watch youself other people will take advantage of you.

      ____ Agree   ____ Disagree   ____ ?

95. It's better not to try to hide anything about yourself; frankness and openness will get you further.

      ____ Agree   ____ Disagree   ____ ?

96. What type of education would you most like to have?

    ____ (1) primary school

    ____ (2) lower-technical school

    ____ (3) clerical or middle-technical school

    ____ (4) partial completion of grammar school

    ____ (5) completion of grammar school

    ____ (6) schooling at the general level of teachers college, higher-technical school, KMA, or social work school

    ____ (7) partial completion of university

    ____ (8) completion of university

    ____ (9) some other type of education not mentioned above. Please give the name of the school type. _____

97. What type of education do you really expect to get?

    ____ (1) primary school

    ____ (2) lower-technical school

    ____ (3) clerical or middle-technical school

    ____ (4) partial completion of grammar school

    ____ (5) completion of grammar school

    ____ (6) schooling at the general level of teachers college, higher-technical school, KMA, or social work school

    ____ (7) partial completion of university

    ____ (8) completion of university

    ____ (9) some other type of education, not mentioned above. Please given the name of the school type. _____

Notes

Notes

Chapter 1
Theoretical Background

1. M. Ginsberg, "Class Consciousness," *Encyclopedia of the Social Sciences*, 3 (1930), 536-538.

2. Dennis Wrong, "Social Inequality Without Social Stratification," Canadian Review of Sociology and Anthropology, Vol 1, pp. 13-14, (1964) reprinted in *Structured Social Inequality*, Celia S. Heller, ed. (New York: The Macmillan Company, 1969).

3. Ibid., p. 515.

4. L. Reissmann, *Class in American Society* (New York: Free Press of Glencoe, 1960), p. 174.

5. T. Parsons, "An Analytical Approach to the Study of Social Stratification," *American Journal of Sociology*, 45 (May 1940), 841-862; R. Merton, "Social Structure and Anomie," *American Sociological Review*, 3 (1938), 677-682; K. Davis and W. Moore, "Some Principles of Stratification," *American Sociological Review*, 10 (1945), 242-249.

6. R.K. Merton, *Social Theory and Social Structure*, rev. ed. (New York: Free Press of Glencoe, 1957), chap. 4.

7. F. Kluckholn, F.L. Strodtbeck, and J. Roberts, *Variations in Value Orientations* (New York: Row, Petersen, 1961).

8. Edwin Lemert, *Human Deviance, Social Problems, and Social Control* (Englewood Cliffs, N.J.: Prentice-Hall, Inc., 1967), p. 5.

9. Ibid., p. 6.

10. E. Mizruchi, *Success and Opportunity* (New York: Free Press of Glencoe, 1964).

11. C. Wright Mills, "Two Styles of Research in Current Social Studies," *Philosophy of Science*, 20 (October 1953), 266-275.

12. T.H. Marshall, *Class, Citizenship and Social Development* (Garden City, N.Y.: Doubleday, 1965), p. 119.

13. Wrong, op. cit., p. 513.

14. Ibid.

15. Ralf Dahrendorf, "Social Structure, Group Interests and Conflict Groups," *Structured Social Inequality*, Celia S. Heller, ed. (New York: The Macmillan Company, 1969), pp. 488-496.

16. Wrong, op. cit., p. 518.

17. Kaare Svalastoga, *Social Differentiation* (New York: David McKay Company, Inc., 1965), pp. 108-109.

18. Norman Ryder, "The Cohort as a Concept in the Study of Social Change," *American Sociological Review*, 30 (1965), 843-861.

19. Svalastoga, op. cit., p. 106.

20. Ibid., pp. 108-109.

21. Talcott Parsons, "The School Class as a Social System," *The Sociology of Education: A Sourcebook*, R. Bell and H. Stubs, eds. (Homewood: The Dorsey Press, 1968), pp. 199-218.

22. Ibid., p. 202.

23. Ibid.

24. Ibid.

25. Ibid.

Chapter 2
Social Selection and Educational
Structure

1. F. Kluckholn, F.L. Strodtbeck, and J. Roberts, *Variations in Value Orientations* (New York: Row, Peterson, 1961).

2. O.D. Duncan and P. Blau, *The American Occupational Structure* (New York: John Wiley and Sons, 1967), p. 8.

3. P. Sorokin, *Social and Cultural Mobility* (New York: Free Press of Glencoe, 1964), p. 195.

4. R.H. Tawney, *Equality* (New York: Capricorn Books, 1961), p. 106.

5. H. Gerth and C.W. Mills, eds., *From Max Weber* (New York: Oxford University Press, 1967), p. 241.

6. R.H. Turner, "Sponsored and Contest Mobility and the School System," *The Sociology of Education: A Sourcebook*, R. Bell and H. Stub, eds. (Homewood: The Dorsey Press, 1968), pp. 219-235.

7. Ibid., p. 219.

8. Ibid., p. 220.

9. Ibid.

10. Ibid., p. 221.

11. Ibid., p. 220.

12. Ibid., p. 222.

13. Ibid., p. 227.

14. Karl Mannheim, *Ideology and Utopia* (New York: Harcourt Brace Jovanovich, n.d.).

15. Turner, op. cit., p. 224.

16. Ibid., pp. 224-225.

17. Mannheim, pp. 265-266.

18. The factual information for the author's description of the Dutch school system was drawn from P.J. Idenburg, *Schets van het Nederlandse Schoolwezen* (Groningen: J.B. Wolters, 1964).

19. Johan Goudsblom, *Dutch Society* (New York: Random House, 1967), p. 31.

20. Turner, op. cit., pp. 228-229.

21. F. Van Heek, *Het Verborgen Talent* (Meppel: J.A. Boom en Zoon, 1968).

22. R.K. Merton and A.K. Rossi, "Reference Group Theory and Social Mobility," *Class, Status and Power*, R. Bendix and S.M. Lipset, eds. (New York: Free Press, 1966).

23. Ibid.

24. Anselm Strauss, *The Contexts of Social Mobility* (Chicago: Aldine Publishing Co., 1971), p. 229.

Chapter 3
Some Methodological Notes

1. Bureau van Statistiek der Gemeente, "Sociale Stratificatie van de Amsterdamse Wijken," *Op Grond Van Cijfers*, 1, no. 2 (1963-1964), 40-48.

2. J.J.M. Van Tulder, *De Beroepsmobiliteit in Nederland van 1919 tot 1954* (Leiden: H.H. Stenfert Kroese, 1962).

3. Ralph H. Turner, *The Social Context of Ambition* (San Francisco: Chandler Publishing Company, 1964), pp. 245-251.

4. Ibid.

5. H.M. In 't Veld-Langeveld, "Maatstaven in de beroepen stratificatie," *Mens en Maatschappij*, 32 (1957), 348.

Chapter 4
Mobility Aspirations and Sponsorship

1. Ralph H. Turner, *The Social Context of Ambition* (San Francisco: Chandler Publishing Company, 1964), p. 36.

2. E.M. Schlatmann, *De Opleiding en Werkgelegenheid Gids* (Zwanenburg: Augustin and Schoonman, 1967).

3. Bureau van Statistiek der Gemeente Amsterdam, "Het onderwijsniveau der Bevolking van Amsterdam en Nederland," *Op Grond van Cijfers*, 1, no. 4 (1963-1964), 108-118.

4. *Jaarverslag van Amsterdam 1960* (Amsterdam: Stadsdrukkerij, 1962).

5. Centraal Bureau voor de Statistiek, *Overgangen binnen het Onderwijs en Intrede in de Maatschappij* (Den Haag: Staatsuitgeverij, 1967).

6. Otis D. Duncan, *The American Occupational Structure* (New York: John Wiley and Sons, 1967), chap. 2.

7. Kaare Svalastoga, *Social Differentiation* (New York: David McKay Company, 1965), p. 106.

8. A.B. Hollingshead, *Elmtown's Youth* (New York: John Wiley and Sons, 1949).

9. L. Empey, "Social Class and Occupational Aspiration: A Comparison of Absolute and Relative Measurement," *American Sociological Review*, 21 (December 1956), 203-709.

10. Turner, op. cit.

11. Turner, op. cit., p. 50.

12. Empey, op. cit.

13. Centraal Bureau voor de Statistiek, op. cit.

14. Ibid.

15. O.D. Duncan, "Path Analysis: Sociological Examples," *American Journal of Sociology*, 72 (July 1966), 1-16.

16. Ibid.

17. O.D. Duncan, *Socioeconomic Background and Occupational Achievement: Extensions of a Basic Model*, U.S. Department of Health, Education, and Welfare, 1968.

Chapter 5
Social Selection and Value Orientations

1. F. Kluckholn, F.L. Strodtbeck, and J. Roberts, *Variations in Value Orientations* (New York: Row, Petersen, 1961).

2. Ibid.

3. Ibid.

4. Joseph A. Kahl, "Some Measurements of Achievement Orientation," *American Journal of Sociology*, 70 (May 1965).

5. Herbert H. Hyman, "The Value Systems of Different Social Classes," *Class, Status and Power*, R. Bendix and S.M. Lipset, eds. (New York: Free Press of Glencoe, 1953), pp. 426-442.

6. Fred L. Strodtbeck, "Family Interaction, Values and Achievement," *Talent and Society*, David C. McClelland, et al., eds. (Princeton, N.J.: D. Van Nostrand and Company, 1959), pp. 135-194.

7. Bernard C. Rosen, "The Achievement Syndrome: A Psychocultural Dimension of Social Stratification," *American Sociological Review*, 32 (June 1967).

8. Ralph H. Turner, *The Social Context of Ambition* (San Francisco: Chandler Press, 1964).

9. Richard A. Rehberg, Walter E. Schafter, and Judie Sinclair, "Toward a Temporal Sequence and Adolescent Achievement Variables," *American Sociological Review*, 35 (1970), 34-48.

10. David C. McClelland, *The Achieving Society* (New York: Free Press of Glencoe, 1961).

11. Rosen, op. cit.

12. John Scanzoni, "Socialization, Achievement, and Achievement Values," *American Sociological Review*, 19 (June 1967).

13. Kahl, op. cit.

14. Strodtbeck, op. cit.

15. Rosen, op. cit.

16. Henrietta Cox, "Study of Social Class Variations in Value Orientations in Selected Areas of Mother-Child Behavior" (unpublished doctoral dissertation, Washington University, St. Louis, 1964).

17. Barry Sugarman, "Teenage Boys at School: A Study of Differential Achievement and Conformity in Four London Secondary Schools" (unpublished doctoral dissertation, Princeton University, 1966).

18. Turner, op. cit.

19. Kluckholn, op. cit.

20. O.D. Duncan, "Path Analysis: Sociological Examples," *American Journal of Sociology*, 72 (July 1966), 1-16.

Bibliography

Bibliography

Almond, A.G., and S. Verba. *The Civic Culture: Political Attitudes and Democracy in Five Nations.* Princeton, N.J.: Princeton University Press, 1963.

Beilin, Harry. "The Pattern of Postponability and Its Relation to Social Class Mobility." *Journal of Social Psychology*, 44 (August 1956), 33-48.

Bordua, David J. "Educational Aspirations and Parental Stress on College." *Social Forces*, 38 (March 1960), 262-269.

Boyle, Richard. *On the Diffusion of Path Analysis to Sociologists.* Unpublished article, 1969.

Bureau van Statistiek der Gemeente. "Sociale Stratificatie van de Amsterdamse Wijken." *Op Grond van Cijfers*, 1, no. 2 (1963-64), 40-48.

Bureau van Statistiek der Gemeente Amsterdam. "Het onderwijsniveau der Bevolking van Amsterdam en Nederland." *Op Grond van Cijfers*, 1, no. 4 (1963-1964), 108-118.

Cayton, Horace R. *Black Metropolis.* New York: Harcourt, Brace, 1945.

Centraal Bureau voor de Statistiek. *Overgangen binnen het Onderwijs en Intrede in de Maatschappij.* Den Haag: Staatsuitgeverij, 1967.

Chinoy, Eli. *Automobile Workers and the American Dream.* New York: Random House, 1955.

Cox, Henrietta. *Study of Social Class Variations in Value Orientations in Selected Areas of Mother-Child Behavior.* Unpublished doctoral dissertation, Washington University, St. Louis, Mo., 1964.

Dahrendorf, Ralf. "Social Structure, Group Interests and Conflict Groups." In Celia S. Heller, Ed., *Structured Social Inequality.* New York: The Macmillan Company, 1969.

Davis, Allison, and Robert J. Havighurst. "Social Class and Color Differences in Child-Rearing." *American Sociological Review*, 11 (December 1946), 698-710.

Davis, K., and W. Moore. "Some Principles of Stratification." *American Sociological Review*, 10 (1945), 242-249.

Dollard, John. *Caste and Class in a Southern Town.* New York: Harper, 1949.

Duncan, Otis D. "Path Analysis: Sociological Examples." *American Journal of Sociology*, 72 (July 1966), 1-16.

_____ *Socioeconomic Background and Occupational Achievement: Extensions of a Basic Model.* Washington, D.C.: U.S. Department of Health, Education, and Welfare, 1968.

_____ *The American Occupational Structure.* New York: John Wiley & Sons, 1967.

Edenburg, P.J. *Schets van het Nederlandse Schoolwezen.* Groningen: J.B. Wolters, 1964.

Empey, L. "Social Class and Occupational Aspiration: A Comparison of Absolute and Relative Measurement." *American Sociological Review*, 21 (December 1956), 203-709.

Freud, Sigmund. "Character and Eroticism." In *Collected Papers*. Vol. II. London: Hogarth, 1925.

Gadourek, I. *Riskante Gewoonten en Zorg voor Eigen Welzijn.* Groningen: J.B. Wolters, 1963.

Gans, Herbert. *The Urban Villagers.* New York: Free Press of Glencoe, 1962.

Gerth, H., and C.W. Mills, Eds. *From Max Weber.* New York: Oxford University Press, 1967.

Ginsberg, M. "Class Consciousness." *Encyclopedia of the Social Sciences*, 3 (1930), 536-538.

Ginzberg, E. "Sex and Class Behavior." In D.P. Geddes and E. Curie, Eds. *About the Kinsey Report.* New York: The New American Library, 1948.

Hodges, Harold M. "Peninsula People: Social Stratification in a California Megalopolis." In W.W. Kallenback and Harold M. Hodges, Eds., *Education and Society: A Book of Readings.* Columbus, Ohio: Charles E. Merril Books, 1963.

Hoggart, Richard. *The Uses of Literacy.* London: Chatto and Windus, 1957.

Hollingshead, August B. *Elmtown's Youth.* New York: John Wiley & Sons, 1949.

Hyman, Herbert H. "The Value Systems of Different Social Classes." In R. Bendix and S.M. Lipset, Eds., *Class, Status, and Power.* New York: Free Press of Glencoe, 1953.

Idenburg, P.J. *Schets van het Nederlandse Schoolwezen.* Groningen: J.B. Wolters, 1964.

In't Veld-Langeveld, H.M. "Maatstaven in de beroepen stratificatie." *Mens en Maatschappij*, 32 (1957), 348.

Jaarverslag van Amsterdam 1960. Amsterdam: Stadsdrukkerij, 1962.

Kahl, Joseph A. "Educational and Occupational Aspirations of 'Common Man' Boys." *Harvard Educational Review*, 23 (Summer 1953), 186-203.

_____ "Some Measurements of Achievement Orientation." *American Journal of Sociology*, 70 (May 1965), 669-681.

Kluckholn, F., F.L. Strodtbeck, and J. Roberts. *Variations in Value Orientations.* New York: Row, Petersen, 1961.

Lemert, Edwin. *Human Deviance, Social Problems, and Social Control.* Englewood Cliffs, N.J.: Prentice-Hall, 1967.

Lerner, Daniel. "Comfort and Fun: Morality in a Nice Society." *American Scholar* 28 (Spring 1958), 157.

Lewis, Oscar. *The Children of Sanchez.* New York: Random House, 1961.

Lipset, S.M., and H. Zetterberg. *Social Mobility in Industrial Society.* Berkeley: University of California Press, 1959.

Mannheim, Karl. *Ideology and Utopia.* New York: Harcourt, Brace and World, n.d.

Marshall, T.H. *Class, Citizenship, and Social Development.* Garden City, N.Y.: Doubleday, 1965.

Matthijssen, M. "Onderwijs en Sociaal Milieu in Zuid-Limberg." *Sociaal Kompas*, 5 (1957-1958).

McClelland, David C. *The Achieving Society.* New York: Free Press of Glencoe, 1961.

Merton, R.K. *Social Theory and Social Structure.* Rev. Ed. New York: Free Press of Glencoe, 1957. Chap. 4.

———— "Social Structure and Anomie." *American Sociological Review*, 3 (1938), 672-682.

Merton, R.K., and A.K. Rossi. "Reference Group Theory and Social Mobility." In R. Bendix and S.M. Lipset, Eds., *Class Status and Power.* New York: Free Press of Glencoe, 1966.

Miller, S.M., and Frank Riessman. "The Working Class Subculture: A New View." *Social Problems*, 9 (Summer 1961), 86-97.

Miller, Walter B. "Social Concerns of Lower-Class Culture." In Ferman, Kornbluh, and Haber, Eds., *Poverty in America.* Ann Arbor, Mich.: University of Michigan Press, 1965.

Mills, C. Wright. "Two Styles of Research in Current Social Studies." *Philosophy of Science*, 20 (October 1953), 266-275.

———— "The Middle Classes in Middle-Sized Cities." *American Sociological Review*, 11 (December 1956), 461-473.

Mizruchi, E. *Success and Opportunity.* New York: Free Press of Glencoe, 1964.

Parsons, Talcott. "An Analytical Approach to the Study of Social Stratification." *American Journal of Sociology*, 45 (May 1940), 841-862.

———— "The School Class as a Social System." R. Bell and H. Stubs, Eds., *The Sociology of Education: A Sourcebook.* Homewood, Ill.: The Dorsey Press, 1968.

Rehberg, Richard A., Walter E. Schafer, and Judie Sinclair. "Toward a Temporal Sequence of Adolescent Achievement Variables." *American Sociological Review*, 35 (1970), 34-48.

Reissmann, L. *Class in American Society.* New York: Free Press of Glencoe, 1960.

Rosen, Bernard C. "The Achievement Syndrome: A Psychocultural Dimension of Social Stratification." *American Sociological Review*, 21 (April 1956), 203-211.

Rosenberg, Morris. *Occupations and Values.* New York: Free Press of Glencoe, 1957.

Ryder, Norman. "The Cohort as a Concept in the Study of Social Change." *American Sociological Review*, 30 (1965), 843-861.

Scanzoni, John. "Socialization, Achievement, and Achievement Values." *American Sociological Review*, 19 (June 1967), 449-456.

Schlatmann, E.M. *De Opleiding en Werkgelegenheid Gids.* Zwanenburg: Augustin and Schoonman, 1967.

Schneider, Louis, and Sverre Lysgaard. "The Deferred Gratification Pattern." *American Sociological Review*, 18 (April 1953), 142-149.

Sorokin, P. *Social and Cultural Mobility.* New York: Free Press of Glencoe, 1964.

Stephenson, Richard M. "Mobility Orientation and Stratification of 1,000 Ninth Graders." *American Sociological Review*, 22 (April 1957), 204-212.

Strauss, Anselm. *The Contests of Social Mobility.* Chicago: Aldine Publishing Co., 1971.

Strauss, Murray. "Deferred Gratification, Social Class and the Achievement Syndrome." *American Sociological Review*, 27 (1962), 326-335.

Strodtbeck, Fred L. "Family Interaction, Values, and Achievement." In David C: McClelland et al., Eds., *Talent and Society.* Princeton, N.J.: D. Van Nostrand and Company, 1959.

Sugarman, Barry. *Teenage Boys at School: A Study of Differential Achievement and Conformity in Four London Secondary Schools.* Unpublished doctoral dissertation, Princeton University, 1966.

Svalastoga, Kaare. *Social Differentiation.* New York: David McKay Company, Inc., 1965.

Tawney, R.H. *Equality.* New York: Capricorn Books, 1961.

Turner, Ralph H. *The Social Context of Ambition.* San Francisco: Chandler Publishing Company, 1964.

_____ "Sponsored and Contest Mobility and the School System." In R. Bell and H. Stub, Eds., *The Sociology of Education: A Sourcebook.* Homewood, Ill.: The Dorsey Press, 1968.

Van Heek, F. *Het Verborgen Talent.* Meppel: J.A. Boom en Zoon, 1968.

Van Tulder, J.J.M. *De Beroepsmobiliteit in Nederland van 1919 tot 1954.* Leiden: H.H. Stenfert Kroese, 1962.

Weber, Max. "Bureaucracy." In H. Gerth and C.W. Mills, Eds., *From Max Weber.* New York: Oxford University Press, 1967.

_____ *The Protestant Ethic and the Spirit of Capitalism.* London: Allen and Unwin, Ltd., 1930.

Wilensky, Harold. "Measures and Effects of Social Mobility." In S.M. Lipset and N.J. Smelser, Eds., *Social Structure and Mobility in Economic Development.* Chicago: Aldine Publishing Co., 1966.

Williams, Robin M. *American Society.* New York: Alfred A. Knopf, 1970.

Wrong, Dennis. "Social Inequality Without Social Stratification." In Celia S. Heller, Ed., *Structured Social Inequality.* New York: The Macmillan Company, 1969.

Index

Ability, differentiation of, 63
  intellectual, 73
  measurement of, 64
  role of, 44
Academici, 87
Achievement, 9, 73
  directiveness of, 133
  emphasis on, 173
  need, 133
  psychological aspects of, 134
  research on, 135
Adolescence, 30, 79
Adolescents, American, 125
  aspirations of, 104
  class position of, 32
  mobility aspirations of, 89, 168
  value of, 144–146. *See also* Students
Advantages, informal, 20
Age, 80
  and aspirations, 120t
  and mobility aspiration, 117f
  values and, 147t, 150f
Age cohort, 79–85
Ambition, 36. *See also* Aspirations
America, classless image of, 62
  mobility patterns in, 100
Americans, aspirations of, 62
Amsterdam, socioeconomic characteristics
    of, 83
Amsterdam Census Bureau, 81
Anthropology, 129
Aristotle, 1
Ascent, social, 9
Aspirations, absolute levels of, 125
  and background, 69, 120t, 121t
  and class, 99–105
  educational, 94–99, 112
  and educational background, 95t
  and educational structure, 77
  of grammar school students, 111
  high-mobility, 60
  indicators of, 115
  lines of cleavage in, 107
  mobility, 31
  occupational, 91–94
  and occupational background, 106t
  and origin, 33
  pattern of, 110
  and persistence, 63
  personal, 89
  ratios of, 102
  realism of, 89–90, 108
  relative rates of, 100

and social selection, 169–173
  stratifier of, 120
  of students, 67
  and values, 61, 145f, 147t, 175
  vertical circulation model of, 105–106t
Attitudes, 15
  shaping of, 32
Authoritarianism, 134
Authority, 139

Background, and aspirations, 69, 120t, 121t
  effect on values of, 60, 147t, 150f
  and expected occupation, 105–106
  index of, 82t
  and mobility aspirations, 116, 117f,
    118–124
  and occupational aspirations, 92t
Behavior, social, 15
Blau, P., 35
Boundaries, class, 21
Bureaucracy, status-order of, 6
Bureaucratization, 16
Burgerij, 49

Calvinists, 52
Career, interruption of, 20
Carpe diem, 137
Catholics, 52, 53, 79
Census, Amsterdam, 84t
  Dutch, 84t
Citizenship, concept of, 13
Class, and aspiration, 99–105, 152
  concept of, 2
  criteria for membership, 22
  cultural characteristics of, 21, 27
  cultural theories of, 7–11
  and culture, 3–7
  of destination, 34, 61, 89
  effect on values of, 149
  indicators of, 85–87
  Marxist theory of, 14, 22
  of origin, 34
  as subculture, 3–5
  and value orientation, 145
Class consciousness, 4, 21
  lack of, 19
Class position, measurement of, 30
  self-awareness of, 14, 20
  transmission of, 102
Clerical schools, 54, 82, 111
Clerical work, 93, 94
Competence, criterion for, 40
Confessional bloc, 78–79

Conformity, 59
Credentials, 18
 educational, importance of, 169
Credentialization, 115, 175
 structure of, 18
Cross-national studies, 85
Cultural pluralism, 165
Cultural variation, 130
Culture, and class, 3-7, 21, 27
 and mobility, 11

Dahrendorf, Ralf, 15
Davis, K., 6
Depression, of 1929, 33
Deprivation, social, 1
Destination, class of, 34, 61, 89
 stratification of, 33
Differentiation, cultural, 73
 in school system, 45
 social, 16
Displaced persons, 17
Distrust, 141
Dominant culture theory, 5-7
Dominant value theory, 9, 22, 31, 32, 33
 problems with, 10
Doubleren, phenomenon of, 80
Dropouts, 64
 in Netherlands, 99
Duncan, Otis D., 35, 100, 101, 115, 121,
  122, 149, 153
Dutch Census Bureau, 85
Dutch National Statistical Bureau, 54

Education, 34
 adaptive, 50, 51
 American, philosophy of, 46
 and class, 26
 desired, 113t
 Dutch, 50
 elite, 58, 71, 157
 expected, 114t
 father's, 84
 grammar school, 54
 high school, 107
 higher, 114
  aspirations for, 64
 in industrial societies, 171
 in the Netherlands, 49
 in nonelite programs, 142
 specialization, 71
 university, 87
  access to, 112
  expectation of, 97. See also School
   systems
Educational system, decentralized, 46
 Dutch, 66. See also School systems

Elites, 44
 in Dutch society, 49
 mobility and, 21
 multiple, 45
 oversupply of, 38, 65
 recruitment of, 45
Elite status, 167
 candidates for, 68, 170
 criterion for, 44
 cultural attributes of, 72
Empey, L., 102, 105
Estrangement, and ambition, 158
Examinations, in Dutch School system, 53

Failure, recognition of, 68
Familism, 136, 140, 146, 157-158
Families, lower-class, 27
 middle-class, 159
Family, and socialization, 24, 26. See also
  Socialization
Feudalism, primary values of, 38
Feudal society, 37
Folk norms, 49, 55
Freedom, 139
Friendships, 59-60, 74
Future orientation, 61, 73, 74

Geleerde stand, 49
Ginsburg, M., 2
Goals, and values, 9
Goudsblom, Johan, 52
Grades, and aspirations, 117f, 120t
Grammar schools, 54, 80, 82
 standards in, 70
 student options at, 111. See also School
  systems
Gratification, achievement, 146, 151,
  158-159
 deferred, 136, 137, 146, 160, 165
 existential, 138
 interpersonal, 140
Group cleavages, patterns of, 60
Gymnasium, Dutch, 49, 50

Hierarchies, organizational, 112
High schools, 60, 62. See also Secondary
  schools
Hollingshead, A.B., 101, 102
Homogeneity, cultural, 7, 11
 intrasocietal, 130
Hyman, H.H., 31, 131

Ideology, "democratic," 172
 mobility, 48, 57
 and mobility norms, 46
 total, 47

Impulsivity, 138
Independence, 139
Index, of anticipated status, 115
   mobility paths, 146
   of values, 161–162
Individualism, 26, 136, 139, 146, 159
Industrialization, and mobility, 169, 170
Industry, personnel departments of, 18
Inequality, 15
   distributive, 21
   and high-mobility rates, 19
   of occupational structure, 19
   social, 1, 2
Inheritance, 35, 101
   of class position, 20
   impact of, 102, 103
   social, 122. *See also* Background; Origins
Instability, expectation of, 20
In't Veld-Langeveld, H.M., 86
Intelligence, 106

James, William, 9
Jannisaries, 17, 38

Kahl, Joseph, 131, 132
Kluckhohn, Florence, 7, 32, 130, 131, 132, 133

Laborers, 101
Ladder model, of mobility, 103
Leiden, University of, 56
Lemert, E., 7, 8
Liberal education, Dutch, 51

Males, adult, 32
Mammoth Law, 57
Managerial positions, aspirations toward, 111
   competition for, 98
Mannheim, Karl, 46, 48
Manual labor, 87, 92
   structural displacement of, 18
Markov chain projections, 23
Marshall, T.H., 12
Marxist theory, 1, 2, 14
Masses, 44
Mastery, 136, 140, 146, 158
McClelland, David C., 133
Membership, in social class, 38. *See also* Class
Meritocracy, 49
Merton, R.K., 6, 59
Methodology, 30. *See also* Questionnaire
Middle-class families, 159
Middle-class schools, Dutch, 49
Middle-class status, criterion for, 40

Miller, S.M., 170
Mills, C. Wright, 10
Mizruchi, E., 10
Mobility, blue-collar, 132
   channels for, 40
   class culture and, 11–28
   and class values, 32–34
   concept of, 34
   contest pattern of, 43, 46
   downward, 127
   high aspirations for, 99
   hydraulics of, 35
   interclass, xv
   intergenerational, 14, 21
   kinds of, 103
   lateral, 20
   mass, 126, 170
   race model of, 65, 103, 105, 125
   rates of, 35, 100
   social control implications of, 47
   and socialization, 66–77
   and social stratification, 16–21
   sponsored system of, 43, 53, 94
   and stratification theory, 15
   upward, 103
   and value formation, 29
   and values, 79
   vertical, 19
Mobility aspiration, determinants of, 115–118, 123t
   indicators of, 122
   six measures of, 118
   and social class, 120
Mobility paths, 156
Money, 34, 45
Moore, W., 6
Morality, and role of school, 25
Multiple regression analysis, 118, 119, 120, 126
Multiple regression coefficients, 104

Need-achievement, 133
Neighborhood, social rank of, 82t
Netherlands, lower-socioeconomic groups in, 81
   occupational structure in, 55, 56
   postsecondary educational institutions in, 54. *See also* School systems

Occupational position, determination of, 27
   differentiation for, 39
   selection for, 40
Occupational structure, mobility in, 17
   in the Netherlands, 55, 56
Occupations, and aspirations, 102
   blue-collar, 87

desired by students, 109
elite, 97
expected, 108
intergenerational continuity of, 19
in the Netherlands, 86
parents', 91
semiprofessional, 86, 91, 110, 125
white-collar access to, 52
Opportunism, 136, 140, 146, 156–157
Organizing norms, 47
Origins, 60
stratification of, 32, *See also* Background
Overachiever, 70
Ownership, 4

Parents, 134
ambitious, 67
higher-status, 121
lower-class, 27, 31
Parsons, Talcott, 6, 24, 25, 26
Passivity, 140
Path analysis, 115, 116, 119, 121, 126–127,
144, 145, 153
failure of, 155, 156
Personality, evolution of, 36
and mobility, 38
motivational dimension of, 133
Pillarization, of Dutch society, 78–79
Popularity, mass, 45
Poverty, culture of, 3
Prestige, identification with, 62
Primitive societies, 7
Professions, 91, 125
choice of, 94, 109
Protestantism, social values of, 132
Psychology, social, 48

Questionnaire, 30, 135, 173
use of, 90, 91

Race, 106
Race model, of mobility, 65, 103, 105, 125,
171
Realism, of aspirations, 89–90, 108
Rehberg, R.A., 131
Reissmann, L., 3
Residence, segregation of, 81
Rosen, B.C., 131, 132, 133
Rossi, A.K., 59

Sample, 77–85
educational level of, 84t
occupational distribution of, 84t
Scanzoni, John, 134
School, and aspirations, 120t
controlled selection in, 53
and desired occupation, 109t

and educational aspirations, 112–115
effect on values of, 150f, 151t
and expected occupation, 110t
influence of, 27
and mobility aspiration, 106–108, 117f,
118–124
and occupational aspirations, 108–112
as socializing agency, 25
values and, 147t
School system, Dutch, 42, 48–57, 77, 168
reform of, 56
English, 45
European, channeling in, 39
graded, 67
shaping of, 43
United States, 46
Secondary education, Dutch, 50, 55, 78
80, 107
classifications of, 169
and father's occupation, 83t
instructors at, 97
Segregation, cultural, 24
residential, 81
Self-employment, 93
Self-expression, 138
Self-reliance, 26, 139
Semiprofessions, 91, 110, 125
aspirations toward, 111
Skilled labor, 125
Social change, 12
Social class, indicators of, 85–87. *See also*
Class
Social climbers, 9
Social controls, 47
Social Darwinism, 5, 50
Socialization, 20
agencies of, 24
anticipatory, 59, 73, 74, 143
theory of, 58–59, 61
childhood, 24
to class values, 35
under contest system, 57–66, 69, 75
control over, 38
familial, 16, 59, 108, 152, 159
institutional, 70, 74, 148, 152, 157, 159,
161, 173, 174
mechanisms of, 163
mechanisms of, 57
of mobile individual, 41
parental, 73
postfamilial, 17
primary, 36
secondary, 24, 36, 37
self, 37
and social selection, 141
under sponsorship, 174
and status transmission, 36

supplementary, 37
Social selection, xvi, 27, 41
  and aspiration, 169–173
  contest systems of, 67, 104
  controlled, 45
  criteria of, 63
  definition of, 35
  and educational structure, 29–75
  ideologies of, 171
  meritocratic logic of, 56
  modes of, xvi
  and socialization, 142–143
  sponsored norms of, 48–57
  sponsored system of, 67, 68, 124
  standard of, 39
  structure of, 41–48
  system of, 34
Social stratification. See Stratification
Social structure, medieval, 38
Society, Dutch, pillarization of, 78–79
  modern, 23
  primitive, 7
Socioeconomic status (SES), 81
Sociology, political, 2
Sorokin, P., 38
Specialization, in school system, 45
Sponsorship system, 169
  adolescent values in, 144
  and aspirations, 124
  mobility aspirations in, 168
  socialization under, 74
  values in, 143
Staffing, of work organizations, 18
Standenhierarchie, 49
Status, allocation of, 23, 27, 62
  anticipated, indices of, 115
  effect on values of, 150f
  hierarchies of, 13
  transmission of, 67
Stratification, 167
  continuum of, 13
  correlates of, 4
  of destination, 33
  functionalist theory of, 5
  of origin, 32
  and social selection, 34–41
  structural bases of, 14
  and values, 144, 162–163
Stratification system, and value orienta-
    tions, 57
Stratification theory, 11, 12–16
Stratum, concept of, 15
Strauss, Anselm, 65
Strodtbeck, F.L., 131, 132
Students, aspirations of, 124–125
  desired occupations of, 93
  Dutch, aspirations of, 31

choices of, 113
  educational aspirations of, 114
educational aspirations of, 94–95
high-status, 127
of lower-class background, 143, 175
nonmobile, 33
parental class background of, 69
secondary school, 77
selection of, 58
socialization of, 107
technical school, 110
values of, 41
Subculture, vs. value pluralism, 144
Subculture theory, 23, 31, 32
Success, 136, 138
Sweden, 171

Talent, 37, 39
  scarcity of, 43
Tawney, R.H., 39
Teachers, in the Netherlands, 72
  secondary school, 87
Technical schools, 82
  Dutch, 50, 54
  standards in, 70
Technology, large-scale changes in, 18
Tradition, 139
Trust, 136, 141, 146, 161
Turner, Ralph H., 43, 43, 44, 45, 46, 47,
    48, 53, 55, 85, 92, 103, 105, 131,
    135, 137, 167

U.L.O. (uitgebreid lager onderwijs), 51
Unions, 93
United States, mobility in, 58. See also
    America
Universities, American, students in, 26
  and aspirations, 98
  attendance at, 99
  competitive standards within, 46

Valuation, contingent, 8
Value differentiation, 129–132
Value orientations, 132–134
  analysis of, 130
  determination of, 147–155
Values, and academic achievement, 26
  achievement, 173
  and aspirations, 145f
  categories of, 136
  class, xv, 74, 132
  composite index of, 161–162
  determination of, 164
  dominant American, 9
  dominant hierarchy of, 6
  and educational structure, 77
  effect of school on, 149

elite, 58
endorsement of, 143
formation of, 148
indices of, 146–147, 164
inference of, 5
internalization of, 36
institutional learning of, 151
learning of, 58, 60, 72
in lower-class environment, 3
measurement of, 30
middle-class achievement, 70
and occupational career, 24
orientations of, 10
social class and, 29
social stratification and, 162–163
stratification of, 66

unitary hierarchy of, 23
Van Tulder, J.J.M., 85
Vertical circulation model, 125
Vocational schools, 51, 96

Weber, Max, 8, 15, 39, 132
Western Europe, elite selection in, 171
Women, values of, 161
Working class, Marxian view of, 1
Wrong, Dennis, 2, 13, 14, 15, 16

Youth, lower class, 101. *See also* Adolescents; Students

Zuilen, 52

About the Author

Cornelis J. Van Zeyl, a native of the Netherlands, received the B.A. in history and the M.A. and Ph.D. in sociology from the University of California at Los Angeles. Presently he is assistant professor of sociology at Columbia University. Professor Van Zeyl is currently engaged in a study of attitudes toward educational credentialization in Venezuela.